The M & E Business Stu

The purpose of this series is to meet the needs of students following business studies courses whether for the Business and Technician Education Council (BTEC) or for the examinations of the major professional institutes. The books have been written to conform with syllabus specifications and are constructed around a series of objectives stated at the beginning of each chapter, with assignments and self-assessment questions where appropriate.

The M&E Business Studies Series

Business Law

G. M. AFFLEY
B.A.(Wales), LL.M.(London)
Senior Lecturer in Law,
Polytechnic of Wales

SECOND EDITION

Macdonald and Evans

Macdonald & Evans Ltd.
Estover, Plymouth PL6 7PZ

First published 1982

Second edition 1985
© Macdonald & Evans Ltd. 1985

British Library Cataloguing in Publication Data
Affley, G. M.
    Business law.—2nd ed.—(The M & E Business
    Studies series, ISSN 0266–9917)
    1. Commercial law—Great Britain.
    I. Title
    344. 106'7   KD1629
    ISBN 0–7121–2405–5

Printed in Great Britain at The Bath Press, Avon

Preface to the Second Edition

This book is intended principally to meet the requirements of students who have chosen the Business Law Option Module under the BTEC National Awards scheme. In this respect, the content of the book is complementary to the Common Core Module, The Organisation in its Environment, but students pursuing non-BTEC courses for which a basic foundation in the law relating to business is required will find it appropriate for their purposes.

The text is divided into four parts: Business Organisations, Business Property, Business Contracting and Non-Contractual Liability. Each chapter is prefaced with its individual objectives and there are self-assessment questions by which readers may measure progress. Assignments are located at the end of each of the four parts of the book requiring readers to consider the legal issues posed by, and law relevant to, different factual situations.

The occasion of this new edition provides an opportunity to amend the text to take account of developments in the law, in particular, in relation to registered companies and the supply of goods and services. In addition, the appendices contain hire-purchase and credit sale agreement forms revised in the light of new regulations made under the Consumer Credit Act 1974.

1985   G.M.A.

Contents

Preface to the Second Edition   v

Table of Cases   xi

Table of Statutes   xxvi

PART ONE: BUSINESS ORGANISATIONS

1 **The Organisation and its Legal Status**   1
Introduction; Unincorporated organisations; Corporate personality; Summary; Self-assessment questions

2 **Partnership**   8
Introduction; Definition and characteristics of the partnership; Relations of partners to each other; Relations of partners to outsiders; Dissolution of partnership; Limited partnerships; Summary; Self-assessment questions

3 **Registered Companies—Formation**   20
Introduction; Classification; Formation; The company's memorandum and articles of association; Share capital; Meetings and resolutions; Summary; Self-assessment questions

4 **Registered Companies—Personnel**   34
Introduction; Members and debenture holders; Directors; Directors and the law of agency; The company secretary; Relationships between the members and the company; Summary; Self-assessment questions

5 **Winding Up and Bankruptcy**   52
Introduction; Winding up; Bankruptcy; Summary; Self-assessment questions

Assignments   63

PART TWO: BUSINESS PROPERTY

6 **The Nature of Business Property**   67
Introduction; Classification of property; Interests in land; Goods; Negotiable instruments; Shares and

debentures; Copyrights, patents and trade marks;
Summary; Self-assessment questions

7 **The Transfer of Business Property**   81
Introduction; Transfer of interests in land; Transfer
(assignment) of contractual rights; Negotiation under
the Bills of Exchange Act 1882; Transfer of shares and
debentures; Transfer of the property in and title to the
goods; Bailment; Summary; Self-assessment questions

8 **Securities**   95
Introduction; Mortgages; Pledges (pawns); Guarantees;
Summary; Self-assessment questions

Assignments   103

PART THREE: BUSINESS CONTRACTING

9 **The Creation of Contractual Relationships**   105
Introduction; Agreement; Consideration and privity of
contract; Capacity; Intention to enter into a legally
binding   relationship;   Summary;   Self-assessment
questions

10 **Contractual Rights and Obligations**   115
Introduction; Nature and importance of the terms of the
contract; Implied terms in contracts for the sale and
supply of goods; Exclusion clauses; Summary;
Self-assessment questions

11 **Voidable, Void and Illegal Contracts**   130
Introduction; Misrepresentation; Duress and undue
influence;   Mistake;   Illegality;   Summary;
Self-assessment questions; Assignments

12 **Performance and Discharge of the Contractual
Obligations**   145
Introduction; Performance; Discharge of the contractual
obligations by breach; Discharge by frustration;
Discharge by agreement and waiver; Summary;
Self-assessment questions

13 **The Carriage of Goods**   158
Introduction; Common carriers; The carriage of goods
by land and air; Carriage by sea; Summary;
Self-assessment questions

14 Agency   **172**
Introduction; Duties of the agent; The agent's rights;
The agent's authority; Relations between the parties;
Summary; Self-assessment questions

15 Banking Transactions   **184**
Introduction; The banker/customer relationship;
Crossed cheques; Statutory provisions protecting
bankers; The Mareva injunction and garnishee
proceedings; Documentary credits; Deposit-taking;
Summary; Self-assessment questions

16 Remedies for Breach of Contract   **196**
Introduction; Damages; Remedies under the Sale of
Goods Act 1979; Equitable remedies; Limitation of
actions; Summary; Self-assessment questions

17 Fair Trading   **204**
Introduction; Consumer trade practices; Restrictive
trade practices; Anti-competitive practices; Monopolies
and mergers; Summary; Self-assessment questions

18 Hire-Purchase and Consumer Credit   **216**
Introduction; Regulated agreements; Hire-purchase,
conditional sale and credit sale agreements; Other forms
of classification of regulated agreements; Entry into
credit and hire agreements; Matters arising during the
currency of credit hire agreements; Exempt agreements;
Extortionate credit bargains; Licensing; Seeking
business; Summary; Self-assessment questions

Assignments   **231**

PART FOUR: NON-CONTRACTUAL LIABILITY

19 Non-Contractual Liability   **234**
Introduction; Liability in tort for defective products;
Liability under the Trade Descriptions Act 1968;
Compensation orders; Summary; Self-assessment
questions

Assignments   **245**

Appendixes   **246**
I Forms of memorandum of association of a public
company

II Specimen credit sale and hire-purchase agreement forms
III Tour Operators' Code of Conduct and Guidelines for Booking Conditions

Index **253**

Table of Cases

Abbatt *v.* Treasury Solicitor and Others [1969] 1 W.L.R. 1575;
  [1969] 3 All E.R. 1175   2
Aberdeen Rail Co. *v.* Blaikie Bros. [1843–60] All E.R. Rep. 249   39
Adamson *v.* Jarvis (1827) 130 E.R. 693   176
Ailsa Craig Fishing Co. Ltd. *v.* Malvern Fishing Co. Ltd. [1983] All
  E.R. 101   127
Alan (W.J.) and Co. Ltd. *v.* El Nasr Export and Import Co. [1972]
  2 Q.B. 189; [1972] 2 All E.R. 127   156
Allam and Co. Ltd. *v.* Europa Poster Services Ltd. [1968] 1 W.L.R.
  638; [1968] 1 All E.R. 826   173
Allcard *v.* Skinner (1887) 36 Ch.D. 145   136
Allen *v.* Gold Reefs of West Africa Ltd. [1900] 1 Ch. 656   29, 48
Aluminium Industrie Vaassen B.V. *v.* Romalpa Aluminium Ltd.
  [1976] 1 W.L.R. 676; [1976] 2 All E.R. 552   55, 89, 92
Andrabell Ltd., *Re* [1984] 3 All E.R. 407   89
Andrews *v.* Gas Meter Co. [1897] 1 Ch. 361   74
Andrews *v.* Hopkinson [1957] 1 Q.B. 229; [1956] 3 All E.R. 422   220
Anglo Overseas Transport Ltd. *v.* Titan Industrial Corporation
  (United Kingdom) Ltd. [1959] 2 Lloyd's Rep. 152   176
Arab Bank Ltd. *v.* Ross [1952] 2 Q.B. 216; [1952] 1 All E.R. 709   190
Archbold's (Freightage) Ltd. *v.* S. Spanglett Ltd. [1961] 1 Q.B.
  374; [1961] 1 All E.R. 417   139
Arcos Ltd. *v.* Ronaasen and Sons [1933] A.C. 470   121
Argent *v.* Minister of Social Security and Another [1968] 1 W.L.R.
  1749; [1968] 3 All E.R. 208   237
Argy Trading Co. Ltd. *v.* Lapid Developments Ltd. [1977]
  1 W.L.R. 444; [1977] 3 All E.R. 785   111
Aries Tanker Corporation *v.* Total Transport Ltd. [1977] 1 W.L.R.
  185; [1977] 1 All E.R. 398   169
Armstrong *v.* Jackson [1917] 2 K.B. 822   174
Asfar *v.* Blundell [1896] 1 Q.B. 123   169
Ashbury Railway Carriage and Iron Co. Ltd. *v.* Riche (1875) L.R.
  7 H.L. 653   27
Ashington Piggeries Ltd. and Another *v.* Christopher Hill Ltd.
  [1972] A.C. 441; [1971] 1 All E.R. 847   122
Ashmore, Benson, Pearce and Co. Ltd. *v.* Dawson Ltd. [1973]
  1 W.L.R. 828; [1973] 2 All E.R. 856   140, 143
Associated Distributors Ltd. *v.* Hall [1938] 2 K.B. 83   221
Automatic Bottlemakers Ltd., *Re* [1926] Ch. 412   76
Automatic Self-Cleansing Filter Syndicate Co. Ltd. *v.* Cunningham
  [1906] 12 Ch. 34   43
B.P. Exploration Co. (Libya) Ltd. *v.* Hunt [1982] 1 All E.R. 925   155

Badeley v. Consolidated Bank (1888) 38 Ch. D. 238   9
Bahia and San Francisco Railway Co., Re (1868) L.R. 3 Q.B. 584   87
Balfour v. Balfour [1919] 2 K.B. 571   113
Bamford v. Bamford [1970] Ch. 212; [1969] 1 All E.R. 969   32, 44
Barclays Bank Ltd. v. Astley Industrial Trust Ltd. [1970] 2 Q.B.
    527; [1970] 1 All E.R. 719   188
Barker v. Hargreaves [1981] Crim. L.R. 262   243
Barron v. Potter [1914] 1 Ch. 895   37, 39
Bartlett v. Sidney Marcus Ltd. [1965] 1 W.L.R. 1013; [1965] 2 All
    E.R. 753   122
Basildon District Council v. J. E. Lesser (Properties) Ltd [1985]
    1 All E.R. 20   117
Baumwoll v. Furness [1893] A.C. 8   163
Bavins, Junr. and Sims v. London and South Western Bank Ltd.
    [1900] 1 Q.B. 270   71
Beale v. Taylor [1967] 1 W.L.R. 1193; [1967] 3 All E.R. 253   121
Bechuanaland Exploration Co. v. London Trading Bank Ltd.
    [1898] 2 Q.B. 658   70, 76
Behnke v. Bede Shipping Co. Ltd. [1927] 1 K.B. 649   202
Belfast Ropework Co. Ltd. v. Bushell [1918] 1 K.B. 210   158, 159, 161
Bell v. Lever Bros. Ltd. [1932] A.C. 161   132, 137
Belsize Motor Supply Co. Ltd. v. Cox [1914] 1 K.B. 244   92
Belvoir Finance Co. Ltd. v. Stapleton [1971] 1 Q.B. 210; [1970]
    3 All E.R. 664   143
Bennett, Waldon & Co. v. Wood [1950] 2 All E.R. 134   175
Bentley (Dick) Productions Ltd. v. Harold Smith (Motors) Ltd.
    [1965] 1 W.L.R. 623; [1965] 2 All E.R. 65   116
Bigos v. Bousted [1951] 1 All E.R. 92   143
Bird v. Brown (1850) 19 L.J. Ex. 154   179
Bird Precision Bellows Ltd., Re [1984] 2 W.L.R. 869   50
Bishopsgate Motor Finance Corporation v. Transport Brakes Ltd.
    [1949] 1 K.B. 322; [1949] 1 All E.R. 37   91
Bissett v. Wilkinson [1927] A.C. 177   131
Boardman v. Phipps [1967] 2 A.C. 46; [1966] 3 All E.R. 721   174
Bock v. Gorrissen (1861) 30 L.J. Ch. 39   176
Bolton v. Mahadeva [1972] 1 W.L.R. 1009; [1972] 2 All E.R. 1322   147
Bolton Partners v. Lambert (1889) 41 Ch. D. 295   178
Bonelli's Telegraph Co., Re (1871) L.R. 12 Eq. 246   39
Bonnard v. Dott [1906] 1 Ch. 740   143
Borden (U.K.) Ltd v. Scottish Timber Products Ltd. [1981] Ch. 25;
    [1979] 3 All E.R. 961   89
Borlands' Trustee v. Steel Bros. and Co. Ltd. [1901] 1 Ch. 279   74
Boston Deep Sea Fishing and Ice Co. v. Ansell (1888) 39 Ch. D. 339   175
Boston Deep Sea Fishing and Ice Co. Ltd., v. Farnham [1957]
    1 W.L.R. 1051; [1957] 3 All E.R. 204   179
Bothe v. Amos [1976] Fam. 46; [1975] 2 All E.R. 321   17
Bottomley v. Nuttall (1858) 28 L.J.C.P. 110   146
Bowmakers v. Barnett Instruments Ltd. [1945] K.B. 65   143

Brace v. Calder [1895] 2 Q.B. 253   198
Brandao v. Barnett and Others [1843–60] All E.R. Rep. 719   99
Branwhite v. Worcester Works Finance Co. Ltd. [1969] 1 A.C. 552; [1968] 3 All E.R. 104   220
Bridge v. Campbell Discount Co. Ltd. [1962] A.C. 600; [1962] 1 All E.R. 385   221
Bridger v. Savage (1885) 15 Q.B.D. 363   142
Brikon Investments v. Carr and Others [1979] Q.B. 467; [1979] 2 All E.R. 754   116, 156
Brinkibon Ltd. v. Stahag Stahl [1982] 1 All E.R. 293   108
British Gas Corporation v. Lubbock [1974] 1 W.L.R. 37; [1974] 1 All E.R. 188   240
British Waggon Co. and Ano. v. Lea and Co. (1880) 5 Q.B.D. 149   85
Brogden v. Metropolitan Railway Co. (1877) 2 App. Cas. 666   108
Brown v. Lewis (1896) 12 T.L.R. 455   3
Buchanan (James) and Co. v. Hay's Transport Services [1972] 2 Lloyd's Rep. 555   93, 161
Burkinshaw v. Nicolls (1878) 3 App. Cas. 1004   87
Bushell v. Faith [1970] A.C. 1099; [1970] 1 All E.R. 53   32, 42
Butler Machine Tool Co. Ltd. v. Ex-Cell-O Corporation (England) Ltd. [1979] 1 W.L.R. 401; [1979] 1 All E.R. 965   106, 107
Butterworth v. Kingsway Motors Ltd. [1954] 1 W.L.R. 1286; [1954] 2 All E.R. 695   120
Butwick v. Grant [1924] 2 K.B. 483   182
Byrne v. Schiller and Others (1871) 6 L.R. Exch. 319   169
Byrne v. Van Tienhoven (1880) 5 C.P.D. 344   106

Campbell v. Thompson [1953] 1 Q.B. 445; [1953] 1 All E.R. 831   3
Car and Universal Finance Co. Ltd. v. Caldwell [1965] 1 Q.B. 525; [1964] 1 All E.R. 290   91, 132
Carlill v. Carbolic Smoke Ball Co. [1893] 1 Q.B. 256   106, 107, 141
Cavendish Woodhouse v. Manley [1984] 82 L.G.R. 376   206
Central London Property Trust Ltd. v. High Trees House Ltd. [1947] K.B. 130   111
Century Insurance Co. Ltd. v. Northern Ireland Road Transport Board [1942] A.C. 509   237
Chapelton v. Barry Urban District Council [1940] 1 K.B. 532   126
Chaplin v. Hicks [1911] 2 K.B. 786   197
City Equitable Fire Insurance Co. Ltd., Re [1925] Ch. 407   41
Clarke v. Dickson (1858) 120 E.R. 463   133
Clarke v. Dunraven [1897] A.C. 59   108
Clarkson, Booker Ltd. v. Andjel [1964] 2 Q.B. 775; [1964] 3 All E.R. 260   182
Clemens v. Clemens Bros. Ltd. [1976] 2 All E.R. 268   49, 50
Clemens (E.) Horst Co. v. Biddell Bros. [1912] A.C. 18   164
Clode v. Barnes [1974] 1 W.L.R. 544; [1974] 1 All E.R. 1166   236, 242
Cohen v. Kittell (1889) 22 Q.B. 680   173
Collen v. Wright (1857) 27 L.J.K.B. 215   181

Commercial Solvents Corporation v. Commission [1974] E.C.R. 225   215
Consten and Grundig v. Commission [1966] C.M.L.R. 418   211
Cottee v. Douglas Seaton (Used Cars) Ltd. [1972] 1 W.L.R. 1408;
   [1972] 3 All E.R. 750   239, 240
Coupe v. Guyett [1973] 1 W.L.R. 669; [1973] 2 All E.R. 1058   242, 243
Coutts and Co. v. Brown-Lecky [1946] 2 All E.R. 207   101
Couturier v. Hastie (1856) 25 L.J. Ex. 253   136
Cox v. Coulson [1916] 2 K.B. 177   10
Craig, Re [1971] Ch. 95; [1970] 2 All E.R. 390   135
Crichton's Oil Co., Re [1902] 2 Ch. 86   75
Crooks and Co. v. Allan and Another (1879) 5 Q.B.D. 38   165
Crouch v. Credit Foncier of England (1873) L.R. 8 Q.B. 374   70
Crowther v. Shannon Motor Co. [1975] 1 W.L.R. 30; [1975] 1 All
   E.R. 139   122, 123
Cuckmere Brick Co. Ltd. and Another v. Mutual Finance Co. Ltd.
   [1971] Ch. 949; [1971] 2 All E.R. 633   96
Cundy v. Lindsay (1878) 3 App. Cas. 459   109
Cutter v. Powell (1795) 101 E.R. 573   147

D. & C. Builders Ltd. v. Rees [1966] 2 Q.B. 617; [1965] 3 All E.R.
   837   111
D.H.N. Food Distributors Ltd. v. Tower Hamlets London
   Borough Council [1976] 1 W.L.R. 852; [1976] 3 All E.R. 462   5
Dafen Tinplate Co. Ltd. v. Llanelli Steel Co. Ltd. [1920] 2 Ch. 124 29
Daniels v. R. White and Sons Ltd. and Tabard [1938] 4 All E.R.
   258   235, 238
Daniels and Others v. Daniels and Others [1978] Ch. 406; [1978]
   2 All E.R. 89   49
Davidson v. Barclays Bank Ltd. [1940] 1 All E.R. 316   187
Davies v. Sumner [1984] 3 All E.R. 831   240
Davis v. Davis [1894] 1 Ch. 393   9, 10, 13, 172
Davis Contractors Ltd. v. Fareham Urban District Council [1956]
   A.C. 696; [1956] 2 All E.R. 145   154
De Francesco v. Barnum (1890) 45 Ch. D. 430   112
De Mattos v. Benjamin (1894) 63 L.J.Q.B. 248   173
Dearle v. Hall [1824–34] All E.R. Rep. 28   84
Debtor, A, (No. 13 of 1964), Re [1980] 1 W.L.R. 263; [1979] 3 All
   E.R. 15   61
Decro-Wall International S.A. v. Practitioners in Marketing Ltd.
   [1971] 1 W.L.R. 361; [1971] 2 All E.R. 216   151
Denny, Mott and Dickson Ltd. v. Fraser and Co. Ltd. [1944] A.C.
   265   154
Derry v. Peek (1889) 14 App. Cas. 337   133
Diestelskamp v. Baynes (Reading) Ltd. [1968] 1 Lloyd's Rep. 431   170
Diggle v. Higgs (1877) 2 Ex. D. 422   142
Doble v. David Greig Ltd. [1972] 1 W.L.R. 703; [1972] 2 All E.R.
   195   241
Donoghue v. Stevenson [1932] A.C. 562   238

Drew v. Nunn (1879) 4 Q.B.D. 661   187
Drury v. Victor Buckland Ltd. [1941] 1 All E.R. 269   220
Dunlop Pneumatic Tyre Co. Ltd. v. New Garage and Motor Co.
  Ltd. [1915] A.C. 79   197
Dunlop Pneumatic Tyre Co. Ltd. v. Selfridge and Co. Ltd [1915]
  A.C. 847   111, 210
Durham Bros. v. Robertson [1898] 1 Q.B. 765   84
Dyson v. Peat [1917] 1 Ch. 99   99

Eastern Distributors Ltd. v. Goldring [1957] 2 Q.B. 600; [1957] 2
  All E.R. 525   90
Ebrahimi v. Westbourne Galleries Ltd. [1973] A.C. 360; [1972] 2
  All E.R. 492   49, 53
Eccles v. Bryant and Pollock [1948] Ch. 93; [1947] 2 All E.R. 865   82
Electric Supply Stores v. Gaywood (1909) 100 L.T. 855   100
Eley v. Positive Government Life Assurance Co. (1876) 1 Ex. D. 88   47
Erlanger v. New Sombrero Phosphate Co. (1878) 3 App. Cas. 1218   23
Esso Petroleum Co. Ltd. v. Commissioners of Customs and Excise
  [1976] 1 W.L.R. 1; [1976] 1 All E.R. 117   106
Esso Petroleum Co. Ltd. v. Harper's Garage (Stourport) Ltd.
  [1968] A.C. 269; [1967] 1 All E.R. 699   140, 141, 208
Esso Petroleum Co. Ltd. v. Mardon [1976] Q.B. 801; [1976] 2 All
  E.R. 5   234
Europemballage Corporation and Continental Can Co. Inc. v.
  Commission [1972] E.C.R. 157   215
Evans v. Triplex Safety Glass Co. Ltd. [1936] 1 All E.R. 283   239

F.G. (Films) Ltd., Re [1953] 1 W.L.R. 483; [1953] 1 All E.R. 615   5
Farnworth Finance Facilities Ltd. v. Attryde [1970] 1 W.L.R. 1053;
  [1970] 2 All E.R. 774   127
Federal Commerce and Navigation Ltd. v. Molena Alpha Inc.
  [1979] A.C. 757; [1979] 1 All E.R. 307   119, 163
Federspiel (Carlos) and Co. S.A. v. Charles Twigg and Co. Ltd.
  [1957] 1 Lloyd's Rep. 240   90
Felthouse v. Bindley (1862) 142 E.R. 1037   108
Fibrosa Spolka Akcyjna v. Fairbairn Lawson Combe Barbour Ltd.
  [1943] A.C. 32   154
Financings Ltd. v. Baldcock [1963] 2 Q.B. 104; [1963] 1 All E.R.
  443   221
Financings Ltd. v. Stimson [1962] 1 W.L.R. 1184; [1962] 3 All E.R.
  386   107, 220
Fisher v. Bell [1961] 1 Q.B. 394; [1960] 3 All E.R. 731   106
Foakes v. Beer (1884) 9 App. Cas. 605   110
Foley v. Hill (1848) 9 E.R. 1002   186
Ford, Re [1929] 1 Ch. 135   60
Ford Motor Co. (England) Ltd. v. Armstrong (1915) 31 T.L.R. 267   197
Forster and Sons Ltd. v. Suggett (1918) 35 T.L.R. 87   140
Foss v. Harbottle (1843) 67 E.R. 189   48, 49

Four Maids Ltd. *v*. Dudley Marshall (Properties) Ltd. [1957]
    Ch. 317; [1957] 2 All E.R. 35   97
Four Point Garage Ltd. *v*. Carter, *The Times*, 19 November 1984   92
Fox, *Re* [1948] Ch. 407; [1948] 1 All E.R. 849   60
Freeman and Lockyer *v*. Buckhurst Park Properties (Mangal) Ltd.
    [1964] 2 Q.B. 480; [1964] 1 All E.R. 630   44
Frost *v*. Aylesbury Dairy Co. Ltd. [1905] 1 K.B. 608   123, 235
Frost *v*. Knight (1872) L.R. 7 Exch. 111   152
Fullwood *v*. Hurley [1928] 1 K.B. 498   174

Galley (Michael) Footwear Ltd. *v*. Iaboni [1982] 2 All E.R. 200   162
Galloway *v*. Galloway (1914) 30 T.L.R. 531   136
General Billposting Co. Ltd. *v*. Atkinson [1909] A.C. 118   149
German Date Coffee Co., *Re* (1882) 20 Ch. D. 169   53
Gibbons *v*. Westminster Bank Ltd. [1939] 2 K.B. 883   187
Gibson *v*. Manchester City Council [1979] 1 W.L.R. 294; [1979]
    1 All E.R. 972   108
Gluckstein *v*. Barnes [1900] A.C. 240   23
Godley *v*. Perry [1960] 1 W.L.R. 9; [1960] 1 All E.R. 36   124
Goldsoll *v*. Goldman [1915] 1 Ch. 292   143
Golodetz (M.) and Co. *v*. Czarnikow–Rionda [1980] 1 W.L.R.
    495; [1980] 1 All E.R. 501   149, 165, 166
Gould *v*. South Eastern and Chatham Railway Co. [1920] 2 K.B.
    186   160
Grant *v*. Australian Knitting Mills Ltd. [1936] A.C. 85   123
Great Northern Railway *v*. L.E.P. Transport and Depository Ltd.
    [1922] 2 K.B. 742   160
Great Northern Railway *v*. Swaffield (1874) L.R. 9 Ex. 132   179
Green *v*. All Motors Ltd. [1917] 1 K.B. 625   100
Greenwood *v*. Martins Bank Ltd. [1933] A.C. 51   186, 187
Greer *v*. Sketchley Ltd. [1979] I.R.L.R. 445   141
Greig and Others *v*. Insole [1978] 1 W.L.R. 302; [1978] 3 All E.R.
    449   141
Griffiths *v*. Peter Conway Ltd. [1939] 1 All E.R. 685   123
Gunsbourg, *Re* [1920] 2 K.B. 426   57, 59

Hadley *v*. Baxendale Ltd. (1854) 9 Exch. 341   198
Halliday *v*. Holgate (1868) L.R. 3 Ex. 299   98
Hamlyn *v*. Houston and Co. (1902) 72 L.J.K.B. 72   15
Hamzeh Malas and Sons *v*. British Imex Industries Ltd. [1958]
    2 Q.B. 127; [1958] 1 All E.R. 262   193
Handel (N.V.) *v*. English Exporters (London) Ltd. [1957] 1 Lloyd's
    Rep. 517   166
Hansa Nord, The [1976] Q.B. 44; [1975] 3 All E.R. 739   119
Harris *v*. Nickerson (1873) L.R. 8 Q.B. 286   106
Harrison *v*. Bank of Australasia (1872) L.R. 7 Ex. 39   170
Harrison *v*. Holland [1921], 3 K.B. 297   196
Hartley *v*. Hymans [1920] 3 K.B. 475   146

Hatton v. Car Maintenance Co. Ltd. [1915] 1 Ch. 621   100
Heald v. Kenworthy (1855) 24 L.J. Ex. 76   182
Hedley Byrne and Co. Ltd. v. Heller and Partners Ltd. [1964] A.C.
    465; [1963] 2 All E.R. 575   133
Helby v. Matthews [1895] A.C. 471   218
Hely-Hutchinson v. Brayhead Ltd. [1968] 1 Q.B. 549; [1967] 3 All
    E.R. 98   44, 177
Hermione, The (1922) 126 L.T. 701   173
Higgins v. Beauchamp [1914] 3 K.B. 1192   15
Highley v. Walker (1910) 26 T.L.R. 685   12
Hill v. James Crow (Cases) Ltd. [1978] I.C.R. 298; [1978] 1 All
    E.R. 812   238
Hill v. William Hill (Park Lane) Ltd. [1949] A.C. 530   142
Hillas and Co. Ltd. v. Arcos Ltd. [1932] All E.R. Rep. 494   109
Hodges and Sons v. Hackbridge Park Residential Hotel Ltd. [1939]
    4 All E.R. 347   175
Hoenig v. Isaacs [1952] 2 All E.R. 176   147, 198
Hogg v. Cramphorn Ltd. [1967] Ch. 254; [1966] 3 All E.R. 420   48
Hollier v. Rambler Motors (AMC) Ltd. [1972] 2 Q.B. 71; [1972]
    1 All E.R. 399   127
Holt v. Heatherfield Trust Ltd. [1942] 2 K.B. 1   84
Holwell Securities Ltd. v. Hughes [1974] 1 W.L.R. 155; [1974] 1 All
    E.R. 161   108
Homer District Consolidated Gold Mines Ltd., Re (1888) 39 Ch. D.
    546   39
Horsley and Weight Ltd., Re [1982] 3 W.L.R. 431   39, 41
Houghland v. R.R. Low (Luxury Coaches) Ltd. [1962] 1 Q.B. 694;
    [1962] 2 All E.R. 159   93
Household Fire and Carriage Accident Insurance Co. v. Grant
    (1879) 4 Ex. D. 216   108
Howe v. Smith (1884) 27 Ch. D. 89   196
Hudgell Yeates and Co. v. Watson [1978] 1 W.L.R. 661; [1978]
    2 All E.R. 363   17
Humble v. Hunter (1842) 17 L.J. Q.B. 350   182
Hutton v. Warren (1836) 5 L.J. Ex. 234   117
Hyde v. Wrench (1840) 49 E.R. 132   106

Importers Co. Ltd. v. Westminster Bank Ltd. [1927] 2 K.B. 297   185
Industrial Development Consultants Ltd. v. Cooley [1972]
    1 W.L.R. 443; [1972] 2 All E.R. 162   40
International Sales and Agencies Ltd. v. Marcus [1982] 3 All E.R.
    551   28, 40
Introductions Ltd. v. National Provincial Bank Ltd. [1970] Ch. 199;
    [1969] 1 All E.R. 887   27

Jarvis v. Swans Tours Ltd. [1973] 1 Q.B. 233; [1973] 1 All E.R. 71   196
Joachimson v. Swiss Bank Corporation [1921] 3 K.B. 110   185, 186
Joel v. Law Union and Crown Insurance Co. [1908] 2 K.B. 863   132

Johnson v. Midland Railway Co. (1849) 4 Ex. Ch. 367   160
Jones (R.E.) Ltd. v. Waring and Gillow Ltd. [1926] A.C. 670   85
Joscelyne v. Nissen [1970] 2 Q.B. 86; [1970] 1 All E.R. 1213   138
Jowitt and Son v. Union Cold Storage Co. [1913] 3 K.B. 1   99

Karak Rubber Co. Ltd. v. Burden and Others (No. 2) [1972] 1
    W.L.R. 602; [1972] 1 All E.R. 1210   187, 189
Keighley, Maxted and Co. v. Durant [1901] A.C. 240   179
Kelner v. Baxter (1866) 36 L.J. C.P. 94   24, 179, 180
Kendall v. Hamilton (1879) 4 App. Cas. 504   16
Kenny v. Preen [1963] 1 Q.B. 499; [1962] 3 All E.R. 814   117
Ketley Ltd. v. Scott [1981] I.C.R. 241   228
Kirkham v. Attenborough [1897] 1 Q.B. 201   88, 89
Kish v. Taylor [1912] A.C. 604   167, 169
Knightsbridge Estates Trust Ltd. v. Byrne [1940] A.C. 613   76
Kopitoff v. Wilson (1876) 1 Q.B.D. 377   167
Koufos v. Czarnikow Ltd. (The Heron II) [1969] 1 A.C. 350; [1967]
    3 All E.R. 686   198, 199
Krell v. Henry [1903] 2 K.B. 740   152
Kum and Another v. Wah Tat Bank Ltd. [1971] 1 Lloyd's Rep. 439   165

Ladbroke and Co. v. Todd (1914) 111 L.T. 43   185
Lakeman v. Mountstephen (1874) L.R. 7 H.L. 17   101
Lamb v. Evans [1893] 1 Ch. 218   175
Lancashire Loans Ltd. v. Black [1934] 1 K.B. 380   135, 136
Laurence and Another v. Lexcourt Holdings Ltd. [1978] 1 W.L.R.
    1128; [1978] 2 All E.R. 810   133
Law v. Law [1905] 1 Ch. 140   12
Lazenby Garages Ltd. v. Wright [1976] 1 W.L.R. 459; [1976] 2 All
    E.R. 770   200, 201
Leaf v. International Galleries [1950] 2 K.B. 86; [1950] 1 All E.R.
    693   132, 137, 203
Lee v. Showmen's Guild of Great Britain [1952] 2 Q.B. 329; [1952]
    1 All E.R. 1175   140
Lee v. Walker (1872) L.R. 7 C.P. 121   173
Lennard's Carrying Co. Ltd. v. Asiatic Petroleum Co. Ltd. [1915]
    A.C. 705   236
L'Estrange v. Graucob Ltd. [1934] 2 K.B. 394   127
Lewis v. Averay [1972] 1 Q.B. 198; [1971] 3 All E.R. 907   91, 109, 130, 133
Liverpool City Council v. Irwin [1977] A.C. 239; [1976] 2 All E.R.
    39   117
Lloyds Bank Ltd. v. Bundy [1975] Q.B. 326; [1974] 3 All E.R. 757 135, 188
London Joint Stock Bank Ltd. v. Macmillan and Arthur [1918]
    A.C. 777   186, 187
Lysaght v. Edwards (1876) 2 Ch. D. 499   82, 99

M.F.I. Warehouses Ltd. v. Nattrass [1973] 1 W.L.R. 307; [1973]
    1 All E.R. 762   242
Macaura v. Northern Assurance Co. [1925] A.C. 619   5, 35

McFadden v. Blue Star Line [1905] 1 K.B. 697   167
McPherson v. Watt (1877) 3 App. Cas. 254   174
McRae v. Commonwealth Disposals Commission (1951) 84 C.L.R.
    377   137
Magee v. Pennine Insurance Co. Ltd. [1969] 2 Q.B. 507; [1969]
    2 All E.R. 891   138
Mahoney v. East Holyford Mining Co. (1875) L.R. 7 H.L. 869   45
Maidstone Buildings Provisions Ltd., Re [1971] 1 W.L.R. 1085;
    [1971] 3 All E.R. 363   46
Malfroot and Ano. v. Noxal Ltd. (1935) 51 T.L.R. 557   234, 235, 238
Manbre Saccharine Co. Ltd. v. Corn Products Co. Ltd. [1919]
    1 K.B. 198   165, 166
Manchester Trust v. Furness [1895] 2 Q.B. 539   164
Mann v. D'Arcy [1968] 1 W.L.R. 893; [1968] 2 All E.R. 172   15
Mareva Compania Naviera S.A. v. International Bulkcarriers S.A.
    [1975] 2 Lloyd's Rep. 509   192
Marfani and Co. Ltd. v. Midland Bank Ltd. [1968] 1 W.L.R. 956;
    [1968] 2 All E.R. 573   191
Matthews (F.P. and C.H.) Ltd., Re [1982] 1 All E.R. 338   56
Medicaments Reference (No. 2), Re [1970] 1 W.L.R. 1339; [1971]
    1 All E.R. 12   210
Megevand, Re (1878) 7 Ch. D. 511   11
Menier v. Hooper's Telegraph Works Ltd. (1874) 9 Ch. App. 350   48, 49
Mercantile Credit Co. Ltd. v. Garrod [1962] 3 All E.R. 1103   14
Merritt v. Merritt [1970] 1 W.L.R. 1211; [1970] 2 All E.R. 760   113
Metro v. Commission and Saba [1978] 2 C.M.L.R. 1   215
Metropolitan Asylums Board v. Kingham and Sons (1890) 6 T.L.R.
    217   179
Microbeads A.G. and Another v. Vinhurst Road Markings Ltd.
    [1975] 1 W.L.R. 218; [1975] 1 All E.R. 529   121
Midland Bank Ltd. v. Reckitt [1933] A.C. 1   191
Mihalis Angelos, The [1971] 1 Q.B. 164; [1970] 3 All E.R. 125   118
Miles v. Clark [1953] 1 W.L.R. 537; [1953] 1 All E.R. 779   13
Mitchell v. Ealing London Borough Council [1979] Q.B. 1; [1975]
    2 All E.R. 779   93
Mitchell (George) (Chesterhall) Ltd. v. Finney Lock Seeds Ltd.
    [1983] 2 A.C. 803   127
Monolithic Building, Re [1915] 1 Ch. 643   77
Montedison SpA v. Icroma SpA [1980] 1 W.L.R. 48; [1979] 3 All
    E.R. 378   169
Moorcock, The (1889) 14 P.D. 64   117
Moore and Co. Ltd. and Landauer and Co., Re [1921] 2 K.B. 519   149
Morris v. C. W. Martin and Sons Ltd. [1966] 1 Q.B. 716; [1965]
    2 All E.R. 725   93
Morritt, Re (1886) 18 Q.B.D. 222   97, 98
Motor Traders Guarantee Corporation Ltd. v. Midland Bank Ltd.
    [1937] 4 All E.R. 90   191
Mullen v. Miller (1882) 22 Ch. D. 194   177

Munro (R. A.) and Co. Ltd. *v*. Meyer [1930] 2 K.B. 312   151
Musselwhite *v*. C. H. Musselwhite and Sons Ltd. [1962] Ch. 964;
    [1962] 1 All E.R. 201   31, 35

Natal Land Co. Ltd. *v*. Pauline Colliery Syndicate Ltd. [1904] A.C.
    120   24
Nathan *v*. Ogdens Ltd. (1905) 93 L.T. 553   71
National Westminster Bank Ltd. *v*. Barclays Bank International
    Ltd. and Another [1975] 1 Q.B. 654; [1974] 3 All E.R. 834   187
National Westminster Bank p.l.c *v*. Morgan (1983) 3 All E.R. 85   135
Nelson *v*. James Nelson and Sons Ltd. (1914) 2 K.B. 770   40
Net Book Agreement, *Re* [1962] 1 W.L.R. 1347; [1962] 3 All E.R.
    751   209
New Zealand Shipping Co. Ltd. *v*. A. M. Satterthwaite and Co.
    Ltd. [1975] A.C. 154; [1974] 1 All E.R. 1015   112
Niblett Ltd. *v*. Confectioners' Materials Co. Ltd. [1921] 3 K.B. 387   120, 121
Nicolene Ltd. *v*. Simmonds [1953] 1 Q.B. 543; [1953] 1 All E.R. 822   109
North Ocean Shipping Co. Ltd. *v*. Hyundai Construction Co. Ltd.
    and Another [1979] Q.B. 705; [1978] 3 All E.R. 1170   110, 134
North and South Insurance Corporation *v*. National Provincial
    Bank Ltd. [1936] 1 K.B. 328   71
Nugent *v*. Smith (1876) 1 C.P.D. 423   159, 166

Official Assignee of Madras *v*. Mercantile Bank of India Ltd. [1935]
    A.C. 53   98
Ooregum Gold Mining Co. of India Ltd. *v*. Roper [1892] A.C. 125   32
Oscar Chess Ltd. *v*. Williams [1957] 1 W.L.R. 370; [1957] 1 All
    E.R. 325   116, 136
O'Sullivan *v*. Management Agency and Music Ltd. [1984] 3
    W.L.R. 448   140
Overbrook Estates *v*. Glencombe Properties Ltd. [1974] 1 W.L.R.
    1335; [1974] 3 All E.R. 511   134, 177
Overstone Ltd. *v*. Shipway [1962] 1 W.L.R. 117; [1962] 1 All E.R.
    52   221

Panama, New Zealand and Australia Royal Mail Co., *Re* (1870) 5
    Ch. App. 318   76
Panorama Developments (Guildford) Ltd. *v*. Fidelis Furnishing
    Fabrics Ltd. [1971] 2 Q.B. 711; [1971] 3 All E.R. 16   46, 177
Parker *v*. South Eastern Railway Co. (1877) 2 C.P.D. 416   126
Parkinson *v*. College of Ambulance Ltd. [1925] 2 K.B. 1   139, 142, 143
Partridge *v*. Crittenden [1968] 1 W.L.R. 1204; [1968] 2 All E.R. 421   106
Payzu Ltd. *v*. Saunders [1919] 2 K.B. 581   198
Peachdart Ltd., *Re* [1983] 3 All E.R. 204   89
Pearce and Another *v*. Brooks (1866) L.R. 1 Exch. 213   139
Peat *v*. Clayton [1906] 1 Ch. 659   87
Peek *v*. Gurney (1873) L.R. 6 H.L. 377   131

Percival v. Wright [1902] 2 Ch. 421   40
Peyton v. Mindham [1972] 1 W.L.R. 8; [1971] 3 All E.R. 1215   17
Pharmaceutical Society of Great Britain v. Boots Cash Chemists
   (Southern) Ltd. [1953] 1 Q.B. 401; [1953] 1 All E.R. 482   106
Phillips v. Lamdin [1948] 2 K.B. 33; [1949] 1 All E.R. 770   83
Phonogram Ltd. v. Lane [1981] 3 W.L.R. 736; [1981] 3 All E.R. 182   24
Photo Production Ltd. v. Securicor Transport Ltd. [1980] A.C.
   827; [1980] 1 All E.R. 556   119, 127, 151
Pike, Sons and Co. v. Ongley and Thornton (1887) 18 Q.B.D. 708   180
Pirie v. Middle Dock Co. (1881) 44 L.T. 426   170
Plaché v. Colburn (1831) 131 E.R. 305   148
Port Jackson Stevedoring Pty. Ltd. v. Salmond and Spraggon
   (Australia) Pty. Ltd. [1981] 1 W.L.R. 138; [1980] 3 All E.R. 257   112
Poussard v. Spiers and Pond (1876) 1 Q.B.D. 410   118
Powell v. Lee (1908) 99 L.T. 284   107
Prager v. Blatspiel, Stamp and Heacock Ltd. [1924] 1 K.B. 566   179
Priestley v. Fernie (1865) 34 L.J. Ex. 172   182

Quistclose Investments Ltd. v. Rolls Razor Ltd. and Ano. [1968]
   1 Ch. 540   186

R. v. Hammertons Cars Ltd. (1977) 75 L.G.R. 4   240
R. v. I.C.R. Haulage Ltd. [1944] K.B. 551   236
R. v. Sunair Holidays Ltd. [1973] 1 W.L.R. 1105; [1973] 2 All E.R.
   1233   242
R. v. Thomson Holidays Ltd. [1974] Q.B. 592; [1974] 1 All E.R.
   823   242, 244
Rahman (Prince Abdul) v. Abu-Taha [1980] 1 W.L.R. 1268; [1980]
   3 All E.R. 409   192
Ramsgate Victoria Hotel Co. v. Montefiore (1866) L.R. 1 Ex.
   109   107
Rawlinson v. Ames [1925] 1 Ch. 96   82
Rayfield v. Hands [1960] Ch. 1; [1958] 2 All E.R. 194   47
Rayner (J.H.) and Co. Ltd. v. Hambros Bank Ltd. [1942] 2 All
   E.R. 694   193
Read v. Astoria Garage (Streatham) Ltd. [1952] Ch. 637; [1952]
   2 All E.R. 292   38
Read Bros. Cycles (Leyton) Ltd. v. Waltham Forest London
   Borough Council (1978) 76 L.G.R. 741   241
Reading v. Attorney General [1951] A.C. 507; [1951] 1 All E.R.
   617   175
Regal (Hastings) Ltd. v. Gulliver [1942] 1 All E.R. 378   40, 174
Regenet OHG Aisenstadt una Barig v. Francesco of Jermyn Street
   Ltd. [1981] 3 All E.R. 327   151
Reid v. Commissioner of Police for the Metropolis [1973] 1 Q.B.
   557; [1973] 2 All E.R. 97   91
Rickards (Charles) Ltd. v. Oppenheim [1950] 1 K.B. 616; [1950]
   1 All E.R. 420   148

Roberts v. Elwells Engineers Ltd. [1972] 2 Q.B. 586; [1972] 2 All
   E.R. 890   176
Robinson v. Graves [1935] 1 K.B. 579   124
Robinson v. Harman (1848) 18 L.J. Ex. 202   196
Rodriguez v. Speyer Bros. [1919] A.C. 59   13
Roith (W. and M.) Ltd., Re [1967] 1 W.L.R. 432; [1967] 1 All E.R.
   427   41
Roscorla v. Thomas (1842) 114 E.R. 496   110
Rose v. Plenty and Another [1976] 1 W.L.R. 141; [1976] 1 All E.R.
   97   237
Rose and Frank Co. v. Crompton Bros. Ltd. [1923] 2 K.B. 261   113
Rosenthal v. London County Council (1924) 131 L.T. 563   160
Rouse v. Bradford Banking Co. [1894] A.C. 586   187
Rowland v. Divall [1923] 2 K.B. 500   120, 201
Rowlandson and Others v. National Westminster Bank Ltd. [1978]
   1 W.L.R. 798; [1978] 3 All E.R. 370   188
Roxburghe v. Cox (1881) 17 Ch. D. 520   84
Royal British Bank v. Turquand [1843–60] All E.R. Rep. 435   45
Ryan v. Mutual Tontine Association [1893] 1 Ch. 116   202

Sachs v. Miklos and Others [1948] 2 K.B. 23   94, 180
Said v. Butt [1920] 3 K.B. 497   182
Salomon v. Salomon and Co. Ltd. [1897] A.C. 22   4, 5
Sandeman v. Scurr (1867) L.R. 2 Q.B. 86   163
Sartoris' Estate, Re [1892] 1 Ch. 11   58
Saunders v. Anglia Building Society [1971] A.C. 1004; [1970] 3 All
   E.R. 961   138
Scammell v. Ouston [1941] A.C. 251   109
Schiffahrt and Kohlen G.m.b.H. v. Chelsea Maritime Ltd. [1982]
   2 W.L.R. 422   166
Schmalz v. Avery (1851) 20 L.J. Q.B. 228   181
Schuler A. G. v. Wickman Machine Tool Sales Ltd. [1974] A.C.
   235; [1973] 2 All E.R. 39   118
Scottish Insurance Corporation Ltd. v. Wilson and Clyde Coal Co.
   [1949] A.C. 462; [1949] 1 All E.R. 1068   75
Scriven Bros. and Co. v. Hindley and Co. [1913] 3 K.B. 564 109, 136
Scruttons Ltd. v. Midland Silicones Ltd. [1962] A.C. 446; [1962]
   1 All E.R. 1   111, 125
Selangor United Rubber Estates Ltd. v. Cradock (No. 3) [1968]
   1 W.L.R. 1555; [1968] 2 All E.R. 1073   187
Sewell v. Burdick (1884) 10 App. Cas. 74   169
Sharpley v. Louth and East Coast Railway Co. (1876) 2 Ch. D. 663 132
Shaw v. Benson (1883) 11 Q.B.D. 563   4
Shaw (John) and Sons (Salford) Ltd. v. Shaw [1935] 2 K.B. 113   43
Shipton, Anderson and Co. v. Weil Bros. and Co. [1912] 1 K.B.
   574   122
Slingsby and Others v. District Bank Ltd. [1932] 1 K.B. 544   186
Smith v. Anderson (1880) 15 Ch. D. 247   10

Smith v. Chadwick (1884) 9 App. Cas. 187   131
Smith v. Land and House Property Corporation (1884) 28 Ch. D. 7   131
Smith and Fawcett Ltd., Re [1942] Ch. 304   86
Smith (Howard) Ltd. v. Ampol Petroleum Ltd. [1974] A.C. 821;
[1974] 1 All E.R. 1126   41
Sobell v. Boston [1975] 1 W.L.R. 1587; [1975] 2 All E.R. 282   18
Solle v. Butcher [1950] 1 K.B. 671; [1949] 2 All E.R. 1107   137
Sorrell and Another v. Finch [1977] A.C. 728; [1976] 2 All E.R. 371   177
Southern Foundries (1926) Ltd. v. Shirlaw [1940] 2 All E.R. 445   42, 48
Spector v. Ageda [1973] Ch. 30; [1971] 3 All E.R. 417   142
Spicer (Keith) Ltd. v. Mansell [1970] 1 W.L.R. 333; [1970] 1 All
E.R. 462   10
Spiers v. Taylor [1984] 271 E.S. 196   175
Spiro v. Lintern [1973] 1 W.L.R. 1002; [1973] 3 All E.R. 319   173
Spurling Ltd. v. Bradshaw [1956] 1 W.L.R. 461; [1956] 2 All E.R.
121   126
Standard Manufacturing Co., Re [1891] 1 Ch. 627   97
Startup and Another v. Macdonald (1843) L.J. Ex. 477   145
Steadman v. Steadman [1976] A.C. 536; [1974] 2 All E.R. 977   82
Stennett v. Hancock and Peters [1939] 2 All E.R. 578   238
Stevenson v. Beverley Bentinck Ltd. [1976] 1 W.L.R. 483; [1976]
2 All E.R. 606   92
Stock v. Inglis (1884) 12 Q.B.D. 564   166
Strongman (1945) Ltd. v. Sincock [1955] 2 Q.B. 525; [1955] All
E.R. 90   116, 143
Suisse Atlantique Société D'Armement Maritime S.A. v. N.V.
Rotterdamsche Kolen Centrale [1967] 1 A.C. 361; [1966] 2 All
E.R. 61   127
Sumpter v. Hedges [1898] 1 Q.B. 673   147, 148
Swaledale Cleaners, Re [1968] 1 W.L.R. 1710; [1968] 3 All E.R.
619   86
Swan, The [1968] 1 Lloyd's Rep. 5   180
Sze Hai Tong Bank Ltd. v. Rambler Cycle Co. Ltd. [1959] A.C.
576; [1959] 3 All E.R. 182   164

Taupo Totara Timber Co. Ltd. v. Rowe [1977] 3 W.L.R. 466;
[1977] 3 All E.R. 123   43
Taylor v. Caldwell (1863) 122 E.R. 309   153
Taylor v. Smith [1974] Crim. L.R. 200   239, 240
Taylor v. Webb [1937] 2 K.B. 283   148
Tesco Supermarkets Ltd. v. Nattrass [1972] A.C. 153; [1971] 2 All
E.R. 127   237, 243
Thomas v. Brown (1876) 1 Q.B.D. 714   82
Thomas v. Thomas (1842) 114 E.R. 330   110
Thompson v. Robinson (Gunmakers) Ltd. [1955] Ch. 177; [1955]
1 All E.R. 154   200
Thompson Trustee v. Heaton [1974] 1 W.L.R. 605; [1974] 1 All
E.R. 1239   12

Thornton v. Shoe Lane Parking Ltd. [1971] 2 Q.B. 163; [1971] 1 All
E.R. 686 — 126

Tiessen v. Henderson [1898] 1 Ch. 861 — 32

Tiverton Estates Ltd. v. Wearwell Ltd. [1975] Ch. 146; [1974] 1 All
E.R. 209 — 82

Tote Investors Ltd. v. Smoker [1968] 1 Q.B. 509; [1967] 3 All E.R.
242 — 142

Toulmin v. Millar (1887) 12 App. Cas. 746 — 175

Tournier v. National Provincial and Union Bank of England [1924]
1 K.B. 461 — 188

Tower Cabinet Co. Ltd. v. Ingram [1949] 2 K.B. 397; [1949] 1 All
E.R. 1033 — 10, 16

Travers (Joseph) and Son Ltd. v. Cooper [1915] 1 K.B. 73 — 159

Tunstall v. Steigman [1962] 2 Q.B. 593; [1962] 2 All E.R. 417 — 5

Tyre Trade Register Agreement, Re [1963] 1 W.L.R. 367; [1963]
1 All E.R. 890 — 209

Underwood Ltd. v. Burgh Castle Brick and Cement Syndicate
[1921] All E.R. Rep. 515 — 89

Union Transport Finance Ltd. v. British Car Auctions Ltd. [1978]
2 All E.R. 385 — 222

United Brands Co. v. Commission [1978] E.C.R. 207 — 214

United Dominions Trust v. Ennis [1968] 1 Q.B. 54; [1967] 2 All
E.R. 345 — 222

United Dominions Trust v. Kirkwood [1966] 2 Q.B. 431; [1966]
1 All E.R. 968 — 184

United Dominions Trust v. Western [1976] 1 Q.B. 513; [1975] 3 All
E.R. 1017 — 139

United Scientific Holdings v. Burnley Borough Council [1978]
A.C. 904; [1977] 2 All E.R. 62 — 146

Universal Guarantee Property Ltd. v. National Bank of Australasia
Ltd. [1965] 1 W.L.R. 691; [1965] 2 All E.R. 98 — 190

Universal Steam Navigation Co. v. McKelvie [1923] A.C. 492 — 180

Wales v. Wadham [1977] 1 W.L.R. 199; [1977] 2 All E.R. 125 — 132

Walker v. Boyle [1982] 1 W.L.R. 495 — 134

Wallersteiner v. Moir (No. 2) [1975] 1 Q.B. 373; [1975] 1 All E.R.
849 — 49

Wallis, Son and Wells v. Pratt and Haynes [1910] 2 K.B. 1003 — 118

Waltham Forest London Borough Council v. T. G. Wheatley
(Central Garages) Ltd. (1978) 76 L.G.R. 195 — 240

Warmington and Another v. Miller [1973] Q.B. 877; [1973] 2 All
E.R. 372 — 202

Warner Bros. Pictures Inc. v. Nelson [1937] 1 K.B. 209 — 202

Watson v. Davies [1931] 1 Ch. 455 — 178

Watteau v. Fenwick [1893] 1 Q.B. 346 — 181

Webb v. Earle (1875) L.R. 20 Eq. 556 — 75

Weiner v. Gill [1906] 2 K.B. 574 — 90

Weiner v. Harris [1910] 1 K.B. 285   178
White and Carter (Councils) Ltd. v. McGregor [1962] A.C. 413;
    [1961] 3 All E.R. 1178   152, 197
Whitwood Chemical Co. v. Hardman [1891] 2 Ch. 416   202
Wickens Motors (Gloucester) Ltd. v. Hall [1972] 1 W.L.R. 1418;
    [1972] 3 All E.R. 248   240
Wilhelm and Others v. Bundeskartellamt [1969] E.C.R. 1   204
Will v. United Lankat Plantations Co. [1914] A.C. 11   75
Williams v. Bayley (1866) L.R. 1 H.L. 200   135
Williams and Another v. Wellingborough Borough Council [1975]
    1 W.L.R. 1327; [1975] 3 All E.R. 462   96
Williamson v. Rider [1963] 1 Q.B. 89; [1962] 2 All E.R. 268   71
Wills v. Wood, *The Times*, March 3 1984   228
Wings Ltd. v. Ellis (1984) 3 All E.R. 577   242, 243
Winn v. Bull (1877) 7 Ch. D. 29   82
Wise v. Perpetual Trustee Co. [1903] A.C. 139   2
With v. O'Flanagan [1936] Ch. 575   131
Wood v. Odessa Waterworks (1889) 42 Ch. D. 636   47, 48
Woodar Investment Development Ltd. v. Wimpey Construction
    U.K. Ltd. [1980] 1 W.L.R. 277; [1980] 1 All E.R. 571   151, 156
Woods v. Martins Bank Ltd. [1959] 1 Q.B. 55; [1958] 3 All E.R. 166   185
Worcester Works Finance Ltd. v. Cooden Engineering Co. Ltd.
    [1972] 1 Q.B. 210; [1971] 3 All E.R. 708   92
Wyatt v. The Marquis of Hertford (1802) 102 E.R. 553   182
Wycombe Marsh Garages Ltd. v. Fowler [1972] 1 W.L.R. 1156;
    [1972] 3 All E.R. 248   240

Yenidje Tobacco Co. Ltd., *Re* [1916] 2 Ch. 426   53
Yeoman Credit Ltd. v. Waragowski [1961] 1 W.L.R. 1124 [1961]
    3 All E.R. 145   221, 222
Yonge v. Toynbee [1910] 1 K.B. 215   181
Young and Martin Ltd. v. McManus Childs Ltd. [1969] 1 A.C. 454;
    [1968] 2 All E.R. 1169   124, 125

Table of Statutes

1677 Statute of Frauds (29 Car. 2, c.3)
    s.4 101
1830 Carriers Act (11 Geo. 4 & 1 Will. 4, c.68)
    s.1 160
1845 Gaming Act (8 & 9 Vict., c.109) 173
    s.18 141
1855 Bills of Lading Act (18 & 19 Vict., c.111)
    s.1 ....165, 168
1874 Infants Relief Act (37 & 38 Vict., c.62)
    s.1 ....101, 113
1878 Bills of Sale Act (41 & 42 Vict., c.31) 97
1882 Bills of Sale Act (1878) (Amendment) Act (45 & 46 Vict., c.43) 97
Bills of Exchange Act (45 & 46 Vict., c.61) 70, 184
    s.2 ....72, 184
    s.3 71
    s.5 72
    s.8 ....72, 85
    s.11 71
    s.17 71
    s.23 73
    s.24 ....85, 187
    s.27 ....85, 86
    s.29 ....85, 86
    s.31 85
    s.34 72
    s.38 85
    s.47 73
    s.54 72
    s.60 190
    s.73 73
    s.74 73
    s.75 187
    s.76 189
    s.77 189

    s.79 189
    s.80 190
    s.81 189
    s.82 191
    s.83 74
1889 Factors Act (52 & 53 Vict., c.45) 91
    s.1 173
    s.2 177
    s.8 ....92, 218
    s.9 92
1890 Partnership Act (53 & 54 Vict., c.39)
    s.1 ....2, 9, 10
    s.2 ....10, 11
    s.3 60
    s.4 9
    s.5 ....11, 14
    s.6 9
    s.7 14
    s.8 14
    s.9 ....2, 15
    s.10 ....15, 236
    s.11 15
    s.14 10
    s.17 16
    s.19 12
    s.20 12
    s.21 12
    s.22 13
    s.23 13
    s.24 ....11, 13
    s.25 12
    s.28 12
    s.29 12
    s.30 12
    s.31 13
    s.32 17
    s.33 ....13, 17, 61
    s.34 17
    s.35 17
    s.36 16
    s.38 17

	s.39	13
	s.42	18
	s.44	18
	s.45	10
1906	Marine Insurance Act (6 Edw. 7, c.41)	170
1907	Limited Partnerships Act (7 Edw. 7, c.24)	18, 19
1914	Bankruptcy Act (4 & 5 Geo. 5, c.59)	52, 56, 57
	s.1	57
	s.3	57
	s.4	57
	s.6	57
	s.7	58
	s.13	58
	s.14	58
	s.15	58
	s.16	58
	s.18	58
	s.20	58
	s.22	58
	s.26	61, 62
	s.28	61
	s.33	60
	s.36	60
	s.37	59
	s.38	59
	s.38A	60
	s.44	59
	s.45	59
	s.62	59
	s.69	61
	s.127	61
1925	Law of Property Act (15 Geo. 5, c.20)	
	s.1	68
	s.40	82
	s.41	146
	s.85	96
	s.86	96
	s.87	96, 97
	s.88	97
	s.89	97
	s.101	96
	s.105	96
	s.126	97
	s.136	83

	Land Registration Act (15 Geo. 5, c.21)	
	s.19	83
	s.22	83
1938	Trade Marks Act (1 & 2 Geo. 6, c.22)	
	s.2	79
	s.4	79
	s.20	79
	s.22	79
	s.68	79
1943	Law Reform (Frustrated Contracts) Act (6 & 7 Geo. 6, c.40)	154, 155
	s.1	148
1948	Companies Act (11 & 12 Geo. 6, c.38)	4
	s.1	21, 22
	s.2	27
	s.5	28, 43
	s.8	29
	s.9	29
	s.10	43
	s.12	22
	s.20	29, 47
	s.26	22, 35
	s.27	35
	s.31	6
	s.38	25
	s.43	23, 25
	s.44	25
	s.47	25
	s.53	26
	s.66	31
	s.73	81
	s.75	86, 88
	s.78	86
	s.80	86
	s.81	87
	s.94	76
	s.95	77
	s.96	77
	s.110	35
	s.116	35
	s.117	87
	s.131	31
	s.132	31
	s.133	31

1948 Companies Act
(*contd.*)
    s.134................................32
    s.136................................32
    s.141................................32
    s.142................................32
    s.165................................50
    s.176........................21, 37
    s.177................................46
    s.180................................45
    s.182................................37
    s.184............32, 42, 43, 50
    s.188................................37
    s.191................................42
    s.194................................43
    s.199................................40
    s.200................................38
    s.212............5, 21, 36, 55
    s.222........................49, 53
    s.224................................53
    s.235................................54
    s.236................................54
    s.238................................54
    s.245................................55
    s.246................................54
    s.252................................54
    s.273................................55
    s.274................................56
    s.278................................54
    s.283................................54
    s.290................................56
    s.293................................54
    s.294................................54
    s.300................................56
    s.303................................55
    s.317................................56
    s.319................................56
    s.320................................56
    s.322................................56
    s.332............................6, 46
    s.353................................56
    s.434..................................4
    s.455........................24, 36
1956 Copyright Act (4 & 5 Eliz. 2,
    c.74) 77
    s.2..................................78
    s.7..................................78
    s.36................................78

    s.49................................78
1957 Cheques Act (5 & 6 Eliz. 2,
    c.36) 184
    s.1................................190
    s.4..................184, 191, 192
1958 Prevention of Fraud (Invest-
    ments) Act (6 & 7 Eliz. 2,
    c.45) 25
    s.13................................26
1961 Carriage by Air Act (9 & 10
    Eliz. 2, c.27) 162
1962 Building Societies Act (10 &
    11 Eliz. 2, c.37) 4
    Transport Act (10 & 11 Eliz.
    2, c.46) 161
1963 Stock Transfer Act (c.18)...86
1964 Hire-Purchase Act (c.53)
   219
    s.27................................92
    s.29................................92
1965 Carriage of Goods by Road
    Act (c.37) 161, 162, 163
1967 Misrepresentation Act (c.7)
    ....25, 234
    s.2................................133
    s.3..........................133, 134
    Companies Act (c.81)
    s.35........................50, 53
    s.120..................................4
1968 Trade   Descriptions   Act
    (c.29) 236, 237
    s.1..........236, 239, 240, 242
    s.2................................239
    s.3................................239
    s.6................................239
    s.11..........................241, 243
    s.14................241, 242, 243
    s.20................................237
    s.23..........................242, 243
    s.24..........................240, 243
    s.26................................243
1969 Family Law Reform Act
    (c.46) 112
    Post Office Act (c.48)............4
    Law of Property Act (c.59)
    s.23................................83
1971 Carriage of Goods by Sea
    Act (c.19) 165, 167, 168

Unsolicited Goods and
Services Act (c.30) 108
1972 European Communities Act
(c.68) s.9 .... 5, 23, 24,
27, 28, 29, 45, 180
1973 Supply of Goods (Implied
Terms) Act (c.13) 117, 206,
220
   s.8 128
   ss.8–10 124
Fair Trading Act (c.41)
   s.2 204
   s.3 205
   s.6 212
   s.7 212
   s.8 212
   s.13 205
   s.14 205
   s.15 205
   s.16 205
   s.17 .... 204, 205, 206
   s.19 205
   s.23 206
   s.26 206
   s.27 207
   s.34 207
   s.35 207
   s.49 213
   s.50 .... 212, 213
   s.51 212
   s.54 213
   s.56 213
   s.58 213
   s.64 213
   s.72 213
   s.73 213
   s.76 213
   s.88 213
   s.130 244
Powers of Criminal Courts
Act (c.62) 244
1974 Consumer Credit Act (c.39)
.... 105, 135, 184, 216
   s.8 217
   s.9 217
   s.10 217
   s.11 224
   s.12 224

s.13 224
s.14 218
s.15 218
s.16 227
s.17 225
s.21 228
s.22 228
s.25 229
s.32 229
s.39 228
s.43 229
s.44 229
s.46 229
s.51 218
s.55 .... 225, 226
s.56 .... 220, 226
s.57 220
s.60 225
s.61 225
s.62 .... 98, 225
s.63 .... 98, 225
s.64 .... 98, 225
s.65 225
s.67 225
s.69 .... 220, 225
s.70 226
s.72 226
s.74 226
s.75 226
s.77–79 227
s.87 .... 222, 226
s.88 .... 222, 223
s.89 223
s.90 .... 223, 226
s.94 .... 222, 226
s.95 222
s.99 .... 222, 223, 226
s.100 222
s.102 221
s.105 101
s.106 101
s.113 102
s.114 98
s.115 98
s.116 98
s.117 99
s.119 99
s.120 98

1974 Consumer Credit Act
      (*contd.*)
         s.137................................228
         s.138................................228
         s.139................................228
         s.145................................219
         s.189......217, 219, 223, 225
      Trade Union and Labour
      Relations Act (c.52) 2
1976 Restrictive Trade Practices
      Act (c.34) 204, 211
         s.1..................205, 207, 208
         s.2.........................142, 208
         s.5...................................204
         s.6...................................208
         s.7...................................208
         s.10.........................208, 209
         s.11...................................208
         s.12...................................208
         s.13...................................208
         s.19.........................208, 209
         s.24...................................207
         s.28...................................208
         s.35...................................207
         s.43...................................208
      Stock Exchange (Comple-
      tion of Bargains) Act
      (c.47) 86
      Resale Prices Act (c.53) ...204
         s.1.........................139, 209
         s.9...................................209
         s.11...................................209
         s.14...................................209
         s.15...................................209
         s.26...................................209
      Insolvency Act (c.60).........61
         s.6.....................................58
         s.9.....................................37
      Companies Act (c.69)
         s.14.....................................32
         s.15.....................................32
         s.21.....................................22
         s.23.....................................23
         s.29.....................................37
1977 Torts (Interference with
      Goods) Act (c.32)
         s.1.....................................99
         s.12.........................100, 180

      Patents Act (c. 37)
         s.1................................78, 79
         s.30...................................79
         s.61...................................79
      Unfair Contract Terms Act
      (c.50) 120, 125, 126,
                     127, 134, 160, 220
         s.1...................................128
         s.2...................................128
         s.3...................................128
         s.5.........................128, 129
         s.6.........................128, 206
         s.7.........................128, 129
         s.9...................................119
         s.11.........................128, 134
         s.12...................................128
1978 Consumer Safety Act (c.38)
         s.1...................................235
         s.2...................................235
         s.3...................................235
         s.6...................................236
      Civil Liability (Contri-
      bution) Act (c.47) 16
1979 Banking Act (c.37).........174,
                               184, 226
         s.1...................................193
         s.2...................................193
         s.3.........................185, 194
         s.21...................................194
         s.22...................................194
         s.23...................................194
         s.28...................................194
         s.29...................................194
         s.36...................................185
      Estate Agents Act (c.38)
         s.14...................................174
         s.18...................................175
         s.21...................................174
      Merchant Shipping Act
      (c.39) 166
      Sale of Goods Act (c.54)....81,
                       117, 124, 151,
                       206, 220, 223
         s.2.....................................89
         s.3.........................112, 113
         s.4...................................105
         s.5.....................................69
         s.6...................................137

s.7 154
s.10 146
s.11 .... 118, 151
s.12 .... 120, 121, 128
s.13 ...... 121, 122, 128, 149
s.14 .... 122, 123, 128
s.15 .... 123, 128
s.16 .... 70, 90
s.17 89
s.18 89
s.20 .... 88, 90
s.21 90
s.22 91
s.24 92
s.25 92
s.27 .... 149, 216
s.28 .... 165, 216
s.29 149
s.30 149
s.31 .... 148, 151
s.32 .... 149, 166
s.34 150
s.35 .... 150, 151
s.36 150
s.39 .... 99, 200
s.41 200
s.44 200
s.48 200
s.49 .... 88, 197, 199
s.50 .... 199, 200, 201
s.51 201
s.52 201
s.53 201
s.54 201
s.57 108
s.61 .... 69, 118,
                                 149, 200
s.62 69
1980 Competition Act (c.21)
.... 204
s.2 211
s.3 212
s.4 212
s.5 212
s.8 212
s.9 212
s.10 212
s.11 214

s.12 214
Companies Act (c.22)
s.1 .... 21, 26
s.2 .... 21, 27
s.3 .... 21, 23
s.4 .... 21, 30
s.5 .... 22, 32
s.6 22
s.14 41
s.15 22
s.16 25
s.17 26
s.20 30
s.21 30
s.22 30
s.24 30
s.29 30
s.32 32
s.34 31
s.39 31
s.47 42
s.54 40
s.68 42
s.72 42
s.75 50
s.78 21
s.79 .... 22, 46
s.87 30
Transport Act (c.34)
.... 161
Magistrates' Courts Act
(c.43) 244
Limitation Act (c.58) 203
1981 Supreme Court Act (c.54)
.... 192
Companies Act (c.62)
s.29 9
s.42 22
s.43 22
s.45 .... 31, 75
s.46 31
s.54 22
s.63 22
1982 Supply of Goods and
Services Act (c.29) 129
s.2 215
s.3 215
s.4 215

1982 Supply of Goods and
      Services Act
      (*contd.*)
         s.5................................215
         s.6................................215
         s.7.................................94
         s.8................................125

         s.9................................125
         s.10...............................125
         s.12...............................150
         s.13...............................150
         s.14...............................150
         s.15...............................150

CHAPTER ONE

The Organisation and its Legal Status

CHAPTER OBJECTIVES

After studying this chapter you should be able to:
* describe the main characteristics of unincorporated associations;
* explain the legal status of such organisations;
* outline the various methods of achieving corporate status; and
* explain the effect of incorporation on the business organisation and its members.

INTRODUCTION

The forms of organisation available to businesses fall into two main categories in law:

(*a*) that in which organisations have no legal status apart from that enjoyed by the individuals of which they are composed and

(*b*) that where organisations are endowed with legal personality having undergone a process of incorporation.

Consequently, a person operating his business as a sole trader or any group of persons associated for the purposes of some common venture, whether it be for business purposes or otherwise, often have a choice between an unincorporated form of association and one which is incorporated or, in other words, possesses corporate personality (*see* p. 3).

UNINCORPORATED ORGANISATIONS

This section is concerned with the nature of unincorporated organisations, the implications of membership and the means by which legal actions involving such associations are commenced and defended.

Definition and characteristics

Unincorporated organisations comprise associations of persons (and, indeed, organisations with a single proprietor) formed with the object of pursuing some business or other activity and possessing no status in law except that which belongs to the participating members. Rights and duties created in the course of the association's activity devolve on the individual members directly. An important form of unincorporated association is the partnership, the essential characteristic of which is that it "subsists between persons carrying on a business in common with a view of profit" (s.1, Partnership Act 1890).

Other examples are those sports and social clubs and friendly societies which have not sought incorporation under the Companies Acts and trade unions. In the latter case, only the unincorporated form of association is possible since the acquisition of corporate status is prohibited (Trade Union and Labour Relations Act 1974 (as amended)).

As an unincorporated association has no recognisable status in law, it is in principle subject to the disability that no action may be commenced or defended in the association's name. This is particularly true of unincorporated clubs, but the Rules of the Supreme Court allow partners to sue or be sued in the firm's name and trade unions have a similar facility conferred by statute (Trade Union and Labour Relations Act 1974). A further difficulty arises with respect to the property of clubs and similar societies which normally belongs to all the members jointly (although it can only be realised by individual members if and when the club is dissolved—*Abbatt* v. *Treasury Solicitor and Others* (1969)). For practical purposes therefore, it is necessary in such cases to vest the title to land and other property in trustees who are permitted to manage it for the members' benefit. The vesting of property in trustees is in fact required by statute in the case of trade unions and registered friendly societies.

There are special rules applicable to partnership property and these will be considered in the next chapter.

Membership
Relationships between the members of unincorporated associations are regulated principally by the law of contract, therefore the rights and duties of each member are to be determined in the first instance by reference to the society's rules or the partnership agreement. It is, however, an implied condition of membership of a club that, in the absence of a contrary provision in the rules, no person may be required to contribute to the funds more than the amount of his subscription (*Wise* v. *Perpetual Trustee Co.* (1903)).

Further, whereas partners are jointly liable for all the debts of the firm (s.9, Partnership Act 1890), an ordinary member of a club will incur no liability in respect of contracts made with outsiders, unless he personally assumes responsibility (for example as a committee member) or in some other way authorises the transaction (*see* the rules relating to agency in Chapter 14). Neither is a member automatically liable for torts arising in the course of the club's activities. Liability is dependent on the aggrieved plaintiff establishing either that the member concerned, whether alone or with other members, committed the act complained of, or is vicariously responsible as the wrongdoer's employer or principal. In fact, in *Campbell* v. *Thompson* (1953), where the plaintiff alleged that injuries she had sustained whilst carrying out cleaning duties resulted from defects in the club premises, the action was allowed to proceed against the defendants as representatives of all the members, because the court took the view that the entire club membership was technically in occupation of the premises.

On the other hand, where a spectator at a football match was injured when a stand collapsed, only the committee members of the offending club were held to blame, because it was they who had employed an incompetent contractor to repair the stand: no liability at all devolved on the non-committee members of the club (*Brown* v. *Lewis* (1896)). The liability of partnerships in tort arises where the wrongdoing has been authorised by the partners or where it is committed in the ordinary course of the firm's business.

Representative actions

In many cases it is clearly not practical to sue all the members of an unincorporated association, especially where the membership is large (there were more than two thousand members in *Campbell's* case, for example). Consequently, there is available in law a procedure whereby a small number of members can be proceeded against, as representatives of the entire membership of the association; this is known as a *representative action*. A basic requirement is, however, that the persons represented should have some common interest in defending the claim, as in *Campbell* v. *Thompson,* where all the members of the club were regarded as both occupiers of the premises and employers of the injured plaintiff.

Where it is necessary to commence an action on behalf of an unincorporated association, similar considerations apply.

CORPORATE PERSONALITY

In this section we consider the methods and effect of incorporation and note how the law will in some cases depart from the principle of separate legal personality

Methods of incorporation

The most common method by which business and other organisations acquire corporate personality and hence full legal recognition is by registration under the Companies Acts. Incorporation by royal charter is also possible but this is an exceptional
procedure. In some cases, the nature of the business may be such
that a particular method of incorporation is prescribed by law.
For example, building societies owe their corporate status to the
Building Societies Act 1962. Further, there are statutes providing
for the incorporation of specific organisations; the Post Office for
instance was established as a body corporate under the Post Office
Act 1969. The European Communities, as supra-national organisations, have legal personality by virtue of the Treaties under which
they have been created (*see*, for example, article 210, EEC Treaty).

Because of legal difficulties inherent in permitting businesses to
be operated by large unincorporated companies, Parliament has
made incorporation compulsory in certain cases. Thus any company, association or partnership which consists of more than
twenty persons and whose business object is the acquisition of gain
must register as a company under the Companies Act 1948, if not
already incorporated in some other way (s.434). Some partnerships, for example those of solicitors and accountants, are
however exempt from this requirement (s.120, Companies Act
1967).

Any association which exceeds the above limitations on
membership and does not obtain incorporation is regarded by the
courts as illegal. In *Shaw* v. *Benson* (1883), the plaintiff sought to
recover on behalf of an unincorporated building society a sum of
money which had been lent to the defendant. The society was
found to be an illegal association because it had a membership in
excess of that permitted by statute. Consequently, the contract for
repayment was also illegal and the loan was deemed irrecoverable.

Effect of incorporation

Whichever method of incorporation is adopted, the effect is to
confer on the association concerned a legal status and personality,
which is different from, and independent of, that enjoyed by each
of its members. Furthermore, the fact that a corporation is under
the control of one person only does not necessarily affect this
position. In *Salomon* v. *Salomon and Co. Ltd.* (1897), Salomon
sold his boot and shoe manufacturing business to a newly formed
limited company which he controlled (various members of his
family were each given a nominal shareholding to comply with
statutory requirements). The company subsequently experienced

difficulties and went into liquidation but the assets were not sufficient to pay all the creditors' claims. In an action brought by the liquidator, the House of Lords reversed the lower court's decision that Salomon should indemnify the company in respect of the money it owed to the creditors. In allowing Salomon's appeal, it was decided that, although a business might be the same after incorporation as it was before, the company was neither the members' agent nor their trustee: a company was in law a different person from its members. It did not follow that a company which was under the absolute control of one person could not be properly incorporated.

Other consequences of incorporation are that the members of the association cease to have any legal or equitable interest in its property (*Macaura* v. *Northern Assurance Co.* (1925)), legal actions may be commenced or defended in the corporate name and, unlike partnerships, the existence of a corporation remains unaffected by the death or bankruptcy of its members. Further, the members of an incorporated association are in principle not responsible for the association's debts (*Salomon* v. *Salomon*) although a partial liability does exist in the case of membership of a limited company registered under the Companies Act 1948, since, on a winding up, members may be required to contribute any sums which have not already been paid in respect of the shares they hold (s.212, Companies Act 1948). In addition, it may be observed that, whereas natural persons and partnerships are under no constraints as to the transactions they can enter into, apart from those imposed by the ordinary law of contract, statutory and registered companies will lack the necessary capacity to carry on their business if their powers are exceeded (subject however to the possible application of s.9, European Communities Act 1972, which is considered in Chapter 3).

Departures from the Salomon principle

We have seen that the courts treat a corporate entity as a different being from its members. This principle is normally rigidly adhered to, but there are occasions on which the courts will abandon the essentially legalistic approach adopted in the Salomon case and give effect to "the reality of the situation" (*Tunstall* v. *Steigman* (1962)). For example, in *F. G. (Films) Ltd.* (1953), the court supported a refusal by the Board of Trade to register a film as British made because the applicant company, albeit incorporated in this country, was nothing more than an agent for an American company which was financing the enterprise. Again, in *D.H.N. Ltd.* v. *Tower Hamlets London Borough Council* (1976), a business operated by three associated companies, A, B and C, was forced to close following the making of a compulsory purchase order on a warehouse owned by B. Although B received substantial compensation in respect of the purchase, the local authority argued that no compensation for disturbance was payable to A, the controlling company, because it owned no legal or equitable interest in the affected premises. The approach of the Court of Appeal however was to treat the three companies as one, and not as separate entities, thereby enabling A's claim to succeed. In the opinion of the court, a strictly legalistic stance was inappropriate given the circumstances of the case.

Finally, it should be noted that departures from the principle of the separate legal personality of a corporate entity are to be found in statute law also. Thus, the remaining member may become personally liable for the debts of a registered company where its membership falls below that required by the Companies Act 1948 (s.31), and the same personal liability may devolve on any persons who are discovered in the course of the dissolution of a company to have been involved in the defrauding of creditors (s.332).

SUMMARY

On completion of this chapter you should be able to:

(*a*) Appreciate the difference between unincorporated organisations and those which have obtained corporate status.

(*b*) Describe the principal characteristics of unincorporated organisations.

(*c*) Explain the meaning of separate legal personality and indicate when the courts are likely to depart from this principle.

SELF-ASSESSMENT QUESTIONS

(Relevant page numbers are given in brackets.)

1. Give two examples of unincorporated organisations. (Page 2)

2. What arrangements must be made with respect to the property of unincorporated organisations? (Page 2)

3. Consider the circumstances in which liability in contract and tort may devolve on the individual members of an unincorporated club. (Pages 2–3)

4. What are the implications for an unincorporated association of persons which infringes the limitation on number of members

contained in the Companies Act 1948? Why are unincorporated clubs not usually caught by this restriction? (Page 4)

CHAPTER TWO

Partnership

CHAPTER OBJECTIVES

After studying this chapter you should be able to:
* understand the principal features of the partnership as a form of business organisation in English law;
* analyse the relations of partners to each other and with respect to outsiders;
* explain the termination of the partnership and its effect.

INTRODUCTION

The main provisions regulating partnerships are to be found in the Partnership Act 1890, although it should be emphasised that, like other associations founded on agreement, this form of business organisation has its basis in the law of contract (*see* pp. 9 and 11).

In Chapter 1, we saw how partnerships differ from incorporated associations with respect to separate legal personality and the limitation of members' liability (*see* p. 4). Further, partnerships are not subject to the statutory requirements relating to formation and publicity which affect registered companies and, unlike shareholders, every partner has the right to take part in the management of the business (*see* p. 11). Partners may normally be regarded as agents of their firm and the implications of this are considered later (*see* p. 13). Readers might also note that a particular feature of the law of partnership is the duty of good faith owed by partners to each other (*see* p. 12).

NOTE: References are to the Partnership Act 1890 unless otherwise stated.

DEFINITION AND CHARACTERISTICS OF THE PARTNERSHIP

This section is concerned with the essential features of a partnership together with the nature of the relationship between the individual members of the firm.

Definition

We noted in Chapter 1 that a partnership is defined as the relation subsisting between persons carrying on a business in common with a view of profit (s.1). Registered companies and other incorporated associations are specifically excluded from this definition and are therefore not partnerships (s.1(2)). It is however possible for a partnership relation to subsist *between* such organisations. Certain partnerships are illegal, for example, those made with enemy aliens.

Partners are known collectively as a firm (s.4) but, in English law, the firm is essentially an unincorporated association with no legal personality apart from that of each of its members (*see* Chapter 1). Nevertheless, partners may commence actions and be sued in the firm name and acts relating to the business of the firm which are carried out in the firm name are binding on all the partners (s.6).

It should be noted that if the partnership name does not consist of the surnames of the partners, the name of each partner must be stated in the firm's business documents (e.g. letters, written orders for goods) and be displayed prominently in the firm's business premises (s.29, Companies Act 1981).

The partnership agreement

The relationship between partners is founded on a contract of agency, since a true partnership only exists where the partners carry on their business as principals and agents for each other (*Badeley* v. *Consolidated Bank* (1888)). This contract may be made informally, e.g. orally, but in many cases there is a formal deed of partnership, making specific provision for such matters as the reference of disputes to arbitration and the circumstances in which the partnership should be dissolved. Even if there is no express contract between the parties, a partnership relationship may be inferred from their conduct. In *Davis* v. *Davis* (1894), for instance, two brothers continued their deceased father's business but never came to any agreement with respect to a partnership. The court decided that there was sufficient evidence of such agreement in that both brothers withdrew equal amounts of money from the business at the same time and invested in the business money which they had jointly borrowed.

The absence of an express or implied partnership agreement does not preclude the possibility of a person becoming liable as a partner to outsiders. Thus, where a person by words or conduct represents himself to be a partner in a particular firm, or knowingly suffers himself to be so represented, he becomes liable as a partner to any person who, on the faith of such representation, gives credit to the firm (s.14). A retired partner was not, however, liable under this section where notepaper containing his name was continued to be used with neither his knowledge nor consent (*Tower Cabinet Co. Ltd.* v. *Ingram* (1949)).

Legal relationships can arise between individuals without agreement in other cases also: the joint ownership of property being but one example, where this is the result of a gift. Consequently, the Act provides that jointly owned property does not of itself create a partnership as to that property (s.2(1)). Although partners as to the business, there was no evidence that the brothers in *Davis* v. *Davis* (above) regarded themselves as partners with respect to houses they had inherited from their father, held by them as tenants in common, and in which the business was carried on.

The business element and participation in profits

An essential requirement for a partnership to exist is that some business activity be carried on (s.1). "Business" is defined in the Act to include every trade, occupation or profession (s.45). Quite clearly, there are many activities in which people participate jointly but which do not amount to a business. For instance, the trustees of a marriage settlement who sell the investments and reinvest are not carrying on a business (James LJ in *Smith* v. *Anderson* (1880)). Moreover, acts which are preparatory to the formation of a registered company are not in themselves indicative of a partnership relation between the promoters (*Keith Spicer Ltd.* v. *Mansell* (1970)).

Note that the definition of partnership requires that the business be pursued for gain (profit) thereby effectively excluding sports and social clubs with no such object.

The Act sets out rules to which regard must be had in determining the existence of a partnership (s.2). Thus, whereas the receipt by a person of a share of the profits of a business is prima facie evidence that he is a partner, the sharing of gross returns does not of itself create a partnership. In *Cox* v. *Coulson* (1916), although the defendant lessee of a theatre shared gross takings with the manager of a touring company, there was no partnership because production expenses were separately allocated. The defendant bore theatre costs and the touring company was responsible for such items as travelling expenses. It was quite possible for one party to make a profit and the other to bear a loss. Another reason for the absence of a partnership in this case was that neither party was authorised to act as agent for the other.

The fact that a person takes a share in the profits of a business is a good indication that he is a partner (s.2(3)) but this should not be regarded as conclusive since of principal importance is the parties' intention and the surrounding circumstances (*Re Megevand* (1878)). A clear distinction is therefore to be made between the person who simply lends money to a businessman and who is repaid from or takes a share of the profits of the business (s.2(3) (*a*) and (*d*)) and the lender who takes no active part in management but on whose behalf the business may be said to be carried on (*Badeley* v. *Consolidated Bank* (1888)). Therefore, a lender's stipulation that he is not to be a partner will have no effect if, in addition to receiving a share of the business profits, he has the right to control the partnership property and shares the losses (*Re Megevand* (1878)). Note that the distinction between the true creditor and the dormant or inactive partner is of crucial importance since the latter will normally be subject to the same liabilities as the active partners (*see* pp. 13–16).

Other instances particularised in the Act which do not in themselves make a person a partner are the receipt by an employee of a share of the profits by way of remuneration and the receipt by way of annuity of a portion of the profits by the widow or child of a deceased partner.

RELATIONS OF PARTNERS TO EACH OTHER

The purpose of this section is to consider the rights and obligations of the individual partners, whether contained in the partnership agreement or determined by the Act.

The partners' rights and duties

These are in the first instance regulated by the provisions of the partnership agreement, whether express or implied. In the absence of agreement, they are to be determined by reference to rules contained in the Act. For example, all the partners are entitled to share equally in the capital and profits of the business and, conversely, must contribute equally to the firm's losses; a partner is an agent of the firm (s.5) and like every agent is entitled to an indemnity in respect of payments made and personal liabilities incurred by him in the ordinary and proper conduct of the business; every partner has the right to participate in the management of the firm's business; furthermore, no partner may be introduced as a partner without the consent of all existing partners (s.24). In addition, the consent of all existing partners is required for any change in the nature of the firm's business (s.24 (8)) but a simple majority is sufficient for resolving differences as to ordinary matters, provided the minority partners are treated fairly. In *Highley* v. *Walker* (1910), the question of the employment by the firm of the son of one of the partners was considered to be an ordinary matter which could be decided by a majority of the partners.

A majority may not, however, expel a partner unless a power to do so has been conferred by express agreement between all the partners (s.25). Similarly, any variation of the partners' rights and duties, whether determined by agreement or set out in the Act, must have the consent of all the partners (s.19).

In their relations with each other, partners are under an obligation to exercise good faith. A partner must therefore account to the firm for any private benefit derived from the use of partnership property or from transactions in which the partnership is involved (s.29). A partner who takes part in some business activity, in competition with his firm, must account for any profits made in that business (s.30). Further, partners are required to render true accounts and full information of all matters affecting the partnership to any partner or his legal representative (s.28). Therefore, a partner who purchases a fellow-partner's share in the business must disclose fully all material facts of which he is aware (*Law* v. *Law* (1905)).

The duty to exercise good faith continues even after the dissolution of the firm if the partnership affairs remain outstanding. In *Thompson Trustee* v. *Heaton* (1974), after the termination of a partnership between A and B, B acquired the freehold interest in premises which the partners had previously occupied as lessees. When B subsequently sold the property the court decided that A was entitled to half the profit. As no provision had been made at the time of termination with respect to the property, neither party was entitled to benefit independently of the other, by virtue of the continuing fiduciary obligations.

Partnership property

The assets of the partnership comprise such items as land, stock in trade and goodwill (i.e. the customer connection), all of which may be brought into the partnership on formation, or acquired subsequently on the firm's behalf. Such property must be held and applied by the partners exclusively for the purpose of the partnership and in accordance with the partnership agreement (s.20). Any property purchased with money belonging to the firm is prima facie deemed to have been acquired on the firm's account (s.21).

It must be emphasised that the use by the partners of any property in the course of the partnership business or for the benefit of the business does not necessarily make it partnership property (*see Davis* v. *Davis*, p. 9.)

On the commencement of a partnership, the partners may specify which property brought in by each should be part of the firm's assets. If however agreement is lacking on this point and a dispute arises, the court will imply only such terms as are necessary to reach a practical solution. In *Miles* v. *Clark* (1953), for example, the partners in a photographers' business never finally decided which of various assets, including the lease of the premises where the business was conducted, should belong to the firm. The court held that it could be assumed that some stock in trade, such as film, was intended to be partnership property because this was necessary for carrying on the business. It was not however necessary for anything else to be brought into the common pool, including the lease. The business could be carried on without the lease simply by the lessee granting his co-partner a licence to use the premises for the purpose of the partnership business.

We have seen that individual partners are entitled to share equally in the partnership property (p. 11 above). What is meant by this is that, upon a dissolution of the partnership, all the partnership assets (including land by virtue of s.22) must be sold and what remains of the proceeds after payment of the firm's debts applied in paying to the partners that which is due to them (s.39). This entitlement to part of the surplus upon a dissolution is, in effect, a partner's share in the partnership property (*Rodriguez* v. *Speyer Bros.* (1919)). It is possible for a partner to transfer his share in the partnership to an outsider but this does not entitle the latter to interfere in the management or administration of the partnership business (s.31). A clear distinction must therefore be made between such a transfer and the introduction of a new partner, to which all existing partners must give their consent (s.24). The assignee is however entitled to receive the share of the profits to which the assigning partner would otherwise be entitled and, in the case of a dissolution, the appropriate share of the partnership assets (s.31).

Note finally that, where a creditor has successfully established a monetary claim against a partner, the court is empowered to make an order charging that partner's interest in the partnership property and profits, with payment of the amount of the judgment debt and interest (s.23). In such a case, the other partners can dissolve the partnership at their option (s.33).

RELATIONS OF PARTNERS TO OUTSIDERS

In this section we consider the contractual and non-contractual liability of the partners to persons dealing with the firm.

Liability in contract

All partners are agents of their firm and each other for the purpose of the partnership business (s.5). Where, therefore, an individual partner enters into a contract with an outsider with the approval of his fellow-partners, that contract will be binding on the firm by reason of the agency relationship. Such approval or authority may arise expressly, be implied from the circumstances of the case, or be acquired by subsequent ratification (*see* the discussion of agency law in Chapter 14).

In the above cases, the contracting partner is said to have *actual authority*. However, in circumstances where he may lack such authority, it by no means follows that the other partners will be under no obligation to the outsider with whom a contract is made. The law is such that a partner acting without actual authority may nevertheless effectively bind his firm and fellow partners where the contract in question is one usually associated with businesses of the kind operated by that firm (s.5). In *Mercantile Credit Co. Ltd.* v. *Garrod* (1962), A and B, partners in a motor garage business, expressly agreed that the buying and selling of motor vehicles should not form part of their activities. Nevertheless, the active partner, B, defrauded the plaintiffs by the sale of a vehicle to a third party. The plaintiffs were able to recover their loss from A, the dormant partner, despite his ignorance of the fraud and the express restriction on B's authority, because it was reasonable for persons dealing with the firm to assume that B had the necessary authority to act. The sale of a motor car was an act associated with businesses of the kind carried on by that firm.

It should be emphasised however that no liability devolves on the firm and the other partners if the outsider is aware that the contracting partner has no authority with respect to that particular transaction, or does not know or believe that person to be a partner (ss.5 and 8). Further, the firm is not bound where one partner, acting without actual authority, pledges the firm's credit for a purpose apparently unconnected with its ordinary business: any personal liability incurred by the partner concerned is however unaffected by this provision (s.7). Clearly, in certain circumstances, a partner may appear to outsiders to have authority to act and this *apparent authority* may or may not coincide with that partner's actual authority. (*Mercantile Credit Co. Ltd.* v. *Garrod* is a case where, because of the restriction, apparent authority exeeded actual authority.) In fact, the courts have come to recognise that membership of a partnership prima facie carries with it the authority to do certain acts. Two examples are, receiving payment of debts due to the firm and selling the firm's goods.

Such instances of apparent authority may however depend on whether the partnership in question is a trading business; that is, one concerned with the buying and selling of goods. Consequently, where the partnership business is not within this category, a partner has no apparent authority to borrow money on the firm's credit (*Higgins* v. *Beauchamp* (1914): the business in this case was that of cinema proprietors). It is not within any partner's apparent authority to bind his fellow partners in partnership with an outsider in another business (*Mann* v. *D'Arcy* (1968)).

Again, it must be emphasised that no apparent authority can arise if the outsider is aware that the contracting partner has no actual authority, or that the authority he does possess is subject to limitations.

Non-contractual liability

An individual partner will of course be liable for loss or damage caused to an outsider by his own wrongful acts, for example, negligence. The firm will also be liable for such loss or damage where the act complained of is committed by the partner, whilst acting in the ordinary course of the firm's business or is authorised by his co-partners (s.10). Thus, in *Hamlyn* v. *Houston and Co.* (1902), a partner bribed a competing firm's employee to divulge confidential information. Despite the illegal conduct, the wrongdoer's firm was held liable in damages in respect of the aggrieved competitor's loss, because the obtaining of information was an act within the ordinary course of the firm's business. Note that where a partner misapplies the money or property of a third person which he has received whilst acting within the scope of his apparent authority, the firm must make good the loss. Similarly, the firm is liable where property, received by the firm in the course of its business, is misapplied by one of the partners whilst in its custody (s.11).

Nature and extent of the partner's liability

Subject to the special rules applicable to limited partnerships (*see* p. 18), a partner is fully liable for the debts and obligations of the firm; therefore his own personal property, in addition to that belonging to the partnership, is potentially subject to the claims of creditors.

A partner's liability in respect of contractual debts and obligations incurred by the firm while he is a partner is said to be *joint* (s.9). The effect of this provision was that, if a creditor commenced an action against one partner but the judgment obtained was unsatisfied because that partner was insolvent, a subsequent action could not be brought against the remaining partners in respect of the firm in question of the same matter (*Kendall* v. *Hamilton* (1879)). In such a case, a creditor can now sue the other members of the firm since the original judgment is no longer a bar to subsequent action (Civil Liability (Contribution) Act 1978).

Liability in respect of the firm's torts is both *joint* and *several*, therefore a person who sued some of the members of a firm once, could always bring a subsequent action against the remainder in relation to the same grievance. As we have already observed partners may be sued in the firm name. If the action is successful, the claimant may normally look to each of the individual partners for payment as well as the partnership property.

In this context, it may be emphasised that a person admitted as a partner into an existing firm is not liable to that firm's creditors in respect of anything done *before* he became a partner. Further, a partner who retires from a firm continues to be liable for debts and obligations incurred before his retirement unless he is discharged from liability under an agreement made between himself, the members of the newly constituted firm and the creditors (s.17).

In principle, a retiring partner should not be liable for debts and obligations of the firm incurred after his retirement, because the other partners will no longer be acting on his behalf. Nevertheless, a person dealing with the newly constituted firm is entitled to assume that its membership comprises those persons whom he knew were partners in the old firm, until he has notice to the contrary. If a person had no dealings with the firm prior to the change, an advertisement in the *Gazette* is sufficient notice (s.36).

On the other hand, a retiring partner is not liable in respect of the firm's subsequent debts to a person who never knew him to be a partner (even though that person might have dealt with the firm previously) (s.36(3)). A case in point is *Tower Cabinet Co. Ltd.* v. *Ingram* (1949) where it was decided that a partner who had retired could not be held responsible for a later debt, where the plaintiff had not previously dealt with the firm and whose only knowledge of that partner's existence was derived from some pre-retirement note-paper, used in the transaction giving rise to the claim.

Finally, the Act provides that the estate of a partner who dies or who becomes bankrupt is not liable for partnership debts contracted after the date of the death or bankruptcy (s.36).

DISSOLUTION OF PARTNERSHIP

This section outlines the means by which a partnership may be terminated and the effect of such termination.

Methods of dissolution

The partnership agreement may make special provision for the circumstances in which the firm can be dissolved. In *Peyton* v. *Mindham* (1971), for example, a case concerning a medical partnership, the partnership deed provided that notice of termination could be given by one of the two partners in the case of the other's incapacity to perform a fair share of the work. If the partners have made no prior arrangements, however, the partnership will be dissolved:

(*a*) on the expiration of a fixed term or by notice if the partnership is for an unspecified period;

(*b*) if the firm has been formed for the purposes of a single venture, on the fulfilment of that venture (s.32); and

(*c*) on the death or bankruptcy of any partner (s.33).

Furthermore, dissolution is an unavoidable consequence where the further prosecution of the firm's business gives rise to an illegality (s.34). Consequently, in *Hudgell Yeates and Co.* v. *Watson* (1978), the court decided that, because it is illegal for an unqualified person to be a member of a solicitor's partnership, the firm was dissolved automatically where one of its members inadvertently failed to renew his practising certificate. In other cases, the partnership business may be interwoven with some other relationship, for example, that of husband and wife. The break-up of the marriage may then result in a corresponding dissolution of the partnership (*Bothe* v. *Amos* (1976)).

It is always open to any partner to apply to the court for a dissolution, in which case the necessary decree of dissolution may be granted in circumstances of mental or other incapacity, conduct prejudicial to the carrying on of the business and wilful or persistent breaches of the partnership agreement. Furthermore, the court can dissolve a partnership where the business can only be carried on at a loss and whenever the court considers that dissolution is a just and equitable course of action having regard to the circumstances of the particular case (s.35). On this latter point, the reader might usefully compare the position with regard to registered companies (*see* Chapter 5, p. 53).

Effect of dissolution

Notwithstanding a dissolution, the authority of each of the partners to bind the firm continues in so far as this may be necessary to wind up the affairs of the partnership and complete unfinished transactions (s.38). Secondly, as we have already discussed (*see* p. 12), dissolution of the firm entitles every partner to demand that the partnership property be applied in paying the firm's debts and liabilities and the surplus distributed to each of the partners (s.39). A partner who retires from the firm may not however insist on a sale of the partnership property where it has been agreed that the business should be continued by the other partners (*Sobell* v. *Boston* (1975)). In such a case, the retiring partner is entitled only to the value of his share at the date of retirement. Pending a satisfactory settlement of the matter, the position is governed by s.42, which provides that the outgoing partner is entitled, at his option, to an appropriate share of the profits or to five per cent interest on the amount of his share of the partnership assets.

The distribution of the partnership assets on a dissolution is governed by s.44. Thus, subject to agreement to the contrary, any losses sustained by the firm must be paid first out of profits, next out of capital and, if necessary, by each partner in the proportion in which profits were shared. The effect is that, if the assets of the firm are insufficient to meet the claims of creditors, each partner will be required to make good the loss from his own property (*see* p. 15).

The assets must be applied, first, in repaying debts and liabilities owed to outsiders; secondly, in the repayment of sums advanced by partners to the firm; and, thirdly, in repaying to each partner what is due to him in respect of capital. Finally, if there is any residue, this must be divided amongst the partners in the proportion in which they are entitled to profits.

LIMITED PARTNERSHIPS

Provision is made in the Limited Partnerships Act 1907 for the creation of a form of partnership comprising both limited and general partners. Whereas general partners are liable to outsiders for all the firm's debts and obligations (as in the case of the ordinary partnership), limited partners incur no such liability beyond the sums they have invested in the firm. A firm made up entirely of limited partners is not possible since the Act requires that there must be at least one general partner.

Limited partners may not take part in the management of the business and have no power to bind the firm. If a limited partner does participate in management, he becomes liable, as if he were a general partner, for all the firm's debts and obligations incurred during this time. The consent of a limited partner is not required for the introduction of a new partner and differences arising with respect to ordinary matters can be decided by a majority of general partners.

It should be noted that a limited partnership must be registered as such with the registrar of companies, failing which its members will be treated as general partners.

Except where excluded by the provisions of the Act of 1907, the law applicable to limited partnerships is that outlined in the previous sections of this chapter.

SUMMARY

On completion of this chapter you should be able to:

(*a*) Outline and appreciate the essential features of the partnership.

(*b*) Describe the rights and duties of the partners and appreciate their position with respect to the partnership property.

(*c*) Understand the nature of the partners' obligations to persons dealing with the firm.

(*d*) Outline the various methods by which a partnership may be dissolved and be aware of the effect of such dissolution.

(*e*) Appreciate the distinction between ordinary partnerships and those which are limited.

SELF-ASSESSMENT QUESTIONS

(Relevant page numbers are given in brackets.)

1. How does the relationship between partners come into being? (Page 9).

2. What are the main characteristics of a partnership? (Pages 8–11)

3. What is the nature of the obligation of good faith owed by partners to each other? (Page 12)

4. Explain what is meant by partnership property. (Page 12)

5. Indicate the circumstances in which a partnership will be dissolved. (Pages 16 and 17)

CHAPTER THREE

Registered Companies— Formation

```
CHAPTER OBJECTIVES
After studying this chapter, you should be able to:
* indicate the different approaches to the classification of
  companies and outline the process whereby registered
  companies are formed;
* discuss some important features of this process, such as
  the status and content of some of the company's principal
  documents.
```

INTRODUCTION

In studying this chapter, it will be useful for readers to bear in mind the comparisons which may be drawn between registered companies and other forms of business organisation. Thus, as explained in Chapter 1, registered companies differ from partnerships and other unincorporated associations in that they possess separate legal personality. This distinguishing characteristic is acquired upon the issue of a certificate of incorporation by the registrar of companies (*see* p. 23). Another feature is that the activities of a company are generally limited to those specified in the objects clause of its memorandum of association. Unauthorised transactions are void and, in principle, are not enforceable against the company. The inconvenience of this rule is however partly remedied by statute and the matter is discussed on p. 28. The principle of limited liability is again of importance but the implications of this, together with other important aspects of company law such as relations between shareholders and the company and the authority and duties of directors, are reserved for subsequent chapters.

References in this and the next two chapters are to the Companies Acts presently in force. It should be noted that Bills consolidating the statutes referred to are scheduled for enactment during 1985.

CLASSIFICATION

Registered companies are those associations which are incorporated in accordance with the provisions of the Companies Acts. It is possible to classify such companies in several ways.

Firstly, a company may be formed with the liability of its members limited to the amount unpaid on their shares or it may be incorporated as an unlimited company (s.1(2), 1948 Act). In the latter case, each member is fully liable to contribute to the company's assets in the event of a winding up in order that the company's debts may be discharged (s.212, 1948 Act).

Secondly, the liability of each member to contribute on a winding up may be limited by the specified amount which he has undertaken to contribute when that situation arises. The company is known in this case as a company limited by guarantee. It has hitherto been possible for a guarantee company to be formed with or without a share capital but the formation of new guarantee companies with a share capital is now prohibited by the 1980 Act (s.1(2)).

Thirdly, and perhaps most importantly, companies may be classified according to whether they are public or private. A public company is defined in the 1980 Act as one limited by shares or by guarantee and having a share capital, being a company whose memorandum of association (*see* below) states that it is to be a public company and in relation to which the registration provisions of the Companies Acts have been complied with (s.1). A private company is, quite simply, one that is not a public company.

Certain differences between the two types of company appear from the statutory definition. Thus, companies which are unlimited and and those guarantee companies with no share capital can only be formed as private companies. Furthermore, the name of a public company must end with the words, "public limited company" or "p.l.c." (ss.2 and 78, 1980 Act) whereas with some exceptions, the last word in the name of a private company must be "limited" or "ltd.".

Other main differences between public and private companies are as follows:

(*a*) The amount of share capital with which a public company proposes to be registered must not be less than the authorised minimum, i.e. £50,000 or such other sum specified by the Secretary of State (s.3 (2), 1980 Act). The share capital of private companies is subject to no such requirement.

(*b*) A public company is prohibited from doing business or exercising borrowing powers until it has received a certificate to do business from the registrar of companies or re-registered (*see* below) as a private company (s.4, 1980 Act).

(*c*) A private company need have only one director whereas a public company (unless registered before 1 November, 1929) must have at least two (s.176, 1948 Act).

(*d*) A private limited company will commit an offence if it offers its shares or debentures to the public (s.15, 1980 Act).

(*e*) The duty of directors with respect to the qualifications of company secretaries (*see* p. 46) does not apply in the case of a private company (s.79, 1980 Act).

(*f*) The limitations on the provision by a company of financial assistance for the purchase of its own shares are less stringent in the case of private companies (ss. 42 and 43, 1981 Act).

(*g*) Persons having interests in the voting shares of public companies may have an obligation to notify their companies of such interests. Persons interested in the shares of private companies are under no such obligation (s.63, 1981 Act).

(*h*) Private companies may redeem or purchase their own shares out of capital (s.54, 1981 Act).

It may be noted that a private company may re-register as a public company provided a special resolution (*see* p. 32) to this effect is passed, application is made in the prescribed way and various conditions are met. For instance, the nominal value of the applicant company's allotted share capital must not be less than the authorised minimum (ss.5 and 6, 1980 Act). Conversely, a public company may re-register as a private company and, again, a special resolution is required.

FORMATION

In this section we discuss the principal issues relating to the formation and registration of a company.

Registration

At least two persons, associated for any lawful purpose, may form a registered company, whether public or private (s.1, 1948 Act, as amended). These persons are required to subscribe their names to the company's memorandum of association and, after registration, they become the company's first members (s.26, 1948 Act).

The process of incorporation is begun by delivering to the registrar of companies, for retention and registration, various documents including the memorandum of association, the articles of association (s.12, 1948 Act) and a statement in the prescribed form containing the names and other details of the company's first directors and secretary (s.21, 1976 Act). This latter statement must be signed by the subscribers of the memorandum and must contain consents by the directors and secretary to act in those capacities. Further, a company must at all times have a registered office and a statement as to its intended situation must be delivered also (s.23, 1976 Act).

The procedure is completed by the registrar issuing a certificate of incorporation and this must state that the newly formed company is a public company if this be the case (s.3, 1980 Act). (For the effect of incorporation, *see* Chapter 1.) The certificate of incorporation is one of the documents the issue of which the registrar must notify in the *Gazette* (s.9(3), European Communities Act 1972).

One important qualification to the above is that a company which is registered as a public company must not commence business or exercise any borrowing powers until the registrar of companies has issued a certificate permitting this (s.4, 1980 Act). No certificate will, for example, be issued unless the registrar is satisfied that the company's allotted share capital is not less than the authorised minimum of £50,000. It is an offence for the company to do business in contravention of this section but the validity of any transaction which it enters into remains unaffected.

Promoters

The promoter of a company is a person who is principally involved in the process of its formation. In many cases, the promoter becomes one of the newly formed company's original members but this is not a necessary consequence.

The promoter is under various obligations both with respect to the company he is about to form and to its members. In the first place, he stands in a fiduciary position towards the company (*Erlanger* v. *New Sombrero Phosphate Co.* (1878)). Where therefore he arranges the sale of his own property to the company, the promoter must either ensure that the company is represented by an independent board of directors who are aware of the circumstances or make full disclosure to the present and future members (for instance, in a prospectus). If he does not do this, the company may be entitled to rescind the contract. Another remedy available to the company is the recovery of any profit arising out of the formation which the promoter might have made and not disclosed (*Gluckstein* v. *Barnes* (1900)).

In addition to the above, the promoter is liable to pay compensation for loss suffered by those persons who purchase shares from the company on the basis of an untrue statement in the prospectus (s.43, 1948 Act).

A problem associated with the promotion of a company is the company's position with regard to contracts purportedly made on its behalf, but before formation. Until it is incorporated, company has no legal existence, therefore it cannot later ratify and become party to such contracts (ratification is considered in Chapter 14). A case illustrating this point is *Kelner* v. *Baxter* (1866). Here, the promoters of an hotel company in the process of formation purchased on credit a quantity of wine from Kelner and claimed to be acting on behalf of the company. The company was ultimately incorporated and did purport to ratify the agreement but went into liquidation before Kelner was paid. The court held that the promoters and not the company were liable for the debt. The promoters' position in this respect is now regulated by statute. Thus, subject to agreement to the contrary, the contract made prior to incorporation has effect as a contract entered into by the person claiming to act for the company or as agent for it, and he becomes personally liable on the contract accordingly (s.9(2), European Communities Act 1972). A case illustrating the application of s.9(2) is *Phonogram Ltd.* v. *Lane* (1981). Prior to the formation of a new company, L negotiated on its behalf a loan of £6,000. In fact, the company was never formed and the Court of Appeal decided that the effect of the subsection was to make L personally liable under the contract for the repayment of the money.

If, on the other hand, the company after incorporation is itself to have the benefit of the earlier contract or be subject to it, it must enter into an entirely new contract on the terms of the old one (*Natal Land Co. Ltd.* v. *Pauline Colliery Syndicate Ltd.* (1904)).

Lastly, it will be clear from this discussion that a promoter can have no claim against the company under a pre-formation contract in respect of his expenses. A limited solution is for the articles of association to include a provision empowering the directors to pay these costs. Thus, if the company's articles are in the form of Table A (referred to below), the directors may pay all expenses incurred in promoting and registering the company (Art. 80).

The prospectus

Any notice, circular, advertisement or other document by which members of the public are invited to subscribe for or purchase a company's shares or debentures is a prospectus (s.455, 1948 Act). A prospectus may be issued by a promoter engaged in the formation of a company, by an already established company or by an issuing house to which the company has agreed to allot its shares for resale to the public (*see* p. 26).

It is important that members of the public should be fully aware of what they are obtaining in return for their investment, therefore a prospectus is required to contain specified information relating to the directors and promoters of the company, the company's share capital and certain financial and business matters (s.38, 1948 Act). For instance, any benefit paid or given to a promoter within the preceding two years must be disclosed, together with particulars of the interest of any director in the promotion of the company or with respect to any property which the company proposes to acquire.

If the company's share capital is divided into different classes of shares, voting rights and those in respect of capital and dividends must be indicated. Other details to be specified are, the amount payable on application and allotment on each share and the minimum amount which, in the directors' opinion, must be raised from the share issue to provide for such matters as the purchase price of any property acquired by the company and preliminary expenses (that is, the minimum subscription). In fact, it should be noted that the allotment of shares is prohibited unless the minimum amount stated in the prospectus has been subscribed (s.47, 1948 Act). Furthermore, in the case of a public company there can be no allotment of share capital at all unless:

(*a*) that capital is subscribed for in full or
(*b*) the prospectus states that shares will be allotted even though the capital might not be fully subscribed (s.16, 1980 Act).

(In conjunction with the above, where a company's shares are to be quoted on the Stock Exchange, the rules of that institution concerning the contents of prospectuses must also be complied with.)

Directors and other persons responsible for the issue of a prospectus may incur civil liability where they fail to specify the matters required by the statute (s.38, 1948 Act). In addition, wherever a prospectus contains misleading or untrue statements, there are both civil and criminal sanctions. Thus, the rules relating to misrepresentation (for which, *see* Chapter 11) operate in the normal way, therefore an aggrieved purchaser of shares may be allowed to rescind the contract he has made with the company and claim damages under the Misrepresentation Act 1967. Further, directors, promoters and others may be liable to pay compensation to those subscribers who have suffered loss by reason or the untrue statement (s.43, 1948 Act) and any person who authorises the issue of a false prospectus will be criminally liable, unless he proves that he had reasonable ground to believe and *did* believe the statement in question to be true (s.44, 1948 Act).

Finally, the provisions of the Prevention of Fraud (Investments) Act 1958 might be noted briefly. This Act makes it unlawful for any person to deal in shares and debentures and to distribute circulars

connected with such dealing, unless he is licensed or exempted by
the Department of Trade. Those not affected by this provision
include the Bank of England, statutory and municipal corporations and members of the Stock Exchange. Further, the distribution of a company prospectus is not prohibited provided it
complies with the requirements of the Companies Act 1948. The
1958 Act makes it an offence for any person (without exception)
to induce another to enter into an agreement for the acquisition
or disposition of shares and debentures by means of a promise,
statement or forecast which is known to be misleading, false or
deceptive (s.13).

The raising of capital

A company may seek the finance it requires in a variety of ways.
As indicated earlier, a company's securities may be offered for
purchase by the public although it should be remembered that this
option is subject to the important limitation affecting private
companies contained in the Companies Act 1980 (*see* p. 22). The
offer may be made to the public directly, or the company may
enter into an arrangement with an issuing house (for example, a
merchant bank) whereby the latter undertakes to dispose of the
securities, either to the public generally or to certain institutional
investors such as insurance companies.

An alternative method is for the company to offer the shares to
its own members in proportion to their existing shareholding. In
fact, it may be noted in this context that the 1980 Act prohibits
both public and private companies from allotting certain shares
without first making an offer to existing shareholders to allot on
similar terms (s.17).

The success of an issue in the above cases may be underwritten.
That is, a specialist underwriter agrees to take any shares which
may remain unsold. In this respect, an underwriting commission
may be paid (s.53, 1948 Act).

An additional source of finance available to a company is its
undistributed profits which it may resort to instead of paying a
dividend. At the same time, the company may use this money to
finance an issue of *bonus* shares which are allotted to its existing
members and credited as fully paid up.

Finally, a company may quite simply borrow the money it needs
from private individuals or institutions such as banks and insurance companies. The loan may be unsecured, or it may be secured
by a fixed or floating charge. The significance of this is considered
in subsequent chapters.

THE COMPANY'S MEMORANDUM AND ARTICLES OF ASSOCIATION

These are the basic constitutional documents of a registered company and, in the following paragraphs, we consider the content and significance of each.

The memorandum of association

This must contain the company's name, state whether the registered office of the company is to be situated in England (including Wales) or Scotland and set out the objects for which the company is established. If the liability of the members is limited, this must be indicated and, in the case of a company limited by guarantee, there is required a statement of the amount which each member is liable to contribute to the company's assets in the event of its being wound up. The amount of share capital with which the company proposes to be registered must be shown, together with the number of shares and the value of each. Further, every person who signs the memorandum must specify the number of shares he is taking (s.2, 1948 Act). If a company is a public company, this fact must be stated also (s.2, 1980 Act and Sched. 1). (*See* Appendix I.) An important feature of the memorandum of association is the *objects clause* since, subject to s.9(1) of the European Communities Act 1972, this effectively limits the lawful activities of a registered company to the matters set out therein. A company lacks the capacity to enter into any transaction which is outside the scope of its permitted objects and, if it does, the transaction is *ultra vires* and void, unless the circumstances are within the above statutory provision. For example, in *Ashbury Railway Carriage and Iron Co. Ltd.* v. *Riche* (1895), a company whose objects included the manufacture and sale of railway carriages and wagons purchased a concession for the construction of a railway and employed Riche to do the work. The financing of railway construction was not one of the company's objects, therefore its subsequent repudiation of the contract was held to be justified by the House of Lords on the basis that the transaction was void.

Again, in *Introductions Ltd.* v. *National Provincial Bank Ltd.* (1970), a company was formed in 1951 with the purpose of providing various facilities for visitors to a festival. Subsequently, the company entered into the business of pig breeding and, in connection with this activity, borrowed a sum of money from the bank giving debentures as security. The court held that the debentures were void because the loan was for an *ultra vires* purpose and the bank was aware of this. Although the company's memorandum contained an express power to borrow money, the bank was prevented from succeeding because, in the view of the Court of Appeal, the borrowing power could only be used in the furtherance of some *intra vires* activity.

The position with respect to *ultra vires* transactions must now be considered in the light of the European Communities Act 1972. This provides that, in favour of a person dealing with a company in good faith, any transaction decided on by the directors shall be deemed to be one which it is within the capacity of the company to enter into. Further, in such a case, the other contracting party need not enquire as to the capacity of the company (by, for example, consulting the company's memorandum) and is presumed to have acted in good faith unless the contrary is proved (s.9(1)).

Consequently, in the above circumstances, an outsider can hold the company to an *ultra vires* transaction unless, for example, he is actually aware at the time of contracting that the company lacks capacity. It must of course be emphasised that the company itself may not take advantage of s.9 and the *ultra vires* rule will continue to apply to those transactions which have not been approved by the directors. Nevertheless, a transaction approved by a single director of the company may be deemed by the courts to have been decided on by all the directors if that director is effectively the sole person in control of the company (*International Sales and Agencies Ltd.* v. *Marcus* (1982)).

A company which wishes to change its objects must comply with s.5 of the 1948 Act. This requires a special resolution (*see* p. 32) and the alteration of the memorandum must be for one of the purposes specified in the section. A company may, therefore, alter its objects in order:

(*a*) to conduct its business more economically or more efficiently;

(*b*) to attain its main purpose by new or improved means;

(*c*) to alter its area of operation;

(*d*) to carry on some business which may be conveniently combined with the company's business;

(*e*) to restrict or abandon any of its stated objects;

(*f*) to sell the whole or part of its undertaking; and

(*g*) to amalgamate with some other company or body of persons.

If there are objections to the alteration, the holders of at least fifteen per cent of the nominal value of the company's issued share capital have twenty-one days, from the passing of the resolution, in which to apply to the court to have the alteration cancelled. No person who has previously consented to, or voted in favour of, the resolution may join in the application. The effect is that the court may confirm the alteration with or without conditions, or may cancel it. Furthermore, the court may if necessary agree to an arrangement whereby the interests of the dissenting members are purchased.

Where the alteration is finally confirmed, the company must deliver a copy of the memorandum as altered to the registrar of companies who is, in turn, required to notify the receipt of this document in the *Gazette* (s.9(3), European Communities Act 1972).

The articles of association
These regulate the internal affairs of a company and provide for such matters as the initial appointment of directors, their powers and duties, the rights of shareholders and the conduct of meetings. A company may draw up its own articles of association or it may adopt wholly or in part those which are set out in Table A of the First Schedule of the 1948 Act. In fact, Table A will apply automatically in the case of a company limited by shares which does not register its own articles (s.8, 1948 Act). A company's articles must be printed, divided into paragraphs, numbered consecutively and signed by each subscriber of the memorandum of association (s.9, 1948 Act). On registration, the memorandum and articles of association constitute a contract between the members and the company (s.20, 1948 Act) and this point is considered in Chapter 4.

The articles of association may be altered by the company subject to the passing of a special resolution and provided the power of alteration is exercised in good faith and for the benefit of the company as a whole (Lindley MR in *Allen* v. *Gold Reefs of West Africa Ltd.* (1900)). Thus, in *Dafen Tinplate Co. Ltd.* v. *Llanelli Steel Co. Ltd.* (1920), the court held an alteration of a company's articles to be void where the effect of the alteration was to allow the majority of the company's shareholders to force any member to sell his shares to a person of their choice. The court felt that such a measure could not be for the company's benefit despite that it might benefit the majority.

SHARE CAPITAL

Definition
The nominal or authorised share capital of a company is that which on registration is required to be stated in the memorandum of association (*see* p. 27 above). Subject to alteration of the memorandum, this sum represents the maximum amount which the com-

pany may divide into shares and issue to its subscribers. A company may choose to leave part of its authorised capital unissued but it should be remembered that, if it is a public company, it will be refused a certificate to do business if the nominal value of its allotted share capital is less than the statutory minimum of £50,000 (s.4(2), 1980 Act). A further possibility is that shareholders may be asked initially to pay only part of the purchase price of their shares. In such a case, the amount unpaid is referred to as uncalled capital, although the shareholders continue to be liable for its payment. On this point, it may be noted that a public company may not normally allot a share without first receiving at least one quarter of its nominal value, plus the whole of any additional amount which may be payable (s.22, 1980 Act).

Payment for shares may be in money or money's worth (for example, by the transfer of property to the company), except that the subscribers to the memorandum of a public company must pay in cash for the shares which, by signing the memorandum, they have committed themselves to take (ss.20 and 29, 1980 Act). Again, a public company may not accept in payment for its shares an undertaking by any person to do work or perform services (s.20(2), 1980 Act).

Regulation

It is clearly in the interests of both creditors and shareholders that a company's share capital should be adequately represented by net assets (defined in s.87(4) of the 1980 Act as the aggregate of the company's assets less the aggregate of its liabilities). Accordingly, there are various rules directed towards ensuring:

(a) that a company receives adequate payment for the shares which it issues; and

(b) that, once the capital fund is established, its value is maintained.

Where, therefore, the shares of a public company are to be paid for otherwise than in cash, the non-cash consideration must be valued by an independent person and a report made to the company within the six months preceding the allotting of the shares (s.24, 1980 Act). The position with regard to private companies is regulated by the common law, but the courts will not normally interfere with a transaction unless, for example, it is fraudulent.

The shares of any company, whether public or private, may not be allotted at a discount (s.21, 1980 Act). Thus, in *Ooregum Gold Mining Co. of India Ltd.* v. *Roper* (1892), the House of Lords decided that an attempt by a company to issue £1.00 preference shares with 75 pence credited as paid up was unlawful. Other restrictions are:

(*a*) a limited company may not reduce its share capital except with the leave of the court (s.66, 1948 Act);

(*b*) dividends on shares must be distributed out of profits available for the purpose, not out of capital (s.39, 1980 Act); and

(*c*) a public company may not finance the purchase or redemption of its own shares out of share capital. The shares must be paid for either out of profits available for dividend or from the proceeds of a fresh issue of shares (ss.45 and 46, 1981 Act).

Finally, it may be noted that where the net assets of a public company fall to half, or less, of the amount of the company's called-up share capital, the directors are required to call an extraordinary general meeting in order to decide how best to deal with the situation (s.34, 1980 Act).

MEETINGS AND RESOLUTIONS

Meetings
Every company must hold an *annual general meeting* and, furthermore, not more than fifteen months may be allowed to elapse between the date of one annual general meeting and the next (s.131, 1948 Act). This meeting is concerned with such matters as the distribution of profits, the accounts and the reports of the company's officers, together with any special business which may be necessary. Special business may also be transacted at an *extraordinary general meeting* which may be convened as the need rises. An extraordinary general meeting must be held:

(*a*) at the request of those members holding at least one-tenth of the company's paid-up capital carrying the right to vote (s.132, 1948 Act); and

(*b*) by a public company where its net assets are reduced to half, or less, of its called-up share capital (s.34, 1980 Act).

Members are entitled to receive at least twenty-one days' notice in writing of the annual general meeting. The same period of notice is required also in the case of any meeting convened for the passing of a special resolution but, in other cases, fourteen days' notice is sufficient (s.133, 1948 Act). Any part of a company's articles of association stipulating shorter periods is void. Subject to the company's articles, every member must be notified, otherwise the meeting may be invalid (*Musselwhite* v. *C. H. Musselwhite and Sons Ltd* (1962)).

Additional provision with respect to notices is normally contained in the articles of association. Thus, where Table A applies, Art. 50 requires that the notice must specify the place, the day and the hour of the meeting and, where special business is to be transacted, the general nature of that business. Further, the general law demands that a notice be sufficiently informative so as to enable a shareholder to decide whether or not he should attend the meeting (*Tiessen* v. *Henderson* (1899)).

In certain cases, special notice is required. For instance, if the proposed business involves the dismissal of a director (*see* Chapter 4), notice of the intention to move the appropriate resolution must be given to the company at least twenty-eight days before the general meeting and the company must then inform its members of the resolution when giving notice of that meeting (s.142, 1948 Act). Special notice is also required if it is proposed to remove an auditor from office before his term has expired (s.15, 1976 Act).

The procedure at a general meeting is in the first instance governed by the articles of association but a minimum requirement is that at least two members must normally be present (s.134, 1948 Act). Article 58 of Table A provides that a resolution may be decided by a show of hands unless a poll is demanded. In the former case, a member has one vote only but, in the case of a poll, every member is entitled to one vote for each share held (s.134, 1948 Act). Any member who is entitled to attend and vote at a meeting of the company can appoint a proxy to attend and vote in his place (s.136, 1948 Act).

Resolutions

(*a*) *Ordinary resolution.* This may be passed by a simple majority of votes (*Bushell* v. *Faith* (1970)) and is sufficient for the removal of a director or auditor from office (s.184, 1948 Act, and s.14, 1976 Act). In addition, a company can by ordinary resolution ratify a director's unauthorised act provided that the act in question is not *ultra vires* the company (*Bamford* v. *Bamford* (1970)).

(*b*) *Extraordinary resolution.* This must be passed by at least a three-fourths majority of the votes at a general meeting of which notice specifying the intention to propose the resolution as an extraordinary resolution has been given (s.141, 1948 Act). This type of resolution is for instance required where it is intended to vary the right of the holders of a particular class of shares in the company (s.32, 1980 Act).

(*c*) *Special resolution.* Here again a three-fourths majority of votes is required with the additional provision that at least twenty-one days' notice of the intention to propose this resolution must be given. A special resolution is necessary in order to alter a company's memorandum and articles of association. It is also one of the requirements where it is proposed to re-register a private company as a public company (s.5, 1980 Act).

SUMMARY

On completion of this chapter you should be able to:

(*a*) State the methods by which registered companies may be classified and indicate the differences between public and private companies.

(*b*) Describe the process of formation of a registered company and understand the rules relating to promoters and the company prospectus.

(*c*) Appreciate the significance of the objects clause in the company's memorandum of association.

(*d*) Understand the meaning of share capital and appreciate the significance of the rules relating to it.

SELF-ASSESSMENT QUESTIONS

(Relevant page numbers are given in brackets.)

1. What are the differences between "limited" companies and those which are "unlimited"? (Page 21)

2. Distinguish between public companies and private companies. (Pages 21–2)

3. What is the position of a registered company with respect to contracts purportedly made on its behalf before its incorporation? (Pages 23–4)

4. What is the effect of the *ultra vires* rule at the present time? (Page 28)

5. Outline the rules relating to the share capital of a company. (Pages 29–31)

CHAPTER FOUR

Registered Companies— Personnel

CHAPTER OBJECTIVES

After studying this chapter you should be able to:
* discuss the main statutory and judicial rules governing the relationships existing between a registered company and the individuals within it;
* describe the duties of directors towards their company;
* understand the circumstances in which a company may be liable in contract to outsiders for the acts of its officials;
* outline the protection available in company law to minority shareholders.

INTRODUCTION

Relationships within the company are regulated principally by the contract contained in the memorandum and articles of association (*see* Chapter 3). In addition, various rights and obligations are contained in the Companies Acts and decisions of the courts, affecting such matters as the functions of directors and the protection of minority shareholders from the improper activities of the majority.

We begin this chapter with a discussion of the company's membership and note the importance of distinguishing between the members *per se* and debenture holders. The chapter continues with an examination of the functions, duties and authority of the directors. Of particular significance are the relationships between the various parties and, in the final section, attention is drawn to that obtaining between the company itself and its membership.

MEMBERS AND DEBENTURE HOLDERS

Shareholders

These are the members of a company limited by shares. Shares may be acquired by the original subscribers of the memorandum of association at the time of the company's incorporation or subsequently, either from existing members or from the company itself in the case of a new issue (*see* p. 26). In the case of persons other than the subscribers, membership is not complete until the shareholder's names are entered in the company's register of members (s.26, 1948 Act). Of significance in this respect is the fact that the directors may be empowered by the company's articles to refuse to register a transfer of shares (*see* Chapter 7).

A decision illustrating the distinction which must be drawn between the ownership of shares and membership of the company is *Musselwhite* v. *Musselwhite and Sons Ltd.* (1962). When the plaintiffs sold their shares in a company, it was arranged that their names should remain on the register of members until the purchasers had paid the price in full. Nevertheless, the company failed to give notice to the plaintiffs of a general meeting. The court decided that the meeting was invalidly held because of the omission to notify all the registered members.

There are certain restrictions on membership. Thus, a subsidiary company may not normally be a member of its holding company and any allotment or transfer of shares made by a company to its subsidiary is void (s.27, 1948 Act).

The register of members

The register must normally be kept at the company's registered office and be available for inspection by any person during business hours. Details to be contained in the register include the names and addresses of the members, the shareholding of each and the date on which a person became a member or ceased to be such (s.110, 1948 Act). The register should not however be regarded as final on the question of membership, since it is open to any aggrieved person to apply to the court to have the register altered, where the necessary justification can be established (s.116, 1948 Act). Where, for example, a person is induced to purchase shares from the company on the basis of a false or misleading statement made by the directors as to the profitability of the company, he may be entitled to repudiate the transaction and request that his name be removed from the register.

Nature of the shareholder's interest

Membership of the company confers on shareholders various rights. There is, for example, the right to receive payment of a dividend if one is declared by the company and members have the right to attend and vote at meetings. Because the company has separate legal personality, the members cannot however be regarded as owners of the company's assets, whether at common law or beneficially. In *Macaura* v. *Northern Assurance Co.* (1925), the plaintiff held all the shares in a company to which he had sold a quantity of timber. He had effected fire insurance policies in respect of the timber, but in his own name. The timber was subsequently destroyed by fire but the House of Lords supported the insurers' refusal to meet the plaintiff's claim, on the grounds of lack of insurable interest in the timber. The timber belonged to the company and the plaintiff stood in no legal or equitable relation to it.

As well as rights, shareholders have obligations. For instance, where a limited company is being wound up (*see* Chapter 5), members are required to contribute towards the payment of the company's debts to the extent of their nominal shareholding (s.212, 1948 Act).

Debenture holders

When a company borrows money, it may issue to the lender a document evidencing the transaction: this is known as a *debenture*, the statutory definition of which includes debenture stock, bonds and other company securities, whether constituting a charge on the assets of the company or not (s.455, 1948 Act). Debenture holders do not have the status of membership, but they are creditors of the company and are therefore entitled to interest on the loan together with repayment of capital. A debenture loan will usually be protected by a charge or mortgage (*see* Chapter 8) on part or all of the company's property and, in the event of the company failing to repay the debt, the lender will have direct rights over that property which is subject to the charge. In this way, "secured" creditors ensure that, where a company is unable to meet all its financial obligations, their right to repayment takes priority over those creditors whose loans are unsecured. (Debentures are considered further in Chapter 6.)

DIRECTORS

In this section, we consider the appointment, qualifications and duties of the company's directors. The authority of directors to act on the company's behalf is considered separately in the following section.

General

The persons with ultimate control of a company are the shareholders, but the articles of association will normally provide for the appointment of directors to manage the company's affairs. Article 80 of Table A for example, provides that the business of the company shall be managed by the directors, who may exercise all the powers of the company that are not required to be exercised by the members in general meeting. Some directors may participate in a company's business on a part-time basis only.

The status of directors is that of officers of the company but they may function also as company employees, in which case separate service contracts may be negotiated. Public companies are required to have at least two directors but private companies need appoint only one (s.176, 1948 Act). Where the articles demand that directors become members of the company by purchasing a specified number of shares (the shareholding qualification), these must be obtained within two months, otherwise the defaulting directors must vacate their office (s.182, 1948 Act).

Appointment
Directors may initially be appointed by being named in the articles of association or their names may be determined in writing by the subscribers of the memorandum. Subsequent appointments are usually by election by the shareholders, in general meeting, with the articles making additional provision for such matters as retirement. If Table A applies, the company may from time to time increase or reduce the number of directors by ordinary resolution (i.e. a simple majority of those members voting). The directors themselves may be empowered by the articles to appoint directors (e.g. to fill a vacancy) but this power will revert to the members in general meeting if for some reason the directors are unable to act. In *Barron* v. *Potter* (1914), a company's articles of association required that there should be a quorum of two directors at meetings of the board. The only two directors were unable to reach agreement and the shareholders convened a meeting at which additional directors were appointed. In the circumstances, the shareholders' action was held to be constitutional, despite a provision in the articles giving the power to make appointments to the directors.

A person may be disqualified by the court from acting as a director for periods of up to fifteen years where he is convicted of an offence in connection with the promotion, formation, management or liquidation of a company or where it appears that, having been a director of insolvent companies, his conduct makes him unfit to be concerned in company management (s.188, 1948 Act and s.9, Insolvency Act 1976 (as amended)). The Secretary of State is required by the Companies Act 1976 to maintain a register of disqualification orders made by the court (s.29).

Every company is required to keep a register containing the names, addresses and other details of its directors and the registrar of companies must be notified within fourteen days of changes in the company's directors or in the contents of the register (s.200, 1948 Act, as amended).

Managing director

A company's articles of association will usually provide for the appointment of a managing director upon whom executive authority to run the company's affairs is conferred. Table A, for example, authorises the directors to assign to the managing director any of the powers exercisable by them with such powers operating to the exclusion of those of the other directors. This means that the managing director may be the only person who may validly exercise the powers concerned.

The articles may also provide for the termination of the managing director's appointment where, for example, he ceases to be a director of the company or where the other directors revoke such appointment. It should be noted though that a dismissed managing director may be entitled to claim damages from the company for breach of a contract of service. Damages were recoverable in *Nelson* v. *James Nelson & Sons Ltd.* (1914) where, under a written contract, the plaintiff was appointed managing director for the time that he remained a director of the company. The board of directors terminated his appointment purporting to act under a power of revocation contained in the articles of association. The Court of Appeal held that, having regard to the terms of the contract, the plaintiff's tenure was not subject to the will and pleasure of the board.

If, on the other hand, there is no separate contract of service regulating the managing director's position and the only relevant provisions are those contained in the articles of association, a dismissal in accordance with the articles will not constitute a breach of contract.

In *Read* v. *Astoria Garage (Streatham) Ltd.* (1952), a company's articles provided for the termination of its managing director's appointment where the members in general meeting so resolved. As there were no contractual provisions (other than the articles) entitling the plaintiff to notice, a resolution by the members that he should be dismissed was valid and effective and did not entitle him to damages for wrongful dismissal.

Directors' meetings

Directors normally exercise their powers at board meetings but the articles may provide for the company's business to be conducted in some alternative way. Where applicable, Article 106 of Table A provides that a resolution in writing signed by all the directors shall be as valid as if it had been passed at a meeting of all the directors.

Furthermore, provided the directors are of one mind, it is unnecessary that they should all meet in the same place. Consequently, the fact that two directors gave their consent to an agreement between the company and a third party at a place different from the other directors did not affect its validity in *Re Bonelli's Telegraph Co.* (1871). Again, the absence of a board resolution will not affect the proper exercise of a power contained in the memorandum where the directors taking the action are themselves the only shareholders in the company (as in *Re Horsley and Weight Ltd.* (1982)).

All the directors are entitled to adequate notice of a board meeting otherwise the proceedings will be unconstitutional. In one case, a company invited the public to apply for a new issue of shares and its five directors resolved that no shares were to be allotted until a minimum number of applications had been received. At a subsequent meeting, two of the directors agreed to make an allotment despite that the required minimum number had not been reached. Two other directors were unable to attend this meeting because they had received only three hours' notice and the fifth director was abroad. The court decided that the meeting was invalidly held and the allotment of shares was void (*Re Homer District Consolidated Gold Mines Ltd.* (1888)).

The articles may stipulate that a minimum number of directors (the quorum) be present at meetings of the board. Where Table A applies, the quorum is two. We have already seen that, where the directors are unable to discharge their functions because of the absence of a quorum, the members in general meeting may be entitled to act in their place (*Barron* v. *Potter* (1914)).

The duties of directors

As individuals

There is a principal of equity that a person in whom trust is placed by another must refrain from acting in his own interests if this would prejudice the interests of the other person. Consequently like trustees, partners and agents, company directors are regarded by the courts as *fiduciaries* and, in the performance of their duties, must avoid conflict between their own interests and those of the company. A director must therefore make full disclosure to the members if he is financially interested in any contract in which the company is involved, otherwise the contract may be voidable at the company's option. In *Aberdeen Railway Co* v. *Blaikie Bros.* (1854) the appellant company wished to repudiate a contract for the purchase of goods from Blaikie Bros. because a member of its own board of directors was also a partner in the firm. The House of Lords decided that the contract was voidable because of the conflict of interest. It should be noted that no fiduciary duty is normally owed by the directors to individual members of the company (*Percival* v. *Wright* (1902)).

The obligation to make full disclosure is now supplemented by statutory provisions. A director is required to disclose at a meeting of the directors of the company the nature of his interest in a contract, transaction or arrangement (or proposed contract etc.) with the company, failure to comply with this provision being a criminal offence (s.199, 1948 Act). Furthermore, with some exceptions, particulars of transactions or arrangements with the company in which a director has a material interest must be disclosed in the company's annual accounts (s.54, 1980 Act).

Apart from being under an obligation to disclose matters in which he is interested, a director's fiduciary position makes him accountable to the company for any financial advantage or business opportunity which he acquires in the course of his duties. *Regal (Hastings) Ltd.* v. *Gulliver* (1942) is a case in point. The directors of Regal formed a subsidiary company to purchase a certain property. Regal took two-fifths of the shares in the new company and the remaining shares were purchased by the directors and their associates. Subsequently, the directors sold all their shares in Regal and the subsidiary, making a profit of £2.80 per share. The new controllers of Regal sought to recover this profit for the benefit of the company. The House of Lords decided that the directors were accountable for the profit in the shares because it had been gained in the course of their management of Regal.

Similarly, in *Industrial Development Consultants Ltd.* v. *Cooley* (1972), the Eastern Gas Board intimated to the defendant that it was unwilling to do business with the plaintiff company of which he was managing director. Subsequently, the board dealt with the defendant privately after he had resigned from the plaintiff's service and the court held that he was under a fiduciary obligation to account for the profit received under the contract; the fact that there was only a remote possibility of the company itself being awarded the contract being regarded as irrelevant.

In another case, *International Sales and Agencies Ltd.* v. *Marcus* (1982), a director was held to be in breach of his fiduciary duty to his company where he arranged for money lent by the defendant to a shareholder to be repaid from company funds after the shareholder concerned had died insolvent.

Duties owed by the directors as a board

The powers conferred on the directors by the articles of association must be exercised for the benefit of the company in accordance with proper management considerations and not for the benefit of the directors themselves. In *Re W. and M. Roith Ltd.* (1967), Roith was the company's controlling shareholder and managing director and he entered into a contract with the company whereby, after his death, a life pension would be paid by the company to his widow. Later, the company was wound up and the question was whether the liquidator was bound by the pension provision. The court decided that the widow's claim should be disallowed because the transaction had not been made for the company's benefit. However, if in such a case there is an independent object in the memorandum of association providing for the pension then it seems that the payments will be regarded as lawful (*Re Horsley and Weight Ltd.* (1982)).

The powers of the directors must not be used improperly even though the directors might honestly believe that they are acting in the best interests of the company. Thus, an issue of shares will be invalid if it is intended to affect the balance of power among the shareholders. A decision illustrating this principle is *Howard Smith Ltd.* v. *Ampol Petroleum Ltd.* (1974). Two rival companies, X and Y, were competing to acquire a controlling interest in company Z. Y was already joint owner of a majority of Z's shares and the directors of Z allotted new shares to X with the result that Y's shareholding became a minority one. The directors had power to issue shares under the articles of association but the court decided that the issue was invalid because it was unconstitutional to use the power in this way.

The Companies Act 1980 in fact prohibits an allotment of shares being made by the directors without the authority of the members in general meeting or a provision in the articles to that effect (s.14).

Duty of care
When discharging their functions, the directors are required to exercise a certain degree of care and skill. However, a non-specialist director need only take such care as is reasonable having regard to his individual knowledge or experience (*Re City Equitable Fire Insurance Co. Ltd.* (1925)).

Insider dealing
A controversial area in the past has been the extent to which a director should be allowed to use information acquired in the course of his duties in order to obtain a personal advantage from share dealings. The position now is that any individual who is knowingly connected with a company (or has been so connected during the preceding six months) is prohibited from dealing in that company's securities where he has information by virtue of his

connection, the information being such that it would not normally be disclosed except in the proper performance of the individual's function, and he knows that it is unpublished, price-sensitive information (s.68, 1980 Act). The prohibition extends to the securities of any other company which is involved in a trans-action with the company with which the individual concerned is connected.

An infringement of the provisions relating to insider dealing is a criminal offence (s.72, 1980 Act).

Removal of directors

Directors can be removed from office on a simple majority of the votes cast at a meeting of the members of the company (s.184, 1948 Act). Further, this statutory power of removal is exercisable despite any provision to the contrary in the company's articles of association or in any agreement between the company and the director concerned. Nevertheless, a provision in the articles re-lating to the adjustment of voting rights in the event of an attempted dismissal may render it difficult if not impossible to remove a director. Such a situation arose in *Bushell* v. *Faith* (1970) where the articles provided that, in the event of a resolution to dismiss a director being proposed, the shares of that director should each carry additional votes. The House of Lords accepted the validity of this provision despite the fact that the effect of the increased voting power meant that two of the company's three shareholders were unable to dismiss the other from his position of director of the company.

A director who is successfully removed is not deprived of any right to claim damages to which he may be entitled. In *Southern Foundries (1926) Ltd.* v. *Shirlaw* (1940), the company's articles of association were altered so as to provide for the dismissal of its managing director who had been appointed to this office for a ten year period under a written agreement. The House of Lords de-cided that, although no company could be prevented from altering its articles of association, action on the basis of such alteration could amount to a breach of contract for which the company could be liable to pay damages.

In this connection, it should be noted that, if a director does have a separate contract of employment, the members in general meet-ing must approve any term which provides for a period of employ-ment in excess of five years. If not approved, the term is void and the contract becomes terminable by the company on the giving of reasonable notice (s.47, 1980 Act).

It is unlawful for a company to compensate a director for loss of office unless particulars of the proposed payment are disclosed to and approved by the members (s.191, 1948 Act). Payments by way of damages for breach of contract and other payments which the company is contractually bound to make (e.g. a lump sum payable on a director's resignation) are not however subject to this provision (s.194, 1948 Act and *Taupo Totara Timber Co. Ltd.* v. *Rowe* (1977)).

Relations between the board of directors and the members in general meeting

We have considered how the articles normally allow for the delegation of managerial powers to a board of directors with there being a possible further delegation of authority to a managing director (*see* p. 36). Certain powers may not however be delegated at all and must be exercised by the members of the company in general meeting: the power to remove a director (s.184, 1948 Act) and the power of alteration of the company's memorandum and articles of association (ss.5 and 10, 1948 Act) are but two examples. Once there has been a valid delegation of power in accordance with the articles any interference by the members in general meeting will be regarded as unlawful. The members are able to recover their power of action only in a constitutional manner: that is, by altering the articles or by dismissing the directors. The relationship of the board of directors to the shareholders in general meeting was considered in *John Shaw and Sons (Salford) Ltd.* v. *Shaw* (1935) where, in the judgment of Greer LJ it was stated that "shareholders may not usurp the powers vested by the articles in the directors any more than the directors can usurp the powers vested by the articles in the general body of shareholders". In this case, the directors wished to commence a breach of contract action against certain members of the company but, at a meeting of the shareholders, it was resolved to discontinue the action. The shareholders had no right to interfere, decided the court, because the matter fell within the scope of the director's powers. Similarly, in *Automatic Self-Cleansing Filter Syndicate Co. Ltd.* v. *Cuningham* (1906), the court refused to allow the shareholders to interfere with the directors' control of the sale of the company's assets because power in this respect had been specifically assigned to the directors in accordance with the articles.

DIRECTORS AND THE LAW OF AGENCY

The wider aspects of the law relating to agency are discussed in Chapter 14.

Actual authority

Unlike partners in relation to the firm, individual directors may not normally be regarded as agents of the company, because the power to bind the company with respect to transactions entered into with other persons is conferred by the articles on the directors as a whole. A person who supplies goods to the company through a director, for example, may only look to the company for payment where the director concerned has been given the necessary authority to create that contract. Such authority may be conferred expressly (e.g. under a provision in the articles) or it may be implied from the circumstances of the case. In *Hely-Hutchinson* v. *Brayhead Ltd.* (1968), R frequently made contracts on the defendant company's behalf which he would subsequently ask the board of directors to approve. He arranged for the company to guarantee money owed to the plaintiff but, when sued on the guarantee, the company argued that R lacked express authority to bind the company. The Court of Appeal held that the necessary actual authority could be inferred from the acquiescence of the company's board of directors in R's conduct over the preceding months.

Further, provided a director's unauthorised act is not *ultra vires* the powers of the company, it may later be ratified and given retrospective validity by the members in general meeting (*Bamford* v. *Bamford* (1970)).

Apparent authority

In the above cases, where authority is express, implied, or the result of ratification, the director is said to have actual authority. Where a director lacks actual authority, he may have nevertheless what is called ostensible or apparent authority, that is, "the authority of an agent as it appears to others" (Lord Denning in the *Hely-Hutchinson* case, above). The company may, for example, through its board of directors represent to an outsider that a particular individual has the authority to bind the company in which case it may subsequently be prevented (estopped) from pleading the absence of such authority. An illustration of this principle is to be found in *Freeman and Lockyer* v. *Buckhurst Park Properties (Mangal) Ltd.* (1964).

K and H formed the defendant company to buy and sell property with daily management being left to K, who engaged the plaintiffs, a firm of architects and surveyors. When the plaintiffs later claimed their fee, the company refused to pay arguing that K had no authority to hire them. Although there was no actual authority, the Court of Appeal decided that the fee was recoverable because, on the facts, the board had suggested to outsiders that K did have the authority to act by permitting him to conduct the affairs of the company in the way he had. It was stated in this case (per Diplock LJ) that the requirements to be fulfilled for apparent agency to arise are:

(a) a representation by persons with actual authority that the agent concerned is empowered to act,

(b) reliance by the other contracting party on such representation, and

(c) the contract which the other party seeks to enforce is neither *ultra vires* the company nor incapable of delegation to the individual concerned.

Procedural defects

Note that a contract created through the agency of a director may be later called into question because of some procedural defect internal to the company. For instance, a decision to enter into the transaction might have been taken at a board meeting convened without proper notice, or without the required quorum of directors. The position with regard to such cases is that persons dealing with the company are entitled to assume, in the absence of contrary evidence, that all the constitutional requirements have been correctly observed. Where therefore a bank advanced money to a company, the loan was recoverable despite the absence of a resolution authorising the transaction (as required by the borrowing company's articles of association) because there were no means whereby the plaintiff bank could establish compliance (*Royal British Bank* v. *Turquand* (1855)).

In another case, a bank paid money from a company's account on the authority of a written instruction of the company's directors. The written instruction appeared to comply with the company's articles of association therefore, on the face of it, everything was in order. The directors had never been properly appointed however and the liquidator of the company (which was in the process of being wound up) sought to recover the payments from an official of the bank. The House of Lords decided that the claim should be disallowed because the bank was justified in assuming that the company's internal requirements as regards the appointment of directors had been met (*Mahoney* v. *East Holyford Mining Co.* (1875)).

This particular form of irregularity (i.e. defective appointment of directors) is now dealt with by s.180 of the Companies Act 1948 which provides that the acts of a director shall be valid despite any defect which may subsequently be discovered in his appointment or qualification.

Finally, it should be noted that, where s.9 of the European Communities Act 1972 applies (i.e. in the case of a transaction decided on by the directors), a person dealing with the company in good faith is affected only by those matters of which he has actual knowledge; he is not fixed automatically with constructive notice of limitations on the directors' authority and procedural requirements contained in the company's memorandum and articles of association (*see also* Chapter 3, p. 28).

THE COMPANY SECRETARY

Every company is required to have a secretary and this function may not be carried out by a sole director (s.177, 1948 Act). The secretary is the chief administrative officer of the company but, whereas his duties and responsibilities include signing contracts relating to day-to-day administration and employing staff, he is not otherwise concerned with company business. In *Re Maidstone Building Provisions Ltd.* (1971), the liquidator of a company brought an action requesting that the directors and company secretary be held personally responsible for the debts of the company on the grounds that they had allowed the company to continue its business despite their knowledge that the company was trading at a loss and could not meet its debts (s.332, 1948 Act). The court decided that the action against the secretary should be discontinued because, in discharging his duties as secretary, he was not a party to the carrying on of the business as required by the statute.

The company secretary's role was considered also in *Panorama Developments (Guildford) Ltd.* v. *Fidelis Furnishing Fabrics Ltd.* (1971) where the defendant company's secretary, acting without authority, hired motor vehicles from the plaintiffs claiming that they were to be used for the purpose of the defendant's business. The vehicles were, in fact, used for the secretary's own purposes and the question for the court was whether the defendant company could be taken to have authorised the transaction. The Court of Appeal decided that the company was liable because the hire of vehicles fell within the ostensible authority of a company secretary, being a matter concerned with company administration. The Companies Act 1980 now requires that, in the case of public companies, persons appointed to the post of company secretary in future must be a chartered secretary, accountant, barrister or solicitor, or have held office as secretary of a company (other than a private company), for at least three of the preceding five years. The duty to ensure compliance with this requirement is imposed on the directors (s.79).

RELATIONSHIPS BETWEEN THE MEMBERS AND THE COMPANY

The contractual relationship

The memorandum and articles of association have a contractual effect because of the statutory provision that these documents when registered shall bind the company and the members as if they had been signed and sealed by each member and contained covenants on the part of each member to observe all the provisions contained therein (s.20, 1948 Act). Where a company's articles provided that a member who wished to sell his shares should inform the directors, who would purchase the shares at a fair value, this provision was upheld in favour of the plaintiff shareholder because of the contractual relationship existing between the plaintiff and the defendant directors as members of the company (*Rayfield* v. *Hands* (1960)).

This contractual relationship does not however benefit a person in some capacity other than that of member, for example a company solicitor: the only rights protected are those which are enjoyed in common with other shareholders. Thus, in *Eley* v. *Positive Government Life Assurance Co.* (1876), the company's articles provided that Eley should be the company's solicitor. When the company failed to employ him, therefore, he commenced an action for breach of contract. The claim was unsuccessful because Eley was not a party to the contract contained in the articles of association. The observance of the articles was a matter between the directors and the shareholders, said the court, not between them and the plaintiff.

As the company is of course a party to the contract, individual members whose personal rights are infringed by the company may seek legal redress. In *Wood* v. *Odessa Waterworks* (1889), instead of paying a dividend on members' shares, a company resolved to give its shareholders interest bearing debenture bonds. Wood successfully applied for an injunction to prevent the company acting on the resolution, because there would have been a contravention of the company's articles of association which provided for the payment of dividends in cash.

Variation of the contract

The terms of the contract between the members and the company are usually contained in the articles of association, the memorandum detailing such matters as the company's objects and share capital (*see* Chapter 3). As the provisions of the articles may be altered by a special resolution (i.e. not less than three-quarters of those shareholders voting at a properly convened meeting) it is possible, in this way, to vary the shareholders' contractual rights. In *Allen* v. *Gold Reefs of West Africa Ltd.* (1900), a company altered its articles in order to acquire a lien (*see* Chapter 8, p. 99) over the fully paid shares of those members who were indebted to the company. The court decided that the revised articles would apply to existing shareholders, provided the power of alteration were exercised in good faith and for the benefit of the company as a whole. It was pointed out, however, that following the alteration, the company might well be in breach of some other contractual obligation (*see*, for example, *Southern Foundries* v. *Shirlaw*, p. 42).

The principle of majority rule

The courts will not normally interfere with the management of a company by the majority of members. A majority in general meeting can in fact pursue whatever course of action it chooses, however "wrongheaded" such a course of action appears to others, provided there is no unfair oppression of other members of the company (*Hogg* v. *Cramphorn* (1967)). Consequently, where a wrong has been done to the company, the courts take the view that the proper plaintiff is the company itself, not individual shareholders. The position is governed by what is known as the rule in *Foss* v. *Harbottle* (1843) where a minority shareholders' action against the defendant directors was disallowed. The allegation against the directors was that they had injured the "whole corporation", therefore, said the court, the right to sue belonged to the company and not to the plaintiffs. The difficulty presented here, however, is that the company itself is unlikely to commence an action against fraudulent or otherwise defaulting directors where the latter are themselves in full control. The rule is therefore subject to a number of exceptions. Individual or minority shareholders are permitted to commence proceedings where either

(*a*) their individual rights are in some way affected (see *Wood* v. *Odessa Waterworks* above) or

(*b*) the action complained of is *ultra vires* the company, or

(*c*) the irregularity is such that it is incapable of ratification by a simple majority of the members, or

(*d*) the persons in control of the company's affairs are acting fraudulently.

For instance, in *Menier* v. *Hoopers' Telegraph Works Ltd.* (1874), a minority shareholders' action was successful where the majority sought to direct their company's business to a competitor and then have the company wound up. More recently, in *Daniels* v. *Daniels* (1978), the court decided that a further exception to the *Foss* v. *Harbottle* rule existed where, albeit in the absence of fraud, a company's directors used their powers in such a way as to benefit themselves at the expense of the company. The allegation in *Daniels'* case was that the company had sold land to one of its two directors at a price below true market value and that the director concerned had subsequently resold the land making a substantial profit. An application to have an action, brought by aggrieved minority shareholders, struck out for being contrary to the rule in *Foss* v. *Harbottle* was unsuccessful.

Actions commenced by individual shareholders on their own behalf and that of other aggrieved persons are said to be *representative*. Where however the plaintiff sues on the company's behalf, because a wrong has been done to the company itself, the action is described as *derivative*. In the latter case, the court may order that the costs of litigation be paid by the company on the principle that it is the company which benefits (in the form of damages) in the event of the action succeeding (*Wallersteiner* v. *Moir (No. 2)* (1975)).

Minority protection

It will be apparent from the foregoing discussion that although the majority of shareholders have ultimate control of the company's affairs, limitations are imposed by the courts on the extent to which they can override the interests of the minority. As we have seen, the principle of majority rule does not justify conduct which is fraudulent (*Menier* v. *Hoopers' Telegraph Works Ltd.* (1874)). Furthermore, in the exercise of their powers, controlling shareholders are required to act, not in their own interests, but in the interests of the shareholders as a general body. In *Clemens* v. *Clemens Bros. Ltd.* (1976), the plaintiff held forty-five per cent of the shares in a company. It was proposed to increase the company's share capital by issuing new shares, the effect of which would be to reduce the degree of control exercised by the plaintiff. The decision of the court was that the majority shareholder was not justified in voting on the matter arbitrarily. Her conduct was subject to equitable considerations and it would be unjust to deprive the plaintiff of existing rights.

The above constraints are supplemented by statute. A company in which oppression or wrongful conduct exists can be wound up where the court considers this to be a just and equitable solution (s.222(*f*), 1948 Act, and *see* Chapter 5). In *Ebrahimi* v. *Westbourne Galleries Ltd.* (1973), the removal of a shareholder from the management of the company was a ground for dissolution because it infringed on earlier understanding that the shareholder concerned would be allowed rights of participation. The removal was effected in the proper manner (*see* s.184, 1948 Act) but the House of Lords pointed out that the exercise of such legal rights of removal was subject to equitable considerations; that it was unfair to use legal rights of expulsion given the circumstances (this decision was in fact relied on in *Clemens* case above).

Where a company's affairs are being conducted in a manner which is unfairly prejudicial to the interests of the members, the court is empowered on the application of an aggrieved member to "make such order as it thinks fit for giving relief in respect of the matters complained of" (s.75, 1980 Act). In particular, the order may regulate the future activities of the company, prohibit the act or omission complained of, authorise the commencement of civil proceedings in the company's name and provide for the purchase of one person's shares by the other members or by the company. This provision was applied in *Re Bird Precision Bellows Ltd.* (1984) where shareholders holding 26 per cent of a company's issued share capital claimed that they had been wrongfully removed as directors by the majority shareholders and prevented from taking part in the company's business. The court found that the company's affairs had been conducted in a manner unfairly prejudicial to the interests of the minority and ordered that their shareholding be purchased at a price fixed on a pro rata basis.

The Secretary of State has power to order an investigation of a company's affairs where there is evidence that these are being conducted fraudulently or in a manner which is unfairly prejudicial to some part of the company's members (s.165, 1948 Act) and, further, may present a winding up petition to the court if it appears following the investigation that it is in the public interest that the company should be wound up (s.35, 1967 Act). Another option available to the Secretary of State in such cases is to petition the court for an order under s.75 of the 1980 Act (above).

SUMMARY

On completion of this chapter you should be able to:

(*a*) Indicate who are the members of a company limited by shares.

(*b*) Appreciate the difference between the ownership of shares and membership of the company.

(*c*) Show an understanding of the different functions of the directors, managing director and shareholders in general meeting and the respective relationships between them.

(*d*) Define and explain the duties of directors towards the company.

(*e*) Understand the rules regulating the contractual liability of a company for the acts of its agents.

(*f*) Know the principle of majority rule and appreciate the limits to which the majority of members can act in defiance of the wishes of the minority.

SELF-ASSESSMENT QUESTIONS

(Relevant page numbers are given in brackets.)

1. Indicate which of the following may be said to have ultimate control of a company's affairs: directors, shareholders, managing director. (Pages 36–43)

2. Who are the members of a company limited by shares: debenture holders, company secretary, shareholders, directors? (Pages 34–7)

3. Distinguish between a director's implied authority and that which is ostensible. (Page 44)

4. Consider whether a company's board of directors can ever:

(*a*) make an allotment of shares,

(*b*) dismiss one of the directors,

(*c*) alter the company's articles of association. (Pages 41, 42 and 47)

CHAPTER FIVE

Winding Up and Bankruptcy

CHAPTER OBJECTIVES

After studying this chapter you should be able to:
* discuss the main provisions regulating the winding up and dissolution of registered companies;
* outline the general characteristics of bankruptcy proceedings; and
* in both cases; consider the rights of creditors.

INTRODUCTION

If a business organisation is unable to meet its financial commitments, one of two sets of rules may be brought into operation for determining the rights of creditors. On the one hand, the position with respect to registered companies is regulated by the Companies Acts. In the case of an unincorporated association such as a sole proprietorship or partnership, the relevant provisions are at present contained in the Bankruptcy Act 1914 (as amended) and Rules made thereunder. In both situations the object is broadly the same; that is, to harness what remains of the organisation's assets (including the private assets of individuals where there is no limitation of liability) and distribute these to the various creditors in accordance with their respective claims.

It should be noted that a new Insolvency Bill (to be enacted during 1985) provides for the repeal of the Bankruptcy Act 1914 and replaces it with provisions relating to the insolvency of both registered companies and individuals (including partnerships).

WINDING UP

Introduction

A registered company which is experiencing financial or other difficulties may be wound up and ultimately dissolved. Winding up, or liquidation, involves essentially the realisation of the company's assets with the object of paying off creditors in the first instance and then distributing whatever sums remain to the company's members. The process may be initiated without the agreement of the company and be subject to the control of the court or it may be effected voluntarily by the members themselves.

Winding up by the court

A petition requesting the winding up of a company may be presented to the High Court (or the county court, provided the company's share capital does not exceed a specified amount) by the company itself, by its creditors or by the members (referred to in this part of the Act as "contributories") (s.224, 1948 Act). In addition, the Department of Trade may request that a company be wound up where it considers this course of action to be expedient in the public interest (s.35, 1967 Act) and the Secretary of State may present a winding up petition where, for example, a public company fails to obtain a certificate to do business under s.4 of the 1980 Act (s.224, 1948 Act, as amended).

Frequently, a company may be wound up if it is unable to pay its debts but it should be emphasised that this is not the only situation in which a winding up order can be made. Thus, the court may also order a winding up where:

(*a*) the company has by special resolution resolved to be wound up by the court,

(*b*) the company's business is not commenced within a year of incorporation or such business is suspended for a year,

(*c*) being an old public company (*see* Chapter 3), the company takes no steps to alter its status,

(*d*) the membership of the company is reduced below two, or

(*e*) the court considers it to be just and equitable that the company should be wound up (s.222, 1948 Act, as amended). Furthermore, a public company can be wound up if it is still without a certificate to do business (*see* Chapter 3) more than a year after registration (s.222(*b*)).

In Chapter 4 (p. 49) it was explained that the "just and equitable" ground referred to above may be used as a form of minority protection where, for instance, a shareholder is denied the right to participate in the management of a small company (*Ebrahimi* v. *Westbourne Galleries Ltd.* (1973)). The application of this particular ground is not however confined to minority protection. In *Re Yenidje Tobacco Co. Ltd.* (1916), two cigarette manufacturers set up a private company in which they were the only directors and shareholders. Subsequently, the two parties fell out and, having regard to the seriousness of their disagreement, the court took the view that the company should be wound up just as a partnership would be dissolved in similar circumstances (*see* Chapter 2, p. 17). A further example is *Re German Date Coffee Co.* (1882) where a company was wound up under the just and equitable rule because the purpose for which it had been formed, the development of a patent for the manufacture of a coffee substitute from dates, could not be fulfilled when the company failed to obtain a grant of the patent.

Responsibility for the conduct of the winding up process is assigned to a liquidator who is appointed by the court. Pending this appointment, the official receiver in bankruptcy may act as provisional liquidator (s.238, 1948 Act). The directors and other officers of the company are required to submit to the official receiver a statement of the company's affairs showing for instance the particulars of its assets, debts and liabilities and the official receiver must report to the court on the causes of the company's failure (ss.235 and 236, 1948 Act). A committee of inspection consisting of representatives of the company's creditors and contributories may be appointed (ss.252, 1948 Act) in which case the liquidator must have regard to its directions when discharging his duties (s.246, 1948 Act).

Voluntary winding up

This form of winding up may occur where:

(a) the company in general meeting resolves to do so when a period fixed in the articles of association for the duration of the company expires,

(b) the company resolves to wind up voluntarily by special resolution, and

(c) the company resolves to wind up by extraordinary resolution because it cannot by reason of its liabilities continue its business (s.278, 1948 Act).

An important distinction must be made in this context between a members' voluntary winding up and a creditors' voluntary winding up. In the former instance, the company's directors are required to declare that they are of the opinion that the company is solvent and will be able to discharge its debts within a period not more than twelve months from the date of the passing of the resolution (s.283, 1948 Act). The directors in fact lay themselves open to criminal proceedings if they lack reasonable grounds for their opinion. If no declaration of solvency is made, the principal effect is that it is the creditors' nominee who is most likely to become liquidator, not that of the company (s.294, 1948 Act). In addition, the directors are required in this event to furnish the creditors with a statement of the company's affairs (s.293, 1948 Act).

Distribution of the company's assets

The liquidator's main function in the winding up of a company is to use its assets in meeting the claims of creditors and then to distribute the remainder to the shareholders. To this end, the liquidator is given various powers, including power to sell the company's property, to raise money on the security of the company's assets, to carry on its business if the winding up necessitates this, and to do all such other things as may be required for winding up the company's affairs and distributing its assets (ss.245 and 303, 1948 Act). Furthermore, he can call upon the shareholders to contribute any sums which may be required in order that the company may pay its debts (s.273, 1948 Act). The basic obligation in this respect is imposed on every past and present member but it is nevertheless subject to some qualifications. Thus, if the company is limited by shares or by guarantee, no member can be required to contribute more than the amount unpaid on his shares or that amount which he has undertaken to contribute in the event of the company being wound up. Again, a past member is under no obligation to pay if his membership of the company ceased one year or more before the commencement of the winding up and, moreover, this obligation is dependent on the existing members being unable to fulfill their commitments (s.212, 1948 Act).

The assets which are available for distribution do not necessarily include all the property which happens to be in the possession of the company at the time of liquidation. A supplier of goods to the company might for instance have stipulated under a reservation of title clause in the contract of sale that ownership should not pass until payment had been made. In fact, in *Aluminium Industrie Vaassen B.V.* v. *Romalpa Aluminium Ltd.* (1976) (considered further in Chapter 7), the effect of the stipulation was such that the supplier's ownership extended also to the proceeds from the sale of manufactured goods by the company to a sub-buyer. In this situation, the supplier's claim to prior payment prevails over the claims of all other creditors, whether secured or unsecured. The order in which the company's assets are applied in settling claims against the company becomes particularly important where there are not sufficient resources to satisfy the demands of the various claimants in full. The creditors who are in the strongest position are those whose claims are secured by a fixed charge; mortgagees of land for example fall into this category. These (secured) creditors may elect to realise their security by selling it and, if the proceeds of the sale do not clear the debt, prove for the balance with the other creditors (s.317, 1948 Act, and Sched. 2,

Bankruptcy Act 1914). The costs and expenses of the winding up must next be discharged and then the assets must be applied in meeting the claims of preferential creditors (s.319, 1948 Act). Payments which are preferential include rates and taxes, wages and salaries in respect of services rendered during the four months preceding the winding up (not exceeding £800 in the case of any one claimant) and amounts due in respect of social security contributions. Preferential claims take precedence over the claims of the holders of debentures secured by a floating charge (described in Chapter 6) which rank next in the order of priority (s.319(5), 1948 Act). This class of secured creditor is in turn followed by those creditors whose claims are unsecured. Finally, the remaining assets, if any, are distributed amongst the members of the company in accordance with their individual entitlements. It may be for example that the holders of preference shares have a right to be repaid their capital before a distribution is made to the ordinary shareholders (*see* Chapter 6).

In concluding this discussion it should be noted that a floating charge (*see* Chapter 6) which is created by an insolvent company within the period of twelve months before the winding up process begins, is invalid if no cash is paid in consideration for it either at the time of, or subsequent to, its creation (s.322, 1948 Act). Furthermore, any conveyance, mortgage, payment or delivery of goods made in favour of any creditor within six months before the winding up may amount to an attempt to give the recipient a preference over other creditors in which case it will constitute a fraudulent preference and be invalid (s.320, 1948 Act). Thus, in *Re F. P. and C. H. Matthews Ltd.* (1982), payments made to a bank by a director of a company, less than three months before the company went into voluntary liquidation, were held to be void and recoverable by the liquidator because the effect of the payments was to give the bank a preference over the other creditors.

Dissolution
This is the final stage in the winding up process and is in effect the termination of the company as a legal person. The dissolution may be ordered by the court or it may be effected by the registrar of companies striking the company's name off the register (ss.274 and 353, 1948 Act). If the winding up is voluntary, the company is deemed to be dissolved three months after the registration of the documents which are required to be furnished to the registrar by the liquidator (ss.290 and 300, 1948 Act).

BANKRUPTCY

The purpose of this section is to outline some of the features of bankruptcy law.

NOTE: References are to the Bankruptcy Act 1914 unless otherwise indicated.

Bankruptcy proceedings

The process whereby a person who is unable to pay his debts may be adjudicated bankrupt and accordingly be subject to all which that entails is described as bankruptcy. The insolvent person is referred to initially as "the debtor" and this term includes a member of a partnership (s.1(2)). Bankruptcy proceedings are normally begun by the presentation to the court of a bankruptcy petition by one or more creditors (s.4) or by the debtor himself (s.6). An important prerequisite is, however, that the petition must be based on an act of bankruptcy (*see* below). Furthermore, the debt owed to the petitioning creditor must amount to at least £750 and be a liquidated sum (*see* Chapter 14), and the act of bankruptcy relied on by the petitioner is required to have occurred within the three months preceding the presentation of the petition (s.4).

The Bankruptcy Act specifies various circumstances in which an act of bankruptcy will occur (s.1). For instance, the debtor commits an act of bankruptcy where he conveys or otherwise disposes of his property to the prejudice of his creditors (that is, fraudulently). Where, therefore, with bankruptcy a distinct possibility, a trader forms a limited company to which he transfers all his assets, the transfer will be regarded as void and in itself amount to an act of bankruptcy (*Re Gunsbourg* (1920)).

The conveyance or assignment of the debtor's property to a trustee for the benefit of his creditors generally, departing the country with intent to defeat or delay creditors, the presentation of his own bankruptcy petition, notification of the suspension of the payment of debts and failure to comply with the terms of a bankruptcy notice served by a judgment creditor also amount to acts of bankruptcy by the debtor. On the presentation of the petition, the court may make a receiving order for the protection of the debtor's estate (s.3).

The receiving order

The immediate effect of this is that the official receiver in bankruptcy is appointed receiver of the debtor's property and the right of any creditor to proceed directly against the debtor in respect of a claim is considerably restricted except that the power of a secured creditor to realise his security (for example, by sale) or deal with it in some other way remains unaffected (s.7).

The official receiver does not at this stage become owner of the debtor's property but he is charged with taking possession of it and receiving any other property to which the debtor may be entitled (*Re Sartoris' Estate* (1892)).

Other consequences of the receiving order are that the debtor must prepare and submit to the official receiver a statement of affairs giving particulars of his assets, his debts and liabilities, and the names of creditors and the details of securities they hold (s.14); the debtor must attend the first meeting of his creditors (s.22 and *see* below); and, furthermore, he is required to submit to a public examination of his conduct, dealings and property (s.15) unless the court orders that this be dispensed with (s.6, Insolvency Act 1976).

The first meeting of creditors is held to consider the most appropriate course of action having regard to the debtor's position. It may be for instance that the creditors are willing to accept a proposal by the debtor for the ordered satisfaction of at least part of the outstanding debt (described as a composition with creditors or scheme of arrangement) in which case the bankruptcy proceedings as such may be discontinued. Alternatively, the creditors may consider it preferable that the debtor be adjudged bankrupt (s.13). Once the composition or scheme is approved by the court, it is binding on all the creditors (s.16).

During their first meeting, the creditors may appoint a committee of inspection for the purpose of supervising the administration of the bankrupt's estate by the trustee (s.20).

The adjudication of bankruptcy

This is a most significant stage in the bankruptcy process in so far as the debtor is concerned, since the effect of adjudication is that he assumes the status of bankrupt together with its attendant disabilities and consequences for his property. The court will adjudge a debtor bankrupt if the creditors at their first meeting resolve this, if the creditors pass no resolution or do not meet, and if a composition or scheme of arrangement is not accepted within a specified period of time (s.18). In addition, the court may order an adjudication where the debtor fails to comply with the requirements of the Act relating to the statement of affairs (s.14) or defaults in the payment of any instalment due under a composition or scheme (s.16).

On the making of an adjudication order, the property of the bankrupt becomes divisible among his creditors and vests in a trustee (that is, the official receiver until a trustee in bankruptcy is appointed by the creditors or a committee of inspection) (s.18). Consequently, the trustee in bankruptcy acquires the ownership as well as possession of the bankrupt's property, which must next be realised and distributed by the trustee in the form of dividends to the creditors (s.62).

The bankrupt's property and its distribution

Subject to certain exceptions, the property which is available to the trustee for realisation and distribution includes all that belonging to the bankrupt at the commencement of the bankruptcy together with any which may be acquired later (s.38). It should be noted however that the bankruptcy is deemed to commence not at the time of adjudication, but when the original act of bankruptcy is committed by the debtor (s.37). By virtue of this principle of relation-back therefore, but subject to s.45, below, the trustee can retrospectively lay claim to property belonging to the bankrupt before the initiation of bankruptcy proceedings. In *Re Gunsbourg* (above), the company to which the bankrupt had fraudulently transferred his property resold part of it to a purchaser for value, who had no notice of the earlier wrongdoing. Nevertheless, because the fraudulent transfer amounted to an act of bankruptcy, the property was deemed to vest in the trustee under the principle of relation back therefore his title prevailed over that of the sub-purchaser. Similarly, transfers and payments made by the bankrupt within the six months preceding the presentation of the bankruptcy petition may be avoided by the trustee in bankruptcy as fraudulent preferences if the intention of the bankrupt was to favour one particular creditor at the expense of the others and he was, at the time, unable to pay his debts (s.44).

Fraudulent transfers and preferences apart, however, payments to creditors and conveyances and assignments for valuable consideration are valid as against the trustee provided:

(*a*) the disposition was made by the bankrupt before the date of the receiving order and

(*b*) the other party was unaware of any act of bankruptcy on which a petition might be based (s.45).

The property available to the trustee for distribution is not strictly confined to that which actually belongs to the bankrupt. In the case of a business, property in this context also includes goods which are at the commencement of bankruptcy in his reputed (apparent) ownership (s.38(*c*)). Thus, the trustee is entitled to those goods which are in the bankrupt's possession with the permission of the true owner, but in respect of which creditors reasonably assume or believe the bankrupt to be the owner.

In *Re Fox* (1948), for example, at issue were materials deposited at a building site and at the yard of a builder who was subsequently adjudicated bankrupt. The materials were in the builder's possession with the consent of their owner and the trustee claimed these as part of the bankrupt's property. The court decided that people dealing with the builder would reasonably assume that the materials at the yard belong to him, therefore the reputed ownership provision applied. The same could not be said of the materials at the building site and the trustee's claim in this respect failed.

It should be emphasised that proof of a trade custom will displace the reputed ownership provision (for example that goods in the bankrupt's possession are usually held on a sale or return basis as in *Re Ford* (1929)) and, further, goods bailed under a hire purchase or consumer hire agreement or agreed to be sold under a conditional sale agreement are not to be treated as the property of the bankrupt during the period between the service of a default notice (*see* Chapter 17) and the date on which the notice expires or is earlier complied with (s.38A). Other property to which the trustee in bankruptcy is not entitled is:

(*a*) that held by the bankrupt in trust for any other person and

(*b*) the tools of the bankrupt's trade together with clothing and bedding to a value not exceeding £250 in all.

The claims of creditors are met in the following order of preference and, clearly, the differences between this and the order in which the assets of an insolvent company are applied (*see* p. 55) are minimal. Thus, secured creditors (i.e. persons holding a mortgage, charge or lien on the debtor's property) have first priority. Payments have then to be made in respect of the costs of the bankruptcy (for example, the expenses incurred by the official receiver and the trustee's remuneration) followed by payments to those creditors whose claims are preferential (i.e. rates and taxes, wages and salaries etc.—*see* p. 56) (s.33). The persons next entitled are unsecured creditors and, after these, the creditors whose claims are postponed must be paid. For instance, a person who lends money to another in consideration of a share of the profits of the latter's business, or a rate of interest varying with the profits, is not entitled to repayment of his loan in the event of the borrower's bankruptcy until the other creditors have first been repaid (s.3, Partnership Act 1890). Similar considerations apply in the case of a wife's claim against her bankrupt husband in respect of loans advanced by her for the purpose of any trade or business carried on by him or otherwise (s.36(2)).

Finally, if there is any surplus remaining after payment of the above, it may be claimed by the bankrupt (s.69).

Partnerships
The bankruptcy provisions considered above apply to both ordinary partnerships and limited partnerships (s.127) subject in the latter case, however, to the rule that the liability of a limited partner is restricted to the amount of his investment in the firm (*see* Chapter 2).

Where all the partners are insolvent, a distinction must be made between the partnership assets (the joint estate) and the separate property or estate of the individual partners since, if the joint estate is deficient, the firm's creditors may not normally claim in respect of their unpaid debts against the separate estates (as noted in Chapter 2, the individual partners are liable to make good partnership losses from their own personal resources) until the separate creditors have received payment in full (s.33(6)). If there are solvent partners, they may pay off the firm's creditors and then claim in the bankruptcy of those partners who are insolvent.

It should be remembered that the bankruptcy of only one partner is a sufficient basis for the dissolution of the entire partnership unless the partners have made provision to the contrary (s.33, Partnership Act 1890).

Discharge
A bankrupt may apply for an order of discharge at any time after the adjudication (s.26). The court may refuse to grant an order or grant one unconditionally, subject to conditions, or suspend its operation for a specified period of time. In one case, for example, a condition of discharge was that the debtor should repay his creditors the sum of £20,000 spread over a period of ten years (*Re a Debtor* (*No. 13 of 1964*) (1980)).

Under the Insolvency Act 1976, provision is made for automatic discharge of a bankrupt in certain circumstances. Thus, when the court concludes (or dispenses with) the debtor's public examination, it may also order that the bankrupt be absolutely discharged on the fifth anniversary of the date of the adjudication. In addition, the court may grant an order of discharge on the application of the official receiver in bankruptcy.

On his discharge, the bankrupt is released from all debts provable in bankruptcy but with certain exceptions. For instance, he remains liable for a debt or liability incurred by means of fraud (s.28). Furthermore, a discharged bankrupt must continue to assist the trustee in bankruptcy in realising and distributing any property which is still vested in the trustee; if he fails to do so, he will be guilty of a contempt of court (s.26).

SUMMARY

On completion of this chapter you should be able to:

(*a*) Distinguish between winding up and bankruptcy and indicate the main legal provisions relating to each.

(*b*) Appreciate the principal objective of both types of procedure.

(*c*) Explain the order of priority in which the claims of creditors are discharged.

SELF-ASSESSMENT QUESTIONS

(Relevant page numbers are given in brackets.)

1. In what circumstances can a petition be presented to the court for the winding up of a company? (Page 53)

2. How does a members' voluntary winding up differ from that of the creditors? (Page 54)

3. What is the order in which a registered company's assets are distributed to creditors on a winding up? (Page 55)

4. What is a fraudulent preference? (Page 59)

5. How are bankruptcy proceedings commenced? (Page 57)

Assignments

1. Linus and Clement are the directors and shareholders of ACZ Ltd., a private company whose principal object is the supply of wild animals to circuses and zoos. Linus is elderly and usually leaves the management of the company to Clement. Clement learns that plastic garden gnomes are likely to be in great demand and, without consulting Linus, in the name of the company obtains on credit a large quantity of gnomes from a local manufacturer, Albert. Clement hopes to sell the gnomes at a considerable profit for himself. Market conditions are unfavourable however, the gnomes remain unsold and Albert is not paid. Albert approaches you for advice on recovering the price of the gnomes supplied to Clement.

(*a*) As his legal adviser, write a memorandum to Albert explaining his position in the light of the relevant law.

(*b*) What would your advice to Albert be if ACZ (*i*) were a partnership or (*ii*) were only in the course of formation as a registered company? (Chapters 2 and 3)

2. MRC Ltd. is a private company manufacturing microcomputers. The directors are Fred and George and they hold the majority (80 per cent) of the company's share capital. Fred also acts as managing director under a separate contract with the company. The remaining shareholder is Tom with a shareholding of 20 per cent. For some time, Fred has been obtaining parts for the microcomputers from a firm of which he is the sole proprietor. (These parts could be obtained much more cheaply from other sources but Fred clearly has no wish to change the present practice.) Tom learns of this and requests that an extraordinary meeting be held to remove Fred as director. Following this request, Fred and George convene a meeting at which they change the company's articles of association so as to force Tom to sell all his shares in MRC Ltd. to Fred.

Write an opinion on:

(*a*) Tom's rights under the Companies Acts;

(*b*) the legality or otherwise of Fred's conduct in supplying parts for the microcomputers from his own firm and the action which might be taken to prevent this; and

(*c*) the company's position if Fred were dismissed from his post as managing director. (Chapters 3 and 4)

3. Philip and Henry are the only directors and shareholders of Slow Ltd., a property development company. Philip is in constant disagreement with Henry over the appropriate method of calculating the value of land and buildings bought and sold by the company. The result is that the business of Slow Ltd. has come to a virtual stop. Because of this, Henry concludes that the company should be wound up and dissolved. Philip is not agreeable to this course of action because he suspects that the available assets of Slow Ltd. are not sufficient to meet the claims of creditors in full and he fears that he and Henry may be required to make good the difference out of their own pockets. The creditors of Slow Ltd. are (*a*) *Joe*, who recently sold a new photocopier to the company for which he has not yet been paid; (*b*) *Bill and Mary*, who, as employees of Slow Ltd., are owed arrears of salary; (*c*) *Frank*, who several years ago loaned £10,000 to the company taking as security a floating charge over the company's assets; and (*d*) *Martin*, a long standing creditor, who has just become mortgagee of the company's office premises.

(*a*) Advise Henry on the action he might take in order to achieve his intention of having the company wound up.

(*b*) Advise Philip regarding his personal liability (if any), comparing his position as shareholder with that of a partner.

(*c*) Explain how the claims of the various creditors should be dealt with if the company were wound up. Would it make any difference in Joe's case if the terms under which the photocopier was supplied to Slow Ltd. included a provision that ownership should not pass until after payment? (Chapter 5)

4. Frank is the sole proprietor of a motor vehicle repair business. His business assets are the premises at which the repairs are carried out, a breakdown vehicle and various tools of trade. Business is very slack and Frank is unable to pay (*a*) local rates, (*b*) an instalment of £400 on a vehicle testing machine which he is acquiring on hire-purchase terms from a finance company, and (*c*) an unsecured debt of £2,000 borrowed from his friend, Andrew, in order to make ends meet.

(*a*) Advise Frank who approaches you to enquire whether he is bankrupt.

(*b*) Assume that Frank gives the breakdown vehicle to Andrew in settlement of the debt and, shortly afterwards, one of Frank's creditors presents a bankruptcy petition.

(*i*) Describe the possible action which the trustee in bankruptcy might take with respect to the breakdown vehicle and indicate which of the assets in Frank's ownership and possession are available for realisation and distribution to creditors.

(*ii*) State the order in which the various creditors' claims will be paid. (Chapter 5)

PART TWO: BUSINESS PROPERTY

CHAPTER SIX

The Nature of Business Property

CHAPTER OBJECTIVES

After studying this chapter you should be able to:
* outline the way in which business property may be classified;
* explain the various forms of property and their respective characteristics.

INTRODUCTION

"Property" is a generic term embracing a variety of forms. We begin this chapter with a brief discussion of the basic distinction between real property and personal property and then consider these different forms of property by reference to their principal features.

It should be noted that we are using the term "property" in this context to represent the tangible or intangible thing which may be the subject matter of a person's ownership or possession. This is to be contrasted with the sense in which "property" is used to represent the fact of ownership itself (*see* Chapter 7).

CLASSIFICATION OF PROPERTY

Property may be broadly classified under two categories: real property (*realty*) and personal property (*personalty*). Real property comprises freehold interests in land. Personal property on the other hand includes leasehold interests in land (chattels real) and all forms of moveable property (chattels personal). Thus, chattels personal consist of those forms of property which are of a tangible nature such as books, motor vehicles and jewellery (things in possession). Other forms of personal property are not capable of physical possession and are therefore intangible. This latter category comprises for instance shares, debts, copyright and negotiable instruments. These are described as *things in action* because the only way in which an owner can assert his rights with respect to them is by legal action.

The reason for the distinction between the two main categories is essentially historical. Real property was such that the specific thing could be recovered (by a real action) if its owner was dispossessed. This was not possible with personal property, where the appropriate remedy was damages. As time progressed, however, leasehold interests in land developed from being merely contractual rights and came to be equated with realty (hence the term, chattels real).

INTERESTS IN LAND

Legal estates

There is no absolute ownership of land as such in English law. The position is that a person is limited to owning an estate or interest in land and it is in this sense that he may be described as a land owner. It is in fact possible for different persons to be interested in the same land simultaneously. An example of this arises where a freeholder grants (as landlord) a leasehold interest to another (the tenant).

The extent of a person's interest in land is reflected by the nature of the estate or interest held. Thus, the most extensive rights are conferred by the estate in fee simple absolute in possession. This is the modern freehold estate and is in fact one of the only two estates which can subsist or be conveyed or created as legal estates in land (the other legal estate being the leasehold or term of years absolute) (s.1, Law of Property Act 1925).

Other freehold interests in land (e.g. the life estate) can take effect only as equitable interests (defined below) and must exist under a trust.

The leasehold estate differs from the freehold since, whereas the latter is of indefinite duration, the leasehold is either limited to a fixed period of time (e.g. twenty-one years) or it is of a periodic nature (e.g. a monthly tenancy) and capable of termination by notice.

Both freeholds and leaseholds are corporeal interests in land, in that they confer on their owners rights of physical possession of the land. These are to be contrasted therefore with various other (incorporeal) interests which do not give rise to a right of possession as such but which do nevertheless enable their owners to exercise certain other rights with respect to the land affected. Easements (e.g. a right of way) and restrictive covenants (*see* below) are examples of this group.

Persons may be interested in land as co-owners or their interests may arise successively. Partners, for example, are co-owners of the partnership property. Successive interests in property will exist where land is given to X for life and then Y. X's interest is said to *vest in possession* whereas Y's interest *vests in remainder* since it does not take effect immediately. It should be noted that neither X nor Y can claim to hold a legal estate, therefore their interests exist only in equity.

Equitable interests

These are interests in land which, although not enforceable under the common law, the courts of equity (pre-1875) were prepared to protect in certain circumstances. The rules of equity are now administered by the ordinary courts. Consequently, despite the fact that a person does not have a legal (i.e. common law) estate in land, his interest may be such that it can be enforced by one of the equitable remedies. An owner of land may, for example, be able to prevent by injunction the use of neighbouring land for a particular purpose (e.g. business use) where that land is burdened by a restrictive covenant. Again, although a person who has entered into a binding contract to purchase land (*see* Chapter 7) cannot regard himself as legal estate owner until the legal estate has actually been conveyed or transferred to him, he will nevertheless in certain circumstances be entitled to an order of specific performance to compel the vendor to comply with his contractual obligation. The attitude of equity in such cases is that the purchaser is the true owner of the land which is subject to the sale.

GOODS

These are defined in the Sale of Goods Act 1979 as including all personal chattels other than things in action and money (s.61). This is a consolidating statute which regulates the sale of goods but the common law rules continue to apply except where they are inconsistent with the provisions of the Act (s.62).

For the purposes of the Sale of Goods Act, goods which are owned or possessed by the seller at the time of the contract of sale are termed existing goods. Where they have to be manufactured or acquired by the seller after the making of the contract of sale, they are called future goods (s.5).

Goods which are identified and agreed upon at the time a contract of sale is made are known as specific goods (s.61). Goods may also be non-specific or unascertained. Thus, if a buyer agrees to purchase a particular make of motor vehicle from a dealer who has a number of vehicles of that make in stock and does not specify the exact vehicle he wants, the vehicle is unascertained. The significance of the distinction between specific and unascertained goods lies in the fact that, until the goods are ascertained, the property in them (i.e. ownership) does not pass to the buyer (s.16). (*See* Chapter 7.)

Another important distinction to be made with respect to goods is that between ownership and possession. Thus, a person who has exclusive rights of enjoyment and disposition may permit another person to have the physical possession of goods. A clear illustration is where a finance company as owner of a motor vehicle allows a hirer to take possession under a hire-purchase agreement (*see* Chapter 18). In some cases, the fact that another person is given possession of goods may lead to the owner losing his rights of ownership completely, in favour of a third party (the position with respect to the transfer of the title to goods is considered in Chapter 7).

NEGOTIABLE INSTRUMENTS

In this section we define the term "negotiable instrument" and discuss the principal features of bills of exchange, cheques and promissory notes.

Definition

A negotiable instrument is a written document conferring on the person who is for the time being in lawful possession of it a contractual right to the payment of money. The chief characteristics of a negotiable instrument are that a person to whom it is transferred may acquire the right to sue under it in his own name and, furthermore, this right to sue is unaffected by any defect in the title of the transferor (*Crouch* v. *Credit Foncier of England* (1873)). In this latter respect, a comparison should be made with the assignment of rights under an ordinary contract since, in such circumstances, the assignee can be in no better position than the person making the assignment (*see* Chapter 7, p. 83).

Bills of exchange, cheques and promissory notes are negotiable instruments and these are subject to the provisions of the Bills of Exchange Act 1882.

Another example of a negotiable instrument is the debenture payable to bearer (*Bechuanaland Exploration Co.* v. *London Trading Bank Ltd.* (1898)). (Debentures are discussed later in this chapter.)

Bills of exchange

A bill of exchange is defined in the Act as "an unconditional order in writing, addressed by one person to another, signed by the person giving it, requiring the person to whom it is addressed to pay on demand, or at a fixed or determinable future time, a sum certain in money to or to the order of a specified person or to bearer" (s.3). An instrument is not a bill of exchange where it does not comply with the requirements of this definition (or where there is demanded some act in addition to the payment of money).

Consequently, there must be an order to pay money; a request is not sufficient. Further, an instrument which directs payment to be made provided a receipt contained within it is properly signed, stamped and dated is not an unconditional order (*Bavins* v. *London and South Western Bank* (1900)). On the other hand, if the direction to sign a receipt is addressed to the payee and not to the drawee (*see* below), it appears that the document may remain within the definition of a bill of exchange (*Nathan* v. *Ogdens Ltd.* (1905)).

As the definition clearly indicates, a bill of exchange may be made payable to, or to the order of, a specified person or to the bearer (i.e. the person into whose lawful possession an instrument payable to bearer comes). A document is not a valid bill of exchange therefore where the instruction is for instance "Pay cash or order" because cash cannot be regarded as a specified person (*North and South Insurance Corporation* v. *National Provincial Bank Ltd.* (1939)). In fact, the court in this case took the view that the words in question constituted a direction to the defendant bank to pay the specified sum of money to the person in possession of the document.

Bills of exchange fall into two main categories. On the one hand, a bill may be payable on demand, in which case the holder (*see* below) is entitled to payment upon presentation to the acceptor. Alternatively, the bill may be payable at a fixed period after date or sight (time bill), or on or at a fixed period after the occurrence of a specified event (e.g. "twenty days after X's death") (s.11). A document which provided for payment "on or before 31 December 1956" was not a valid bill of exchange because of the uncertainty with respect to time of payment (*Williamson* v. *Rider* (1963)).

The first parties to a bill of exchange are the drawer, drawee and payee. The drawer is the person directing payment and the drawee is the person to whom the direction is addressed. If the drawee accepts the bill, he becomes the acceptor. The acceptance of a bill of exchange is defined in the Act as "the signification by the drawee of his assent to the order of the drawer". Such assent must be effected by the drawee signing the bill (s.17).

The person to whom the amount specified in the bill is initially payable is the payee, but he may indorse the bill (i.e. sign it on the reverse side) and deliver it to another party (indorsee or bearer). A person who is in possession of a bill, whether as payee, indorsee or bearer, is described as the holder (s.2).

In the following illustration, the function of each party is indicated in brackets.

```
┌─────────────────────────────────────────────────────────┐
│                                                         │
│   £400                          Cardiff, January 1st, 198–  │
│                                                         │
│                                                         │
│   Three months after date pay ABC Ltd. (payee) or order │
│   the sum of Four Hundred pounds for value received.    │
│                                                         │
│                                                         │
│   To: XYZ Ltd.                              Paul S.     │
│                                                         │
│   Glasgow (drawee)                          (drawer)    │
│                                                         │
└─────────────────────────────────────────────────────────┘
```

It is possible for different parties to a bill of exchange to be one and the same person. A bill may be for instance drawn payable to the order of the drawer himself or it may be payable to the drawee (s.5).

An important distinction must be made between order bills and those which are payable to bearer, because in each case the method of negotiating the bill to another person differs. Thus, an order bill is one which is expressed to be so payable or which is payable to a particular person. A bill is not an order bill if it contains words prohibiting transfer or indicating an intention that it should not be transferable.

A bearer bill on the other hand is one which is expressed to be payable to bearer or on which the only or last indorsement is an indorsement in blank (s.8). The point about this distinction is that an order bill is negotiated by indorsement and delivery, whereas a bearer bill is negotiated simply by delivery. For example, if A draws a bill on B in favour of C, C may indorse the bill without specifying an indorsee (indorsement in blank) or he may indorse and specify the person to whom the bill is to be payable (special indorsement) (s.34). A bill which is indorsed in blank becomes payable to bearer, whereas a bill which is specially indorsed continues to be an order bill.

Liability under the bill devolves in the first instance on the drawee once he has indicated his acceptance (s.54). If the bill is dishonoured, however, the person who is entitled to payment can seek recovery from the drawer and any person who has indorsed the bill (s.47). Nevertheless, no person may be liable under a bill of exchange, whether as drawer, indorser or acceptor, unless he has signed it (s.23).

Bills of exchange have an important commercial function, in particular with respect to the financing of international trade. Thus, an importer of goods may undertake to pay for them by accepting a bill drawn on him by the exporter in return for the bill of lading and other documents (*see* Chapter 13, p. 164). If the bill is a time bill (*see* p. 71), the buyer will have a breathing space before payment is required but the seller will usually have already obtained payment for the goods by negotiating the bill (at a discount) to a bank or specialist institution which now becomes entitled to demand payment at the appropriate time. (The negotiation of bills of exchange is considered in Chapter 7.)

Cheques

A cheque is a bill of exchange drawn on a banker (*see* Chapter 15) and which is payable on demand (s.73). With certain exceptions, the rules applicable to bills of exchange also operate with respect to cheques. Thus, although a banker is the drawee, banks do not in practice accept cheques within the meaning of s.17 (*see* p. 71). Consequently, it is the drawer of a cheque who is primarily liable under it. An example of a cheque is given below, and the significance of the crossing—the two parallel lines—is considered in Chapter 15, p. 189.

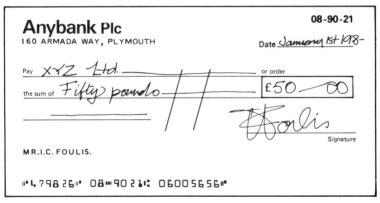

If a cheque is not presented for payment within a reasonable time of issue, a drawer who suffers actual damage as a result of the delay is discharged to the extent of such damage (s.74) (for instance, the drawer's account is in credit but his bank goes into liquidation before presentation for payment by the holder: the drawer would be unduly penalised if he were not protected by this provision).

(Cheques are discussed further in Chapter 15.)

Promissory notes

This type of negotiable instrument is defined as "an unconditional promise in writing made by one person to another signed by the maker, engaging to pay, on demand or at a fixed or determinable future time, a certain sum in money, to, or to the order of a specified person or to the bearer" (s.83).

Essentially, then, a promissory note is a promise by one party to pay a sum of money to another. In the first instance, there are two parties, the maker and the payee or bearer. The principal difference between promissory notes and bills of exchange is that with the former there is no acceptance. The note can of course be negotiated with the maker remaining primarily liable to subsequent holders.

SHARES AND DEBENTURES

In this section, we consider the two main classes of securities issued by registered companies.

Shares

It was stated by Farwell J in *Borland's Trustee* v. *Steel Bros. and Co. Ltd.* (1901) that a share is "the interest of a shareholder in the company measured by a sum of money". A share does not however confer on its holder any rights with respect to the company's property (except on a dissolution) but it does give rise to contractual rights and obligations (*see* Chapter 4, p. 35).

The articles of association may provide for a company's share capital (*see* Chapter 3) to be divided into different classes of shares. Table A for instance provides that any share in the company may be issued with such preferred, deferred or other special rights or such restrictions as regards dividend, voting, return of capital or otherwise, as the company may from time to time by ordinary resolution determine. Further, it was held by the Court of Appeal in *Andrews* v. *Gas Meter Co.* (1897) that it was lawful for a company to alter its articles so as to provide for the issue of shares having a preference to existing shares.

(*a*) *Preference shares.* These are shares which confer a preference over other (ordinary) shareholders with respect to the payment of a dividend (out of profits) and the return of capital if the company is wound up (*see* Chapter 5). Dividends may be cumulative or non-cumulative. In the former case, a dividend not paid in any one year will be made up in a subsequent year. In the absence of specific provision, dividends on preference shares are presumed to be cumulative (*Webb* v. *Earle* (1875)). Nevertheless, cumulative preference shareholders are not entitled to arrears of dividends once winding up proceedings have commenced (*Re Crichton's Oil Co.* (1902)).

If shares are made preferential with respect to the payment of a dividend, the preference shareholders are not entitled to a further share of the profits (i.e. after receiving the agreed rate of dividend) unless their shares are participating. If non-participating, the agreement with respect to the preferential dividend is deemed to be exhaustive of the preference share holders' rights (*Will* v. *United Lankat Plantations Co.* (1914)). Similarly, where by the terms of the issue of their shares, preference shareholders are entitled on a winding up to a return of their capital before repayment of capital to the ordinary shareholders (*see* below) they have no automatic right to an additional share of the surplus assets (*Scottish Insurance Corporation Ltd.* v. *Wilsons and Clyde Coal Co.* (1949)).

(*b*) *Ordinary shares.* The holders of ordinary shares are entitled to their dividend (or capital repayment on a winding up) after the claims of the preference shareholders have been met. Apart from this, a principal difference between the two classes of shares is that ordinary shareholders are subject to no limitations as regards their right to a share of the company's profits.

A company's articles of association may provide for the issue of shares which are redeemable. Certain requirements must be complied with. For instance, the shares must be fully paid up and, except in the case of a private company, the shares may only be redeemed out of profits available for distribution to the company's members or out of the proceeds of a fresh issue of shares made for the purpose of the redemption (s.45, Companies Act 1981).

Debentures

As described in Chapter 4, a debenture is essentially a document representing a loan of money made to the company. The lender, as debenture holder, is a creditor of the company and is therefore entitled to be repaid his capital (with interest) in due course. In addition to this contractual right to repayment, the lender may have the security of a mortgage or floating charge on some or all of the company's assets (*see* below).

A borrowing may be covered by a single debenture (e.g. a mortgage of the company's freehold property as in *Knightsbridge Estates Trust Ltd.* v. *Byrne* (1940)) or the company may issue a series of debentures or debenture stock, in which case the issue may be accompanied by a trust deed created between the company and trustees, acting on behalf of the debenture or stock holders as a whole. In the deed, the company will undertake to repay the loan and, further, may effect a mortgage of its freehold and leasehold property and create a floating charge (*see* below) on its other assets. Other matters which may be provided for in the trust deed are the circumstances in which the loan will become immediately repayable (e.g. in the event of the company being unable to pay its debts) and the appointment of a receiver to safeguard the interests of the debenture holders with respect to the charged property. In the case of an issue of debenture stock, the individual lender is given a debenture stock certificate evidencing his particular entitlement.

Debentures may be payable to a specified person or they may be expressed to be payable to bearer. In the latter instance, the debenture is a negotiable instrument and may therefore be transferred by delivery free from defects in the title of the transferor (*Bechuanaland Exploration Co.* v. *London Trading Bank Ltd.* (1898)).

Where a floating charge is given as security to debenture holders, it may relate to part or all of the company's assets (e.g. the company's stock in trade). The basic advantage of this form of security is that, unlike a fixed charge such as a mortgage, it enables the company to continue dealing with the property which is subject to the charge. Consequently, this property is allowed to change with the business needs of the company. Nevertheless, circumstances may arise where the floating charge "crystallises" and becomes attached to the company's existing assets as a fixed charge. Such circumstances may be provided for in the debenture or trust deed (e.g. on the appointment of a receiver) or crystallisation may occur automatically as on a winding up of the company (*Re Panama, New Zealand and Australian Royal Mail Co.* (1870)).

The significance of crystallisation is that the debenture holders become entitled to be repaid their loan out of the property which is subject to the charge in priority to unsecured creditors (subject however to the claims of preferential creditors (s.94(5), Companies Act 1948, and *see* Chapter 5, p. 56).

Subject to the rules concerning registration of charges (*see* below), a floating charge once created has priority over a later floating charge over the same assets (*Re Automatic Bottle Makers Ltd.* (1926)). However, if the assets are later subjected to a fixed charge or mortgage, the latter does have priority, unless the later mortgagee is aware of a provision in the debenture or trust deed creating the floating charge restricting the company's power to create further charges.

Fixed and floating charges must be registered with the registrar of companies within twenty-one days of creation otherwise they are void as against the liquidator of the company and any creditor (s.95, Companies Act 1948). The company is under a duty to furnish the relevant particulars of a charge to the registrar but registration may also be effected on the application of any person interested (e.g. the debenture holder) (s.96).

The effect of a charge becoming void is that the money secured by it becomes immediately repayable to the lender. Furthermore, although normally a fixed charge has priority over a floating charge for winding up purposes (*see* Chapter 5, p. 55), if a fixed charge is created but not registered and is then followed by a floating charge which is properly registered in accordance with the statutory requirements, the later charge has priority even though the debenture holder is aware of the earlier charge (*Re Monolithic Building Co.* (1915)).

It may be noted that one of the options usually open to debenture holders is the appointment of a receiver to take possession of the asset or assets which are subject to the charge and the circumstances in which they become entitled to this will be specified in the debenture or trust deed. The position here should be contrasted with that obtaining on the appointment of a liquidator (*see* Chapter 5) since the winding up of a company is not necessarily a cause or consequence of the appointment of a receiver.

COPYRIGHT, PATENTS AND TRADE MARKS

In this section we consider three forms of property which are created and protected by statute.

Copyright
This is governed by the Copyright Act 1956 (as amended). Copyright is a type of personal property which confers on its owner exclusive rights with respect to the reproduction and publication of original literary, dramatic, musical and artistic works. Copyright may also subsist in sound recordings, cinematograph films, and television and radio broadcasts. Essentially, the copyright owner (usually the author of the work) is given protection (by means of an injunction and damages for instance) against specified unauthorised acts. These

(*a*) reproducing the work in any material form,
(*b*) publishing the work,
(*c*) performing the work in public,
(*d*) broadcasting the work and
(*e*) making an adaptation (s.2(5)). In order to constitute an infringement, however, an act must relate to a substantial part of the work (s.49).

Furthermore, certain acts are exempted from restriction. These include:

(*a*) fair dealing with a literary, dramatic or musical work for the purposes of research or private study or for the purpose of criticism or review provided, in the latter case, the review is accompanied by a sufficient acknowledgment;
(*b*) fair dealing for the purpose of reporting current events;
(*c*) reproduction for the purpose of judicial proceedings; and
(*d*) provided certain conditions are met, the inclusion of a short passage of material in a collection intended for the use of schools (s.6).

Libraries are given special exemption with regard to the copying of articles (s.7).

Copyright subsists in a work until the expiration of a period of fifty years following the death of the author or artist (s.2(3)).

Being a form of property, copyright is of course assignable but an assignment will have no effect unless in writing and signed by or on behalf of the assignor (s.36).

Patents

A patent is personal property and is granted by the crown in respect of patentable inventions. The Patents Act 1977 applies to patents granted after its commencement and, under this statute, an inventor may acquire for a twenty year period the sole right to develop a product or process commercially. A patentable invention is one that is new, involves an inventive step and is capable of industrial application (s.1(1)). Certain developments are not inventions for the purpose of the Act. These include:

(*a*) a discovery, scientific theory or mathematical method;
(*b*) a literary, dramatic, musical or artistic work or any other aesthetic creation whatsoever;
(*c*) a scheme, rule or method for performing a mental act, playing a game or doing business, or a computer program; and
(*d*) the presentation of information.

In addition, a patent will be refused where the publication or exploitation of an invention would be likely to encourage offensive, immoral or anti-social behaviour (s.1(2) and (3)).

The remedies available for an infringement of the patent include an injunction, damages and an account of the profits derived by the wrongdoer (s.61).

Patents may be assigned or mortgaged but such transactions are void unless made in writing and signed by or on behalf of the parties (s.30).

Trade marks

These are governed by the Trade Marks Act 1938 which establishes a system of registration. A trade mark is defined in the Act as "a mark used or proposed to be used in relation to goods for the purpose of indicating, or so as to indicate, a connection in the course of trade between the goods and some person having the right either as proprietor or as registered user to use the mark . . ." (s.68). A trade mark, in essence, is a means whereby a consumer may differentiate one manufacturer's products from those of another manufacturer and with which he may associate a particular level of quality. Registration confers on the proprietor of a trade mark the exclusive use of that mark and other persons are prohibited from using marks which are identical with it or which are so similar as to be likely to deceive or cause confusion (s.4). The fact that a trade mark is not protected by registration does not prevent its owner from bringing an action for breach of the common law tort of passing off (s.2).

Registration is in the first instance for a period of seven years and is then renewable for periods of fourteen years (s.20).

Both registered and unregistered trade marks may be assigned (s.22).

SUMMARY

On completion of this chapter you should be able to:

(a) Appreciate the different forms of business property.

(b) Understand the distinction between things in possession and things in action.

(c) Explain the principle of negotiability.

(d) Outline the characteristics of shares and debentures.

SELF-ASSESSMENT QUESTIONS

(Relevant page numbers are given in brackets.)

1. Distinguish between legal and equitable interests in land. (Pages 68 and 69)

2. What is the significance of the distinction between specific goods and unascertained goods? (Page 69)

3. Indicate the characteristics of a bill of exchange. (Page 70)

4. How does an order bill differ from a bearer bill? (Page 72)

5. How do preference shares differ from ordinary shares? (Pages 74 and 75)

6. What is the extent of the protection afforded by the law relating to copyright? (Page 77)

CHAPTER SEVEN

The Transfer of Business Property

CHAPTER OBJECTIVE

After studying this chapter you should be able to:
* explain the methods by which different forms of business property may be transferred or assigned by one person to another.

INTRODUCTION

It will be clear from the discussion in this chapter that the appropriate method of transferring business property depends upon the type of property under consideration. Shares in a registered company for example are transferable in the manner provided in the company's articles (s.73, Companies Act 1948) (*see* p. 86). Similarly, special rules apply with respect to the transfer of interests in land (*see* below) and bills of exchange (*see* below).

Also dealt with in this chapter is the transfer of property in and title to goods under a contract of sale, the rules concerning which are to be found in the Sale of Goods Act 1979 and other relevant statutes.

TRANSFER OF INTERESTS IN LAND

The transfer or conveyance of an interest in land commonly involves two basic stages. In the first instance, the parties enter into a contract for the transfer of the relevant interest and this is eventually followed by the actual transfer of that interest from the vendor to the purchaser.

The contract

This is usually comprehensively formulated on the basis of standard terms and conditions (e.g. the National Conditions of Sale) but, exceptionally, the contract may be an "open" contract where only the essential details (e.g. as to price, a description of the property) are agreed. In both cases, the ordinary principles of contract law (as considered in subsequent chapters) apply subject to an additional and important requirement. A contract for the sale or other disposition of an interest in land should be evidenced by a written note, or memorandum, signed by the person being sued, or by his lawfully appointed agent. In the absence of such written evidence, the agreement is unenforceable (s.40(1), Law of Property Act 1925). The note or memorandum must contain details of the parties, the property which is subject to their (oral) agreement, and the price together with any other material terms which may have been agreed (*Tiverton Estates Ltd.* v. *Wearwell Ltd.* (1975)).

An agreement which is not evidenced in writing in accordance with the statute is not void: it is merely unenforceable by action. Where therefore a purchaser pays a deposit to the vendor but then seeks to repudiate the agreement on the grounds of lack of written evidence, the vendor has no basis on which to sue the purchaser but he is entitled to keep the deposit (*Thomas* v. *Brown* (1876)).

This requirement of written evidence with respect to the transfer of an interest in land does not affect the law relating to part performance (s.40(2), Law of Property Act 1925). Consequently, if the plaintiff can establish a sufficient act of part performance under the oral agreement (e.g. that he already has possession of the property), he may be entitled to the remedy of specific performance (*see* Chapter 16, p. 201) to compel performance by the other party of his contractual obligations. Thus in *Rawlinson* v. *Ames* (1925), the plaintiff orally agreed to lease a flat to the defendant and in fact carried out work to the premises under the latter's supervision. The court held that there was a sufficient act of part performance entitling the plaintiff to have the contract specifically enforced. It has been held that, in appropriate circumstances, a payment of money may constitute an act of part performance (*Steadman* v. *Steadman* (1974)—payment by husband of £100 maintenance under an oral separation agreement, which included a promise by his wife to transfer to him for £1,500 her interest in their jointly owned house).

The parties' initial agreement may be expressed to be made "subject to contract" (or "subject to the preparation and approval of a formal contract" as in *Winn* v. *Bull* (1877)) and the effect of this is that neither party has any contractual rights until a formal contract is drawn up. Furthermore, it may be necessary for the parties to exchange signed contracts (whether by post or otherwise) before a binding contract will come into being (*Eccles* v. *Bryant and Pollock* (1948)).

The effect of a binding contract for the transfer of an interest in land is that, provided the remedy of specific performance is available, the purchaser acquires the beneficial or equitable ownership, with the vendor continuing as legal owner but as trustee for the purchaser (*Lysaght* v. *Edwards* (1876)). The relevant principle is that, despite the absence of a formal conveyance at this stage, equity regards *as* done that which *should be* done. The vendor is therefore under an obligation to ensure that the property is maintained in a reasonable state (*Phillips* v. *Lamdin* (1948)—vendor required to reinstate an ornate and valuable door which he had removed after the conclusion of the contract of sale).

The conveyance
This stage of the transaction differs according to whether the vendor's title to the land is unregistered or registered.

In the former case, it is necessary for the vendor to establish his title (ownership of the legal estate) to the property. He does this by producing documents arising out of dealings with the land over at least the previous fifteen years (unless otherwise agreed) (s.23, Law of Property Act 1969) beginning with a good *root of title* (e.g. a conveyance on a sale of the land). The procedure is completed by the vendor executing (i.e. signing and sealing) a deed of conveyance and delivering this to the purchaser with the relevant title deeds.

The process of land transfer is somewhat simplified in the case of registered land (now embracing much of England and Wales) since an investigation of the vendor's title is unnecessary, given that the vendor's position can be ascertained by an inspection of the register which is kept at the Land Registry. The transfer of registered land (a statutory form of transfer is used) must be completed by registration because, until this is done, the transferor is deemed to remain proprietor of the land (ss.19 and 22, Land Registration Act 1925).

TRANSFER (ASSIGNMENT) OF CONTRACTUAL RIGHTS

Statutory assignments
A right arising under a contract (e.g. a right to the payment of money for goods supplied) is a thing in action (*see* Chapter 6, p. 67). With some exceptions, a contractual right may in certain circumstances be assigned by its owner (the assignor) to another person, (the assignee) thereby enabling the latter to pursue a claim directly against the person who is subject to the obligation (the debtor). The requirements are that:

(*a*) the assignment must be in writing;
(*b*) it must be an absolute assignment (*see* below); and
(*c*) notice in writing of the assignment must be given to the debtor (s.136, Law of Property Act 1925).

An assignment is absolute where the assignor effects a transfer of his interest in its entirety without any conditions being imposed. For instance, in *Durham Bros.* v. *Robertson* (1898), a firm of builders were owed £1,080 by R. As security for a loan of money advanced to them by D, they assigned their interest in R's debt to D "until the money with added interest be repaid to you". The assignment was held by the Court of Appeal to be conditional and therefore not an effective statutory assignment.

Assignment in equity

Where the statutory requirements are not met it does not necessarily follow that an assignment will be ineffective, since there may be a valid equitable assignment. No formality is necessary and all that is basically required is an intention on the part of the assignor to effect a transfer of his interest. The difference, however, is that the assignee must join the assignor to any action he may bring against the debtor. Thus, in *Durham Bros.* (above) the court held that there was a valid equitable assignment but the assignee's action against the debtor was unsuccessful because the assignor had not been made party to the action.

Nevertheless, in the case of an absolute assignment of an equitable *thing in action* (e.g. an interest under a trust fund) the assignee is permitted to sue the debtor in his own name.

For the purposes of an equitable assignment, it is not necessary to give notice to the debtor (*Holt* v. *Heatherfield Trust Ltd.* (1942)). Notice is desirable however for two basic reasons. In the first place, the debtor is discharged from liability where he pays off the assignor without knowing of the assignment. Secondly, the assignor may (perhaps fraudulently) make successive assignments of the debt to different parties. Priority in such a case is not dependent on the order in which the assignments are made, but is determined by the order in which notice is given to the debtor (*Dearle* v. *Hall* (1828)).

Both statutory and equitable assignments are "subject to equities". This means, in effect, that the defences which the debtor might have pleaded against the assignor (e.g. the latter's fraud) can also be pleaded against the assignee. It may be for instance that goods supplied under the (assignor/debtor) contract giving rise to the debt are defective in which case the debtor can rely on the fact when sued for the price by the assignee. Again, the debtor may have the right to set off against the assignee's claim a debt owed to him by the assignor under some other transaction. In this respect, though, the debtor's claim must have arisen before he received notice of the assignment (*Roxburghe* v. *Cox* (1881)).

At this juncture, the assignment of a contractual right may be compared with the transfer of a negotiable instrument, which may be effected free from defects in the title of the transferor (*see* Chapter 6, p. 70) and the following section).

Limitations

Certain contractual rights may not be assigned, in particular those arising under a contract for personal services where the preferences of the person who is subject to the obligation (e.g. an artist) must first be considered.

Similarly, and in concluding this section, it must be emphasised that the *obligations* created by a contract may not be assigned unless the other contracting party agrees in which event there is said to be a novation (*see also* Chapter 12, p. 155). It may be possible however to delegate to another person the function of performing the obligation provided the identity of the performer is not a material factor (*British Waggon Co. and Another* v. *Lea and Co.* (1880)).

NEGOTIATION UNDER THE BILLS OF EXCHANGE ACT 1882

The negotiation of a bill of exchange is effected by transferring it to another person in such a manner as to make that person the holder of the bill (s.31) except that a person to whom a bill is transferred cannot acquire rights under it if it contains words prohibiting transfer (s.8).

As indicated in the previous chapter, a bearer bill is negotiated quite simply by delivery but an order bill is negotiated by indorsement and delivery (in the latter case, the negotiation is ineffectual if the indorsement is forged or unauthorised (s.24)).

The effect of negotiation is to enable the transferee to sue on the bill in his own name provided he is a holder for value (i.e. value as defined below has at some time been given for the bill although not necessarily by the current holder (s.27(2)). Furthermore, if the transferee becomes a holder in due course, his title to the bill is acquired free from any defects in the title of the transferor or a previous holder (s.38).

In essence, a holder in due course is a person who takes a bill, complete and regular on the face of it, in good faith and for value without notice of any defect in the title of the person negotiating it (s.29). The definition does not include the original payee since it is presupposed that the bill must first be negotiated (*R. E. Jones Ltd.* v. *Waring and Gillow Ltd.* (1926)).

Value is defined to mean valuable consideration (*see* Chapter 9) and includes an antecedent debt or liability (e.g. a debt already owed by the drawer of the cheque to the payee) (s.27). The point is that a holder of a bill may have rights under it, provided value has at some time been given but, unless he is a holder in due course, he takes the bill subject to possible defects in the title of previous holders. Nevertheless, a holder (whether for value or not) who derives his title to the bill through a holder in due course has all the rights of the latter provided he is not himself a party to any fraud or illegality affecting the bill of exchange (s.29(3)).

TRANSFER OF SHARES AND DEBENTURES

Restrictions on the transfer of shares

A shareholder may normally transfer his shares to another person (e.g. under a contract of sale) but the company's articles of association may place restrictions on his freedom to do this. For instance, if Table A applies, the directors have power to decline to register the transfer of a share not fully paid up to a person of whom they may disapprove. Any power of refusal which the directors have in this respect must however be exercised in good faith (*Re Smith and Fawcett Ltd.* (1942)). Further, the company has two months from the receipt of the transfer document (for which, *see* below) in which to notify the transferee of a decision to refuse to register a transfer of shares (s.78, Companies Act 1948). In addition, the power to refuse a transfer may be lost if its exercise is subject to undue delay (*Re Swaledale Cleaners* (1968)).

Procedure

A company may not register a transfer of shares until there has been delivered to it a proper instrument of transfer (s.75, Companies Act 1948). The shares of a registered company which are fully paid up may be transferred by means of the form of transfer contained in Schedule 1 (as amended) of the Stock Transfer Act 1963 and this document need only be signed by the transferor. Both the instrument of transfer and the relevant share certificate (*see* below) must be delivered by the transferee to the company in order that he may be registered as a member. The company then has two months in which to complete and have ready, for delivery a new share certificate (s.80, Companies Act 1948) but this requirement does not apply (in the case of stock exchange transactions) where the shares are transferred (temporarily) to a nominee of the Stock Exchange (Stock Exchange (Completion of Bargains) Act 1976).

The share certificate is a document issued by the company certifying that the person named is registered owner of specified shares. It is furthermore prima facie evidence of ownership of the shares (s.81, Companies Act 1948) and its object is to give share-holders "the opportunity of more easily dealing with their shares in the market . . ." (Cockburn CJ in *Re Bahia and San Francisco Railway Co.* (1868)).

The statement in the share certificate as to ownership may give rise to liability on the company's part since it will be prevented from denying the truth of a representation which has been relied upon by another. Thus, if A fraudulently obtains a share certificate from the company, having forged a transfer in favour of himself, and then sells the shares to B who relies on the representation in the certificate that A is the lawful holder of the shares, the company will be *estopped* (i.e. precluded) from denying this fact and will be liable in damages to B if his name is subsequently removed from the register of members in favour of the original true owner (*Re Bahia*, above). Similarly, where a company issues a share certificate stating that the shares specified are fully paid up, the liquidator may be prevented from claiming from a subsequent purchaser any unpaid amounts if the shares are in fact only partly paid up (*Burkinshaw* v. *Nicolls* (1878)).

The significance of registration

A person to whom shares are transferred does not become a member of the company until the transfer is registered (*see* Chapter 4, p. 35). Pending this, the transferee has only an equitable or beneficial interest in the shares which he holds. The effect of this is that any claim in respect of the shares which the transferee may wish to assert must be made against the transferor as continuing legal owner, since the company is not concerned with the fact that the latter has parted with the beneficial interest (s.117, Companies Act 1948). (If Table A applies, the transferor is deemed to remain holder of the shares until the transferee's name is entered in the register of members.) Consequently, dividends are payable only to the transferor as regis-tered member, but the latter is, of course, accountable for these sums to the transferee as beneficial owner.

Where a transferor (fraudulently) makes several dispositions of the same shares to successive transferees, each one of whom pur-chases without notice of the previous transfer, the rule is that the interest which is prior in time prevails. Thus, in *Peat* v. *Clayton* (1906), X assigned shares to trustees for the benefit of his creditors but retained the share certificate. X subsequently sold the same shares to Y to whom he also delivered the share certificate. The court held that the trustees were entitled to the shares because their (equitable) claim was prior in time.

It should be noted that, irrespective of the order in which he may have purchased his interest, an innocent transferee will obtain priority once he has secured registration as a member.

Debentures

These are subject to s.75 of the 1948 Act (above) therefore a proper instrument of transfer must be produced before the company may register a transfer from one person to another. If the debentures are in bearer form, they are of course transferable simply by delivery to the transferee.

TRANSFER OF THE PROPERTY IN AND TITLE TO GOODS

References are to the Sale of Goods Act 1979 except where otherwise specified.

Introductory

In this section, the transfer of the ownership of goods is examined from two different standpoints. On the one hand, we consider the circumstances in which the "property" in goods (to be distinguished from the physical goods themselves) will pass from the seller to the buyer under a contract of sale. The passing of the property in goods is significant because, unless the parties agree otherwise, the risk of loss or damage to the goods devolves upon the buyer (irrespective of delivery) once the property in them is transferred to him (s.20). In addition, the seller's right to sue for the price of the goods sold (as opposed to a claim for damages) can only be maintained after the property in the goods has passed to the buyer (s.49).

The transfer of ownership is also important where there are competing claims to the title to goods (*see*, for instance, the discussion of *Kirkham* v. *Attenborough* below). Further, it should be noted that there are (exceptionally) circumstances in which it is possible for a person to obtain a good title to goods under a contract where the seller is not the true owner and, in so doing, defeat the claim of the original owner (*see* p. 90).

NOTE: The transfer of ownership is of course to be distinguished from delivery of the goods to the buyer. The seller's obligations in this respect are discussed in Chapter 12, p. 149.

The transfer of the property in goods

A contract of sale of goods is defined as one by which the seller transfers or agrees to transfer the property in goods to the buyer (s.2). Where the goods are specific or ascertained (defined in Chapter 6, p. 69), the property in them passes to the buyer when the parties intend this to occur (s.17). Thus, it is possible for the seller to prevent the passing of the property until a particular condition is fulfilled (s.19). For instance, in *Aluminium Industrie Vaassen BV* v. *Romalpa Aluminium Ltd*. (1976), the plaintiff supplier of aluminium foil stipulated that the property in the goods should not be transferred to the buyer until they had been paid for. The effect of this stipulation was that, on the occasion of the buyer's insolvency, the supplier had priority over other creditors and could recover aluminium foil still in the buyer's possession. Nevertheless, such a reservation of title clause may not be effective to retain title to the goods once they have been mixed with other goods in the production process (*Borden (U.K.) Ltd*. v. *Scottish Timber Products Ltd*. (1981)) and, further, the clause may give rise to a charge merely which will then be void if not registered under the Companies Act (*Re Peachdart Ltd*., (1983) and see Chapter 6, p. 77). In addition, the seller will be unable to claim the proceeds from a sale to a sub-buyer if (unlike in the *Romalpa* case above) there is no fiduciary relationship between seller and buyer (*Re Andrabell Ltd*. (1984)).

The Act lays down the rules for ascertaining the parties' intention with respect to the transfer of property where such intention cannot otherwise be determined (s.18).

(*a*) The property in specific goods is deemed to pass when the contract is made provided the contract is unconditional and the goods are in a deliverable state (Rule 1). In one case, for example, a thirty ton condensing engine was held not to be in a deliverable state where, at the time of sale, it was still bolted to the floor of the seller's premises (*Underwood Ltd*. v. *Burgh Castle Brick and Cement Syndicate* (1921)).

(*b*) Where it is necessary for specific goods to be put in a deliverable state or, being in a deliverable state, they have to be weighed, measured, etc. in order to ascertain price, the property does not pass until this is done and the buyer has been informed (Rules 2 and 3).

(*c*) In the case of goods delivered to the buyer on approval or on sale or return, the property in them passes to him when he signifies his approval or acceptance to the seller, or does any other act adopting the transaction. If no approval or acceptance is signified and the goods are retained without notice of rejection being given to the seller, the property passes on the expiration of the time fixed for return or, otherwise, on the expiration of a reasonable time (Rule 4). In *Kirkham* v. *Attenborough* (1895), K delivered jewellery to W on a sale or return basis following which W pledged the goods with A, a pawnbroker. The goods were not paid for and the issue was whether they were recoverable from A. The Court of Appeal decided that the pledging of the goods by W constituted an act adopting the transaction, the effect of which was to pass the property in them to W; therefore the sellor's claim to the jewellery failed. In a similar case, on the other hand, the seller's action succeeded because he had clearly stipulated that the property in the goods was to remain with him until they had been paid for. Consequently, the buyer's act of pledging the goods made no difference to the seller's rights with respect to them (*Weiner* v. *Gill* (1906)).

(*d*) If the contract is one for the sale of unascertained goods (*see* Chapter 6, p. 69) no property in them is transferred to the buyer until they are ascertained (s.16). This will occur where the goods are appropriated to the contract (Rule 5). For instance, if a buyer agrees to purchase by description a particular type of motor vehicle, there will be an appropriation (and, hence, a transfer of property) when the dealer chooses that vehicle which is to comprise the subject matter of the contract provided the buyer assents and the choice is irrevocable (*Carlos Federspiel and Co. SA* v. *Charles Twigg and Co. Ltd.* (1957)).

As indicated earlier, the goods will normally be at the seller's risk until the property in them is transferred to the buyer (s.20). However, in *c.i.f.* contracts (*see* Chapter 13, p. 165) . . . the goods are at the buyer's risk from the time of shipment despite that the property in them does not pass until the shipping documents are delivered to the buyer. Again, the risk of any loss resulting from a delay in delivery must be borne by the person responsible for the delay (s.20(2)).

The transfer of the title to goods

It is a basic principle of English law that no person is capable of transferring to another a better title to property than he has himself (*nemo dat quod non habet*). Consequently, if goods are sold by a person other than the true owner, the buyer will acquire no better title than the seller had (s.21). To this basic rule there are exceptions. Clearly, if the seller is acting under the actual authority of the owner, the buyer does acquire a good title. Furthermore, although there may be no actual consent to the sale, the true owner may be precluded (i.e. estopped) by his conduct from denying the seller's authority. An illustration is afforded by *Eastern Distributors Ltd.* v. *Goldring* (1957) where A permitted B, a car dealer, to represent that he owned A's motor vehicle which B then proceeded to sell to the plaintiff finance company. Subsequently, A purported to sell the same vehicle to C, but the court held that A could not deny the dealer's authority to sell and therefore the plaintiff's title prevailed.

(It should be noted in this context that a disposition by a mercantile agent under the Factors Act 1889 may also operate to pass a good title and this particular point is considered in Chapter 14.)

The other main exceptions to the *nemo dat* rule are as follows:

(*a*) If goods are sold in *market overt* (open) in accordance with the usage of the market, the buyer will acquire a good title provided he buys the goods in good faith and without notice of any defect or want of title on the seller's part (s.22). "Market overt" includes shops within the City of London and every other legally constituted market. The sale does not necessarily have to be effected by a trader as such. Thus, in *Bishopsgate Motor Finance Corporation* v. *Transport Brakes Ltd.* (1949), a person in possession of a motor vehicle under a hire-purchase agreement took it to Maidstone Market (established by Royal Charter), where he sold the vehicle privately to a purchaser who was acting in good faith and without notice. The court decided that the purchaser obtained a good title because the sale took place in accordance with the usage of the market. Because it is important for such transactions to be conducted openly, the sale must take place between sunrise and sunset (*Reid* v. *Commissioner of Police of the Metropolis* (1973)).

(*b*) A buyer may acquire good title to goods which he purchases from a seller whose title to them is *voidable*, but not yet *avoided* (*see* Chapter 11, p. 130, for a definition of these terms) provided he purchases the goods in good faith and without notice of the defect. It will be seen, for instance, that a contract may be avoided by an innocent party where he has been induced to enter into it as the result of a misrepresentation (Chapter 11). Until such steps are taken by the innocent party, the guilty party can effectively transfer to another a good title to property which he has obtained under the voidable contract. Thus, in *Lewis* v. *Averay* (1972), a crook obtained possession of the plaintiff's motor vehicle in return for a worthless cheque. Because of the fraud, the crook's title to the vehicle was voidable, yet he was able to pass a good title to an innocent purchaser because of the plaintiff's failure to avoid the original contract in time. (Compare *Car and Universal Finance Co. Ltd.* v. *Caldwell* (1965), discussed in Chapter 11, p. 132).

(*c*) In some circumstances, a seller may continue in possession of goods (or the documents of title relating to them) after a sale to the buyer. In this event, any subsequent delivery or transfer of the goods (or documents of title) under any sale, pledge, or other disposition, to another person who receives them in good faith and without notice of the previous sale, is as effective as if the seller were acting under the first buyer's authority (s.24, Sale of Goods Act

1979, and s.8, Factors Act 1889). In *Worcester Works Finance Ltd.* v. *Cooden Engineering Co. Ltd.* (1971), the defendants sold a motor vehicle to a car dealer and in return received a cheque for £525. The dealer then sold the vehicle to the plaintiff finance company but continued in possession of it. The cheque given to the defendants was dishonoured and therefore, being unaware of the other transaction, they retook possession of the vehicle with the dealer's consent. The Court of Appeal held that the defendants and not the finance company were entitled to the vehicle because, after the sale to the finance company, the dealer was a seller who continued in possession and the retaking by the defendants, whilst forgoing their rights under the cheque, constituted a delivery of the vehicle to them under a disposition within the meaning of the statute.

(*d*) The converse of (*c*) above is the situation where a buyer is given possession of the contract goods before the property in them is transferred to him. For instance, the seller might have stipulated that no property in the goods should pass until they have been paid for (*see* the *Romalpa* case, p. 89). Nevertheless, provided the person in possession has bought or agreed to buy the goods and has possession with the seller's consent, a sale and delivery of the goods (or the relevant documents of title) to a person who takes them in good faith and without notice of the original seller's rights, can effectively confer on the latter a good title (s.25, Sale of Goods Act 1979, and s.9, Factors Act 1889). In *Four Point Garage Ltd.* v. *Carter* (1984), a reservation of title clause did not prevent the ownership of a motor car passing to a sub-buyer.

This exception does not apply where the goods are in a person's possession under a hire-purchase agreement (for which *see* Chapter 18) because he is not one who has "bought or agreed to buy" (*Belsize Motor Supply Co. Ltd.* v. *Cox* (1914)) and similar provision is made in this respect by statute where the buyer holds the goods under a conditional sale agreement (s.25(2), Sale of Goods Act 1979, and *see* Chapter 18).

(*e*) It should be noted finally that a person in possession of a motor vehicle under a hire-purchase or conditional sale agreement who disposes of it (unlawfully) to a private purchaser will pass a good title provided the purchaser takes the vehicle in good faith and without notice of the agreement under which the vehicle is held (s.27, Hire-Purchase Act 1964 (as amended)).

A private purchaser is one who neither deals in motor vehicles nor provides finance for the acquisition of vehicles under hire-purchase and conditional sale agreements (s.29). If a person operates a car dealer's business on a part time basis, he is not a private purchaser despite that he acquires the disputed motor vehicle for his own private use (*Stevenson* v. *Beverley Bentinck Ltd.* (1976)).

BAILMENT

A bailment is the entrusting of the possession of goods by one party (the bailor) to another (the bailee) but with the property in the goods remaining with the bailor. The arrangement under which the goods are bailed may be *contractual* or *gratuitous*. Examples of the former are contracts of hire-purchase (*see* Chapter 18) and contracts for the carriage of goods (considered in Chapter 13). The relationship of bailor and bailee is not however dependent upon a contractual relationship between the parties. For example, in *Morris* v. *C.W. Martin and Sons Ltd.* (1966), the plaintiff's mink stole was sent to a furrier for cleaning and, with her consent, was sent on to the defendants to whom the work was subcontracted. Whilst in the defendant's possession, the fur was stolen by one of their employees. The Court of Appeal decided that the defendants were sub-bailees for reward and as such were directly responsible to the plaintiff for the loss of the fur.

The duties owed by a bailee with respect to the goods in his custody are basically twofold. First, the bailee is under an obligation to take reasonable care of the goods and, secondly, he must return them (on demand in the case of a gratuitous bailment) unless the parties have arranged otherwise (note the position with regard to hire-purchase contracts and see Appendix II).

The standard of care required is determined by the circumstances of the case. Furthermore, it is for the bailee to establish that the required degree of care has been observed. In *Houghland* v. *R. R. Low (Luxury Coaches) Ltd.* (1962), the plaintiff passenger's suitcase was deposited in the boot of the defendant's coach. During the journey, passengers and their luggage were transferred to a relief coach. At the journey's end, the suitcase was found to be missing. The Court of Appeal decided that it was for the defendants to rebut a presumption of negligence and this burden they were unable to discharge (*see also James Buchanan and Co.* v. *Hay's Transport Services* (1972) discussed in Chapter 13, p. 161).

It should be noted that the bailee is strictly liable for loss or damage to the goods which may occur after he has been requested by the bailor to return them and fails to do so. In *Mitchell* v. *Ealing L.B.C.* (1979), the defendant local authority evicted the plaintiff squatter from one of their properties but agreed (gratuitously) to store his furniture in a lock-up garage. The furniture was not re-delivered at the time arranged and was subsequently stolen from the premises. The court held that, following their failure to return the furniture at the proper time, the defendants remained in possession as "insurers"; that is, they became liable for its loss irrespective of whether they had exercised reasonable care or not.

A bailee is liable in conversion where he wrongfully disposes of the goods which have been entrusted to him (*see Sachs* v. *Miklos* (1948), Chapter 14, p. 180).

Where a contract is one for the hire of goods (excluding hire-purchase), there is an implied condition on the part of the *bailor* that he has a right to transfer the possession of the goods for the period of the bailment (s.7, Supply of Goods and Services Act 1982, and *see* Chapter 10, p. 125).

SUMMARY

On completion of this chapter you should be able to:

(*a*) Explain the rules relating to the assignment of rights under a contract.

(*b*) Understand the meaning of negotiation in relation to bills of exchange.

(*c*) Outline the basic steps involved in the transfer of (*i*) interests in land, and (*ii*) company securities.

(*d*) Understand the different standpoints from which the ownership of goods may be considered.

(*e*) Explain the *nemo dat* rule and list and discuss exceptions to it.

SELF-ASSESSMENT QUESTIONS

(Relevant page numbers are given in brackets.)

1. Distinguish between part performance and the remedy of specific performance. (Page 82)
2. Distinguish between (*a*) registered, and (*b*) unregistered title to land. (Page 83)
3. State the requirements for a valid statutory assignment of a right arising under a contract. (Page 83)
4. What is a "holder in due course"? (Page 85)
5. Describe the duties of a bailee of goods. (Page 93)

CHAPTER EIGHT

Securities

CHAPTER OBJECTIVES
After studying this chapter you should be able to:
* understand the nature of a mortgage transaction and the principal rights and obligations of the parties thereto; and
* describe and distinguish the various other forms of security which are available to a creditor.

INTRODUCTION

A person who advances money to another on loan or provides credit in some other way (e.g. on a sale of goods) may require the borrower to provide some security for repayment, additional to the usual contractual obligation to pay the debt. In Chapter 6, we noted how a person supplying credit to a registered company could secure the advance by means of a mortgage or floating charge. In this chapter, we examine first the characteristics of a mortgage and then consider other methods whereby advances of money and claims to its payment may be secured.

MORTGAGES

Introductory

Mortgage transactions may relate to both real property and personal property (including things in action, e.g. shares in companies). The essence of a mortgage is that the person providing the loan or credit (the mortgagee) is given a legal or equitable interest in the property comprising the security until the debt is repaid. It is not necessary that there should also be a transfer of possession which may be retained by the borrower (the mortgagor). Because the whole point of a transaction is to provide the lender with a security, the arrangement between the parties cannot be regarded as permanent and the mortgagor is prima facie entitled to redeem the mortgage at any time by paying off whatever sums of money are outstanding.

Mortgages of land

The creation of a land mortgage differs according to whether the mortgage is legal or equitable. A legal mortgage of the freehold estate in land requires a deed (a document under seal) and is effected either:

(a) by granting the mortgagee a leasehold estate in the land (but subject to termination of the lease upon repayment of the loan); or

(b) by granting the mortgagee a charge expressed to be by way of legal mortgage (s.85, Law of Property Act 1925).

Although the legal chargee does not acquire a leasehold estate he is given the same protection, powers and remedies as if he had a three thousand year lease (s.87, Law of Property Act 1925).

Where the mortgagor's interest in the land is itself leasehold, the loan is secured by granting the mortgagee either a sublease (again determinable upon redemption of the mortgage) or a legal charge (s.86, Law of Property Act 1925). Again, the position of the legal chargee with respect to powers and remedies is equated by s.87 to that of the mortgagee by sublease.

A mortgage is equitable where the secured property is an equitable interest in land (e.g. a life interest). Further, a mortgage may be equitable by virtue of the method by which it is brought into being. Thus, an equitable mortgage of land may arise

(a) where the parties enter into a contract to create a legal mortgage, and

(b) provided a mortgage is intended, by the borrower simply depositing his title deeds with the mortgagee.

In the event of the mortgagor defaulting under the agreement, several remedies are available to the legal mortgagee in addition to the right he may have to sue the mortgagor on personal undertakings to repay the sums advanced and observe other terms of the mortgage. An important remedy is the power of sale (s.101, Law of Property Act 1925) on the exercise of which the mortgagor's interest in the property is relegated to a claim against the proceeds of sale after various payments (including for instance the mortgagee's advance) have been deducted (s.105, Law of Property Act 1925). It should be noted that the mortgagee must exercise the power of sale with sufficient care so as to obtain the proper market price for the property at the time he chooses to sell it (*Cuckmere Brick Co. Ltd. v. Mutual Finance Co. Ltd.* (1971)). Building societies in particular are under a statutory obligation to ensure that the sale price is the best that can reasonably be obtained (s.36, Building Societies Act 1962).

A mortgagee is not permitted to exercise the power of sale in his own favour (*Williams* v. *Wellingborough Borough Council* (1975)).

Another remedy is foreclosure, the effect of which is to enable the mortgagee to acquire the mortgagor's freehold estate or leasehold estate as the case may be (ss.88 and 89, Law of Property Act 1925). Further, a legal mortagee has the right to take possession of the mortgaged land and this right is exercisable independently of any breach on the mortgagor's part (*Four Maids Ltd.* v. *Dudley Marshall (Properties) Ltd.* (1957)).

It is usual however for the mortgagee to take advantage of this right only in connection with the exercise of the power of sale.

The principal remedies available to an equitable mortgagee are foreclosure and, provided the mortgage is contained in a deed, a power of sale.

The above remedies must be considered in the light of the Consumer Credit Act 1974, where the mortgage agreement falls within the definition of regulated agreement contained in that Act (*see* Chapter 18, p. 217). Thus, the mortgagee is required to serve a default notice on the mortgagor before he becomes entitled to enforce his security or recovery possession of that land (s.87, and *see* Chapter 18, p. 222). Furthermore, the mortgagee's power of sale and right to take possession of the land are affected by s.126 of the Act, which provides that a land mortgage securing a regulated agreement is enforceable by court order only. Finally, mortgages as credit agreements are subject to the provisions of the Act relating to extortionate credit bargains and are liable to be reopened by the court if the mortgagor is required to make "grossly exhorbitant" payments or the bargain "grossly contravenes the ordinary principles of fair dealing" (*see* Chapter 18, p. 228).

Mortgages of goods

A legal mortgage of goods is effected by the transfer of the title to goods to the mortgagee as security for the debt (Cotton LJ in *Re Morritt* (1886)). The transfer of ownership may or may not be accompanied by a delivery of the goods themselves.

Because the mortgagor retains an equity of redemption, the mortgagee is obliged to retransfer the title upon repayment of the debt.

If a mortgage of goods is comprised in a document, it constitutes a bill of sale and must therefore comply with the requirements of the Bills of Sale Acts 1878 and 1882 as regards form and content and registration. Further, and importantly, there must be annexed to a bill of sale a schedule listing the goods to which the agreement relates (s.4, 1882 Act).

It should be noted that the Bills of Sale Acts do not apply to debentures issued by registered companies (s.17, 1882 Act) and *Re Standard Manufacturing Co.* (1891)).

PLEDGES (PAWNS)

Characteristics

A pledge is constituted by one person (the pledgor or pawnor) transferring the possession of goods to another (the pledgee or pawnee) as security for a loan of money. The goods which are subject to the pledge may be physically delivered to the pledgee or delivery may be constructive: for example, by the handing over of the keys of a room in which the goods are stored (Lord Wright in *Official Assignee of Madras* v. *Mercantile Bank of India Ltd.* (1935)).

The principal distinction between a pledge and a mortgage of goods is that the mortgagee is given the owership of, or general property in, the goods whereas a pledgee acquires only a special property (Cotton LJ in *Re Morritt* (1886)) or that which is "necessary to secure the debt" (Willes J in *Halliday* v. *Holgate* (1868)). The effect of this is that, after giving notice to the pledgor, the pledgee has a common law right to sell the goods in the event of the pledgor defaulting on the loan and then recoup the amount of his advance out of the proceeds of sale.

Pledges under the Consumer Credit Act 1974

The provisions of the Act relating to pledges apply where articles are taken in pawn under a regulated agreement (defined in Chapter 18, p. 217—and *see* this chapter for the provisions affecting regulated agreements generally which must be complied with in addition to those discussed in these paragraphs).

A person who receives an article in pawn (i.e. the pawnee) must give to the pawnor a "pawn-receipt" (s.114); failure to do so is an offence (s.115). Further, an offence is committed where the creditor (pawnee) fails to observe the provisions of the Act with respect to copies of the pledge agreement (ss.62 and 63) and notification to the debtor (pawnor) of his right of cancellation (s.64).

The article which is subject to the pledge (the pawn) may be redeemed at any time within the period of six months following the date on which it was taken by the pawnee under the regulated agreement (a longer period may be fixed by the parties by agreement) (s.116). A failure by the pawnor to redeem within the redemption period entitles the pawnee to realise the pawn by sale on giving at least fourteen days notice. Further, if the redemption period is six months only and the pawn is security for fixed-sum credit not exceeding £15.00 or running-account credit with a credit limit not exceeding this sum, the general property in the pawn (i.e. ownership) is transferred to the pawnee (s.120).

Redemption of the pawn is effected by the pawnor surrendering the pawn receipt and paying the amount outstanding under the regulated agreement (s.117). It is an offence for the pawnee to refuse to allow the pawn to be redeemed without reasonable cause (s.119).

It should be noted that the specific provisions of the Act relating to pledges do not apply to (*a*) a pledge of documents of title or (*b*) a non-commercial agreement (described in Chapter 18, p. 225).

LIEN

Definition

A lien at common law is the right a person may have to retain property which is lawfully in his possession until his demands are met by the person to whom the property belongs (*Dyson* v. *Peat* (1917)).

This "possessory" type of lien must be distinguished from an equitable lien which is not dependent on possession, but which nevertheless confers on the person entitled to it a right against real or personal property. For instance, a purchaser of land has an equitable lien against the land in respect of the amount of the deposit he has paid. Similarly, a vendor has an equitable lien against the land until he has received the full purchase price (*Lysaght* v. *Edwards* (1875)). The holder of an equitable lien has the right to have the property which is subject to it sold and this is in contrast with the position obtaining in the case of common law, or possessory, liens where a right of sale is not normally conferred. In fact, if the holder of a possessory lien does sell without justification, he may be liable in damages for wrongful interference with goods (s.1, Torts (Interference with Goods) Act 1977).

A lien may be granted by statute. Thus, an unpaid seller of goods has the right to retain possession of them by virtue of s.39, Sale of Goods Act 1979 (for the unpaid seller's rights generally, *see* Chapter 16, p. 199).

General and particular possessory liens

A general lien confers the right to retain property in respect of all claims the person in possession may have against the owner of the property. This type of lien may arise by custom, as in the case of the banker's lien (*Brandao* v. *Barnett* (1846)), or the parties to a contract may provide for a general lien expressly. In *Jowitt and Son* v. *Union Cold Storage Co.* (1913), for instance, the defendants acquired a general lien under their conditions of storage and this consequently enabled them to retain the plaintiff's meat against charges outstanding in respect of their storage of other goods.

The holder of a particular lien has a right of retention only in respect of charges or other sums relating to the specific property in his possession. For example, common carriers (*see* Chapter 13, p. 158) have a lien against the goods they carry in respect of unpaid charges (*Electric Supply Stores* v. *Gaywood* (1909)). Again, a particular lien arises where goods are held for the purpose of repairing and improving them (*Green* v. *All Motors Ltd.* (1917)). On the other hand, a person who merely carries out work of maintenance without improving the goods does not acquire a particular lien (*Hatton* v. *Car Maintenance Co. Ltd.* (1915)—plaintiffs agreed to garage and maintain a motor vehicle for its owner; the court refused to recognise a right of lien in respect of expenditure on maintenance where there was no element of improvement).

Sale

There is usually no right to sell goods which are subject to a possessory lien. A power of sale may however be conferred by statute. Thus, repairers and other bailees (e.g. persons with whom goods have been deposited for valuation or appraisal) may sell uncollected goods provided (*inter alia*):

(*a*) the bailor is under an obligation to take delivery of the goods, and

(*b*) the bailee has notified the bailor of his intention to sell or, despite taking reasonable steps to do so, has failed to trace or communicate with the bailor in order to give him the proper notice (s.12 and Sched. 1, Torts (Interference with Goods) Act 1977).

The purchaser of the goods obtains a good title to them as against the bailor (s.12(6)) but the bailee must account to the bailor for the proceeds of the sale less the costs of the sale and (provided notice of intention to sell has been given) any sums payable by the bailor in respect of the goods (s.12(5)).

GUARANTEES

The essence of this form of security is that one person (the guarantor or surety) enters into an arrangement with another (the creditor) whereby he becomes answerable to the creditor for the debt of a third person (the principal debtor). X may for instance contract with Bank Y to guarantee a loan advanced to Z. If the undertaking is construed as a guarantee proper (as opposed to an indemnity; see below) the guarantor's liability is secondary merely in that it is dependent upon the principal debtor failing to comply with his primary obligation to repay the debt. There is no question of the guarantee operating for instance if the primary obligation is legally non-existent. Thus, in *Coutts and Co.* v. *Brown-Lecky* (1946), the defendant guaranteed an overdraft granted by the plaintiff bank to a minor. Because the primary credit transaction was void by virtue of the Infants Relief Act 1874 the guarantee itself was ineffectual and could not be enforced (s.1 of the Act provides that contracts made with minors for repayment of money lent or to be lent shall be "absolutely void").

Promises to answer for the debt, default or miscarriage of another must be evidenced in writing and the document signed by the guarantor or his agent (s.4, Statute of Frauds 1677). If the statutory requirement is not complied with, the contract of guarantee is unenforceable. It is for this reason that a distinction must be drawn between a contract of guarantee and a contract of indemnity which may be made orally. A person is deemed to indemnify the creditor (as opposed to guaranteeing the creditor against another's default) where he undertakes a direct responsibility for money advanced to or services provided for another. If, for instance, the guarantor orally advises the creditor that he will ensure payment, he will be primarily liable if there is no principal debtor from whom the creditor could otherwise recover (*Lakeman* v. *Mountstephen* (1874)).

Another situation in which written evidence is not necessary is that of a *del credere* agency. A *del credere* agent receives a special commission for undertaking or guaranteeing that customers whom he introduces to his principal will pay for the goods with which they are supplied.

Under the Consumer Credit Act 1974 a guarantee or indemnity which is provided in relation to a regulated agreement must be expressed in writing (s.105). Moreover, the "security instrument" must comply with regulations made under the Act as to form and content, be signed by or on behalf of the surety, embody all the terms of the security other than implied terms, and be readily legible when presented for signature. In addition, the surety is entitled to copies of the security instrument and the executed regulated agreement. If these requirements are not met, the security is enforceable by court order only (s.105(7)). Further, if the application for a court order is dismissed, the security is to be treated as if it never had effect (s.106).

It should be noted finally, that a creditor or owner (in the case of a consumer hire agreement) may not benefit from a security to a greater degree than would be the case if there were no security and the creditor or owner were to recover from the debtor or hirer to the extent permitted by the Act only (s.113).

SUMMARY

On completion of this chapter you should be able to:

(*a*) Explain the nature of a mortgage transaction.

(*b*) Outline the remedies available to a mortgagee of land in the event of the mortgagor's default.

(*c*) Distinguish between mortgage, pledge and lien.

SELF-ASSESSMENT QUESTIONS

(Relevant page numbers are given in brackets.)

1. What is the purpose of a mortgage? (Page 95)

2. How are land mortgages created? (Page 95)

3. What is the nature of the mortgagee's power of sale? (Page 96)

4. Explain the difference between a pledge and a mortgage. (Page 98)

5. What is the significance of the distinction between a contract of guarantee and a contract of indemnity? (Page 101)

Assignments

1. Arthur draws a cheque for £50.00 in Brian's favour in payment for goods supplied. Brian indorses the cheque in blank and gives it to his sister, Carole, as a birthday present. Before Carole can cash the cheque, it is stolen by Dennis who then transfers it to Edwin in settlement of a debt. Edwin is unaware of the theft. Edwin sends the cheque to his bank but it is later returned with a note stating that Arthur has placed a stop on payment.

Explain to Edwin the legal position of each person through whose hands the cheque has passed. Would Edwin's own position be any different if the cheque were stopped by Arthur because the goods supplied by Brian had been stolen? (Chapters 6 and 7)

2. Vic agrees orally to sell his freehold dwelling house to Paul who pays Vic 10 per cent of the total purchase price. Later, but before the agreed completion date, Vic permits Paul to enter the property and construct a swimming-pool in the garden. Subsequently, Vic decides not to sell the house and he repudiates the agreement with Paul. Vic is prepared to reimburse Paul's 10 per cent deposit and will pay the cost of constructing the swimming-pool.

(*a*) Advise Paul on whether he can enforce the agreement for the sale of Vic's dwelling house. Would your advice differ if, the day after the oral agreement, Vic had written a letter to Paul confirming the sale?

(*b*) On the assumption that there is an enforceable agreement between Vic and Paul, (*i*) explain to Paul what his rights are pending completion of the sale and specify the remedy he should seek to compel completion; and (*ii*) indicate the further steps Vic must take in order to transfer the dwelling house to Paul. (Chapter 7)

3. Basil contracts to transfer his ordinary shares in X Ltd. to Frank but the directors of X Ltd. refuse to register the transfer. A dividend is declared by the company and the money is sent to Basil.

(*a*) Write a memorandum to Frank outlining his position and indicating whether or not he has any claim to the dividend.

(*b*) Advise the directors of X Ltd. on the validity of their action. (Chapter 7)

4. Simon deals in "Gabra" motor vehicles and has ten of these on display in his showroom. Ted contracts to purchase a "Gabra"

vehicle but does not specify the particular vehicle he requires. Delivery and payment are arranged for the following day. Overnight, Simon's showroom and all the vehicles are destroyed by fire. The fire is purely accidental without fault on any person's part. Subsequently, Simon sends Ted a bill for the price of one "Gabra" motor vehicle.

Advise Ted regarding his contractual relationship with Simon with special reference to the ownership of the vehicle and the request to pay the purchase price. (Chapters 6 and 7)

5. Lucy has recently lent £20,000 to MNY Ltd., taking as security for the loan a legal mortgage of the company's factory premises. Lucy wishes to know (a) whether there is anything further which must be done in order to safeguard her rights under the mortgage against the claims of other creditors in the event of the company being wound up, and (b) what her principal remedies against the company would be if the loan were not repaid.

Draft a memorandum to Lucy explaining the nature of a mortgage transaction and answering the particular questions she has raised. (Chapters 6 and 8)

CHAPTER NINE

The Creation of Contractual Relationships

CHAPTER OBJECTIVE

After studying this chapter you should be able to:
* summarise the main rules relating to the formation of contracts.

INTRODUCTION

The rights and obligations of the parties to a contract have their origin in agreement but the binding nature of such agreement is dependent on other elements. These are:

(*a*) consideration,
(*b*) capacity of the parties to contract,
(*c*) legality of purpose (discussed in Chapter 11), and
(*d*) intention of the parties to enter into a legally binding relationship.

In some circumstances, the contracting parties must formulate their agreement in a particular way. For instance, regulated agreements as defined by the Consumer Credit Act 1974 (*see* Chapter 18) are required to be expressed in writing. In addition, although their terms are not required to be set out in a written document, contracts for the transfer of interests in land (*see* Chapter 7) and contracts by which one person promises to answer for the debt, default or miscarriage of another (considered in Chapter 8) must be evidenced in writing, otherwise they are unenforceable.

In the absence of any specific requirement to the contrary however, no particular formality is necessary and contracts may therefore be made orally, or in writing or under seal. In fact, in relation to contracts of sale of goods, the Sale of Goods Act 1979 provides that contracts "may be made in writing (either with or without seal), or by word of mouth, or partly in writing and partly by word of mouth, or may be implied from the conduct of the parties" (s.4).

AGREEMENT

Offer and invitation to treat

The traditional method of establishing an agreement is to consider whether one party has made an offer which has become incorporated in a binding contract by the acceptance of the other (on the assumption of course that the other essential elements are also present). In this respect, it is first necessary to discount any words or conduct on the offeror's part which are not intended to be legally binding and which are, essentially, steps leading towards an offer. Such preliminary steps may be nothing more than invitations to treat and hence be incapable of conversion into a binding agreement. The courts have decided that this is the position in fact with regard to goods displayed in shop windows with price tags attached (*Fisher* v. *Bell* (1961)) and goods set out on the shelves of self-service stores (*Pharmaceutical Society of Great Britain* v. *Boots Cash Chemists (Southern) Ltd.* (1953)). Similarly, an advertisement announcing that an auction would be held did not make the defendant auctioneer liable for the plaintiff's expenses, following the withdrawal of certain items from the sale in *Harrison* v. *Nickerson* (1873). Further, in *Partridge* v. *Crittenden* (1968), an advertisement for the sale of brambelfinches in a magazine was held not to amount to an offer for sale contrary to the (now repealed) Protection of Birds Act 1954.

It is not possible to be categoric about whether a particular form of conduct amounts to an offer since much depends upon the particular circumstances. Thus, in *Carlill* v. *Carbolic Smoke Ball Co.* (1892) an advertisement in which the defendants promised to pay £100 to any person who should contract influenza after using their product was held to constitute a binding offer because "it was intended to be understood by the public as an offer which was to be acted upon" (Bowen LJ). Again in *Esso Petroleum Ltd.* v. *Commissioners of Customs and Excise* (1976), posters advertising world cup coins with every four gallons of petrol purchased were held to be an offer which could be accepted by the motorist driving on to a garage and purchasing the appropriate quantity of petrol.

Provided he is under no contractual obligation to keep the offer open, the offeror can revoke or withdraw his offer at any time before acceptance. The offeree must be advised of such revocation however otherwise he may validly accept and thereby create a contractual relationship (*Byrne* v. *Van Tienhoven* (1880)). An offer can also be terminated by the offeree simply rejecting it or by making a counter-offer (*Hyde* v. *Wrench* (1840)).

In *Butler Machine Tool Co. Ltd.* v. *Ex-Cell-0 Corporation*

(England) Ltd. (1979), X offered to sell goods to Y for £75,000 subject to their terms and conditions of sale which were to prevail over Y's. One of the terms was a price variation clause which provided that the relevant price should be that operating at the time of delivery. Y placed an order for the goods but subject to their own terms and these contained no price variation clause. X used Y's form by which to acknowledge the order and this stated that the sale was to be subject to Y's terms and conditions. On the question whether X were entitled to increase their price, the Court of Appeal decided that Y's order amounted to a counter-offer thereby rejecting the seller's offer. X's subsequent acknowledgment constituted the necessary acceptance and there came into being a binding contract subject to Y's terms.

An offer will lapse if not accepted within a reasonable period of time (assuming no expiry date has been specified) (*Ramsgate Victoria Hotel Company* v. *Montefiore* (1866)—defendant held entitled to reject shares which had not been allotted to him by the plaintiff company within a reasonable time following his application). Furthermore, if made subject to a condition, an offer will cease to be effective if the condition should not be met. In *Financings Ltd.* v. *Stimson* (1962), an offer by the defendant to acquire a motor vehicle from the plaintiff hire-purchase company was deemed to be subject to an implied condition that the vehicle would be in the same state when the offer was accepted. Consequently, when some time later the plaintiffs purported to accept, their acceptance was held to be ineffectual because the vehicle had in the meantime been stolen from the dealer's premises and damaged.

Acceptance

An agreement is concluded by the person to whom the offer is made communicating to the offeror his willingness to accept the offer. The acceptance must be in the same terms as the offer otherwise it will amount to a counter-offer (as in the *Butler Machine Tool* case above). A decision to accept is not in itself sufficient since the fact of acceptance must usually be communicated to the offeror (*Powell* v. *Lee* (1908)) unless the circumstances show that the offeror has dispensed with the need to communicate—as is the case where the offeror makes a promise in return for the offeree performing a certain act (for instance, the purchase and use in the specified manner of the product advertised in *Carlill's* case, above). These latter transactions are commonly called unilateral contracts, as distinct from bilateral contracts which consist of reciprocal promises. Acceptance can then be inferred from the parties' conduct (*see also Brogden* v. *Metropolitan Railway Co.* (1877)), but the acceptance of an offer cannot be inferred from mere silence (*Felthouse* v. *Bindley* (1862)) although a person who is sent unsolicited goods may become their absolute owner notwithstanding his silence (Unsolicited Goods and Services Act 1971). In connection with the sale of goods by auction, a sale "is complete when the auctioneer announces its completion by the fall of the hammer, or in other customary manner; and until the announcement is made, any bidder may retract his bid" (s.57(2), Sale of Goods Act 1979).

Where the parties conduct their negotiations by post, or it is understood that the postal service may be used, a valid acceptance may be effected at the time the acceptance letter is posted, despite the fact that the letter might not arrive at its destination (*Household Fire and Carriage Accident Insurance Co.* v. *Grant* (1879). Nevertheless, the offeror may stipulate that he be given notice of the offeree's acceptance in fact in which case the postal rule is displaced (*Holwell Securities Ltd.* v. *Hughes* (1974)). Similarly, contracts made by telephone or teleprinter are complete only upon receipt by the offeror of the offeree's acceptance. Thus, in *Brinkibon Ltd.* v. *Stahag Stahl* (1982), an offer made by an Austrian company to an English company was accepted by the latter by a telex message sent from England. The House of Lords decided that the contract came into being at the place where the acceptance was communicated to the offeror, in Austria.

The traditional method of analysing agreement in terms of offer and acceptance may be difficult to apply in some cases. In *Clarke* v. *Dunraven* (1897), for example, the rules of a yacht race contained a provision whereby damages were payable in full if one vessel collided with another. The appellant's yacht collided with that of the respondent's and, when sued, the former sought to limit his liability under statute. Despite the apparent absence of offer and acceptance as between the parties, the House of Lords decided that there was a contractual relationship between them enabling the respondent to recover in full. This relationship had come about by each entrant agreeing to be bound by the rules of the race.

A traditional approach towards the discovery of agreement was adopted in *Gibson* v. *Manchester City Council* (1979). A council tenant applied to his local authority to purchase his council house. The local authority replied stating that they might be "prepared to sell" and invited the tenant to "make formal application to buy". This the tenant did but, before the transaction could be completed, political control of the local authority changed and further sales of council houses were stopped. On the question whether the tenant was entitled to the remedy of specific performance, the House of Lords decided that no offer and acceptance was disclosed by the parties' correspondence. In particular, the wording of the local authority's letter made it impossible to regard it as an offer capable of acceptance.

Certainty of terms

A contract cannot be regarded as concluded if there is substantial uncertainty as to what the parties have agreed to (*Scammell v. Ouston* (1941)—agreement for the purchase of a motor vehicle on "hire purchase terms" held to be too vague). Nevertheless, the contract may be enforced if the uncertainty can be resolved by reference to the parties' previous dealings (*Hillas and Co. v. Arcos Ltd.* (1932)). Furthermore, if on the facts it is clear that there is nothing further for the parties to agree about (which was not the case in *Scammell v. Ouston*), meaningless terms will be simply ignored and the contract given full legal effect (*Nicolene Ltd. v. Simmonds* (1953)).

Mistake

In some circumstances, the parties may conduct their negotiations in a way which renders it impossible to conclude that they have reached agreement. In *Scriven Bros. and Co. v. Hindley and Co.* (1913), for example, the defendants agreed at an auction to buy a quantity of tow under the mistaken impression that they had bid for hemp. The clear intention of the plaintiffs was to sell tow. The court held that there was no concluded contract because there was no *consensus ad idem* (meeting of minds) on the question of the subject matter of the sale. There will be a similar lack of *consensus* and, hence, no concluded contract where one party to the negotiations is able to establish to the satisfaction of the court that he was mistaken as to the identity of the other contracting party and that he intended to deal not with that person but with somebody else (as in *Cundy v. Lindsay* (1878)). This may be a difficult thing to establish, however, especially where the parties are not conducting their affairs by correspondence but are negotiating in each other's presence, since there is in such cases a presumption of an intention to deal with the person physically present and not with the person whom the latter might (fraudulently) represent himself to be. Thus, in *Lewis v. Averay* (discussed also in Chapter 7, p. 91), the plaintiff motor car owner was induced by a fraudulent purchaser to believe that he was selling his vehicle to a famous film and television star. The cheque which he had received in exchange for the vehicle was subsequently dishonoured, therefore the plaintiff sought to assert title to the vehicle against the innocent third party to whom the crook had in the meantime sold it. The plaintiff's argument, that there was no agreement between himself and the crook because of a mistake as to identity and that, consequently, the crook had no title to the vehicle which could pass to the innocent purchaser, was unsuccessful because the plaintiff was unable to displace the presumption that he intended dealing with the person to whom he had transferred the vehicle.

CONSIDERATION AND PRIVITY OF CONTRACT

Consideration

If a promise is to be legally enforceable, it must be supported by consideration unless made under seal. Consideration is essentially the reciprocal element in a contract and is required to be furnished by the person to whom the promise is made. Consequently, the promisee must establish either that he has made a counter-promise (executory consideration) or that he has already performed some act (executed consideration) in exchange for the promise which he is seeking to enforce. Further, both the consideration and the promise must form part of the same contract (*Roscorla* v. *Thomas* (1842)—guarantee of the fitness of a horse unenforceable because it was given after completion of the sale of the animal and without fresh consideration in return). The consideration which is supplied must be of some value (i.e. must be sufficient) yet the common law does not require that it be of equivalent value to the defendant's promise. In *Thomas* v. *Thomas* (1842) a promise to pay £1.00 per annum and keep the premises in repair was held to be sufficient consideration for a promise to grant the plaintiff a life interest in a dwelling house.

Consideration will not be regarded as sufficient however where it amounts to nothing more than the performance of an existing obligation, whether contractual or otherwise. Thus, in *North Ocean Shipping Co. Ltd.* v. *Hyundai Construction Co. Ltd.* (1979) an obligation to construct an oil tanker under a pre-existing agreement did not amount to sufficient consideration for a promise by the owners to pay an additional 10 per cent following a devaluation of the US dollar (the currency in which the price was payable). However, the builders' promise to increase the value of a letter of credit opened under the agreement did amount to sufficient consideration in this case (and *see* the discussion in Chapter 11, p. 134).

A promise to repay part of a debt is not acceptable consideration for a promise by the creditor to release the debtor from his obligation to pay the balance (*Foakes* v. *Beer* (1884)) unless, at the creditor's request, some fresh element is introduced (for example, earlier payment).

It should be noted, however, that, even in the absence of sufficient consideration, a person may be held to his promise under the doctrine of promissory estoppel (as stated in *Central London Property Trust Ltd.* v. *High Trees House Ltd.* (1947)). This doctrine is very similar to the principle of waiver (discussed in Chapter 12, p. 155). The essence of the doctrine is that a plaintiff may be prevented from enforcing his contractual rights where he has promised the other contracting party that such rights would not be enforced and the latter has relied on the promise. It must be emphasised that the doctrine will only operate to provide a defence to an action (*Argy Trading Co. Ltd.* v. *Lapid Developments Ltd.* (1977)) and it must be inequitable for the promisor to seek to revoke his promise (*D. and C. Builders Ltd.* v. *Rees* (1966)).

Privity of contract
Closely associated with any discussion of consideration is the basic common law rule that only the parties to a contract may have the right to sue under it. An important decision is *Dunlop Pneumatic Tyre Co. Ltd.* v. *Selfridge and Co. Ltd.* (1915) where in a contract between X and Y, Y promised to obtain from his customers a commitment not to resell X's tyres at less than list prices. Y then resold to Z who, in return for a 10 per cent discount, undertook to observe the restriction. Z in fact resold the tyres in breach of his undertaking. In a subsequent action brought by X, the House of Lords decided that there was no basis on which X could succeed against Z in respect of the breach because he was neither party to the Y/Z contract nor had he furnished consideration in return for Z's promise.

In a later case, *Scruttons Ltd.* v. *Midland Silicones Ltd.* (1962), a firm of stevedores damaged a drum of chemicals whilst unloading it from a ship. In accordance with the above basic rule, the House of Lords held that the stevedores were not entitled to the benefit of a limitation of liability clause in the contract of carriage between the carriers who had employed them and the plaintiff cargo owners (the consignees). Nevertheless, Lord Reid stated that stevedores and others might have protection in such circumstances provided:

(*a*) the bill of lading (*see* Chapter 13) stated that they were to have the benefit of protection;

(*b*) it was clear that in this connection the carrier was contracting with the owner of the goods on behalf of the stevedores;

(*c*) the stevedores had provided the necessary agency authority for this to be done; and (*d*) the stevedores furnished consideration.

These requirements were found by a majority of the Privy Council to be present in *New Zealand Shipping Co. Ltd.* v. *A. M. Satterthwaite and Co. Ltd.* (1975) where stevedores were held to have obtained the benefit of an exclusion clause in the bill of lading through the agency of their employer, the carrier. The performance of their function in unloading the vessel was regarded as sufficient consideration for the consignee's agreement to their being brought within the exclusion.

A similar decision was reached by the Privy Council in *Port Jackson Stevedoring Pty. Ltd.* v. *Salmond and Spraggon (Australia) Pty. Ltd.* (1981) where stevedores were given the benefit of an exclusion clause contained in the bill of lading in respect of goods stolen from a shed for which they were responsible at the port of discharge.

An important exception to the privity of contract rule is the doctrine of privity of estate in land law. Thus, provided certain conditions are fulfilled, the covenants in a lease (for example, to pay rent, covenants for repair) will bind not only the original parties to the transaction but their successors in title. Even where there is no privity of estate, land may be burdened by a restrictive covenant (*see* Chapter 6, p. 69) in which case successors in title of the parties who originally agreed the covenant may have the benefit and burden of the restriction respectively.

CAPACITY

Minors
These are persons under the age of eighteen (Family Law Reform Act 1969). Whether or not a minor has the capacity to contract depends upon the nature of the particular contract. Minors can for example enter into binding contracts of employment and similar arrangements provided they are to the minor's benefit and are not substantially unreasonable (*De Francesco* v. *Barnum* (1890)). In addition, contracts for necessary goods and services are valid and binding although a minor need only pay a reasonable sum for necessary goods which have been sold and delivered to him (s.3, Sale of Goods Act 1979). Necessary goods are defined in the Sale of Goods Act as those which are suitable to the condition in life of the minor and to his actual requirements at the time of the sale and delivery (s.3).

Other contracts are voidable in that they bind the minor unless he chooses to repudiate them before his majority or within a reasonable time thereafter. This category includes contracts concerning interests in land (for example, tenancy agreements), contracts for the purchase of shares and partnership agreements.

Certain other contracts when made with minors are deemed to be absolutely void by statute. These are:

(a) contracts for the repayment of money lent or to be lent;

(b) contracts for goods supplied or to be supplied (other than necessaries); and

(c) accounts stated (that is, acknowledgments that a sum of money is owed) (s.1, Infants Relief Act 1874).

Mental incapacity and drunkenness

In these cases, if the person concerned is unable to appreciate the significance of his actions, the contract is voidable provided the other contracting party is aware of the disability. A contract for the sale of necessary goods (as defined above) is nevertheless binding but only a reasonable price is payable (s.3, Sale of Goods Act 1979).

Corporations

The contractual capacity of corporations is dependent upon the method of their creation (for which *see* Chapter 1, p. 4). Whereas charter corporations are subject to no restriction, statutory companies are limited by the provisions of their enabling statute or, in the case of registered companies, the memorandum of association. The position is governed by the *ultra vires* doctrine which is considered in relation to registered companies in Chapter 3, p. 27.

INTENTION TO ENTER INTO A LEGALLY BINDING RELATIONSHIP

The necessary intention to create a legally binding agreement will be presumed with respect to contracts of a business or commercial nature but the presumption may be rebutted by the parties to the contract clearly providing to the contrary (*Rose and Frank Co.* v. *Crompton Bros. Ltd.* (1923)—clause in contract that parties' arrangement was not entered into as a formal or legal agreement and should not be subject to litigation in the courts). Conversely, there is a presumption that no binding agreement is intended in the case of social, family and domestic transactions (*Balfour* v. *Balfour* (1919)) but the presumption will be displaced here also, in appropriate circumstances. Thus, in *Merritt* v. *Merritt* (1970) an agreement between a husband and wife who were separated whereby the husband promised to convey to the wife his interest in their jointly owned house, provided she completed the mortgage repayments, was held to be binding.

SUMMARY

On completion of this chapter you should be able to:

(*a*) State the necessary elements of a binding contract.
(*b*) Explain the nature of agreement.
(*c*) Understand and appreciate the significance of consideration, capacity to contract, and intention to create a binding relationship.

SELF-ASSESSMENT QUESTIONS

(Relevant page numbers are given in brackets.)

1. Distinguish between "offer" and "invitation to treat". (Pages 106–7)
2. How can an offer terminate? (Page 106)
3. Can there be a valid acceptance of an offer without communication with the offeror? (Page 107)
4. To what extent does mistake nullify agreement? (Page 109)
5. Explain the doctrine of privity of contract. (Page 111)

CHAPTER TEN
Contractual Rights and Obligations

CHAPTER OBJECTIVES
After studying this chapter you should be able to:
* understand the nature and importance of the various rights and obligations of the contracting parties;
* indicate the circumstances in which the terms of a contract may be created by implication of law; and
* explain the effect of common law and statute on the validity of exclusion clauses.

INTRODUCTION

The rights and obligations of the parties to a contract are determined in the main by what has been expressly agreed. In addition, depending on the nature of the particular contract, the parties' position may be affected by implied terms (*see* p. 117). Whatever the method of their creation, the provisions of a contract may differ in importance and this aspect is considered on pp. 117–19). The reader should be aware of the important implied obligations affecting contracts for the sale and supply of goods and these are examined in some detail on p. 120. The terms of a contract may provide for the limitation or exclusion of obligations or liability for their breach and this chapter concludes with a discussion of the effectiveness of such exclusion clauses.

NATURE AND IMPORTANCE OF THE TERMS OF THE CONTRACT

In this section we consider how the terms of a contract may arise expressly or by implication of law and we examine the differing degrees of importance of such terms.

Express terms

The respective rights and obligations of the contracting parties are governed by the terms of the contract. Such terms may be created expressly, whether orally or in writing, or they may arise by implication of law. In the steps towards the conclusion of their agreement, the parties will often make statements which are not intended to be contractually binding. Not everything said or written in the formation of a contract can be automatically categorised as a contractual term. Consequently, the usual remedies for a breach of contract (*see* Chapter 14) will be inapplicable if a statement with no contractual status is subsequently shown to be false. Nevertheless, there are various remedies available for false statements amounting to a misrepresentation and these are discussed in the next chapter.

Whether or not a statement has the force of a contractual term depends upon what may be reasonably concluded as to the parties' intention having regard to their words and conduct. In *Oscar Chess Ltd.* v. *Williams* (1957), for example, the defendant sold a motor vehicle to a car dealer having innocently stated that it was a 1948 model, whereas the vehicle was in fact manufactured in 1939. The Court of Appeal adopted the view that the seller's statement as to age was merely one of belief and not a term of the contract since he had no special knowledge apart from the details contained in the registration book.

On the other hand, the necessary intention that a statement should become a part of the contract will be inferred if its maker is well placed to verify the accuracy of the information on which that statement is based. In *Dick Bentley Productions Ltd.* v. *Harold Smith (Motors) Ltd.* (1965), a car dealer informed the purchaser of a Bentley motor car that it had travelled only 20,000 miles whereas the actual mileage was much higher. This statement was held to be a contractual term, thereby entitling the aggrieved purchaser to recover damages for breach of contract.

It should be noted that a representation or assurance which does not form part of the principal transaction may nevertheless be comprised in a collateral contract and be equally effective. A case in point is *Strongman (1945) Ltd.* v. *Sincock* (1955). A building firm carried out work for the defendant under a contract which lacked proper governmental authorisation. The contract was illegal, therefore the builders were unable to recover the agreed sum. Despite this, the builders were awarded damages for breach of a collateral promise made by the defendant that he would obtain the necessary authorisation. It was in consideration for this promise that the builders had entered into the illegal agreement. Similarly, in *Brikom Investments* v. *Carr and Others* (1979), the occupants of various flats were offered 99 year leases of the accommodation by their landlords. The latter promised to pay the cost of structural repairs which had become necessary. After the leases had been granted, the tenants were asked to pay a contribution in respect of the same repairs. The Court of Appeal decided that the landlords were precluded from recovering under the leases having regard to their earlier assurances.

Implied terms

In addition to being bound by terms which have been expressly agreed, the contracting parties may be subject to obligations incorporated in the contract by the courts or under some statutory provision. The courts will in fact imply terms to give effect to a well established custom, to enable a contract to operate more effectively and where the nature of the transaction itself requires that a particular term be included. Essentially, the courts are in these cases giving effect to the presumed intention of the parties (*The Moorcock* (1889)). In *Hutton* v. *Warren* (1836), an agricultural lease was held to be subject to a local custom that, on his leaving the premises, the tenant was entitled to an allowance in respect of seeds and labour. Again, in *The Moorcock*, the defendants agreed to allow the plaintiff's ship to discharge its cargo alongside their jetty. The contracting parties knew that the ship would be grounded at low water but were unaware of a ridge of hard ground beneath the mud. When the ship did settle, it was damaged. As the parties had made no express provision for this event, the Court of Appeal decided that the jetty owners were in breach of an implied obligation to make reasonable efforts to ensure the suitability of the berth for the plaintiff's ship. Similarly, in *Basildon District Council* v. *J. E. Lesser (Properties) Ltd.* (1985), a case concerning a contract for the construction of dwelling houses, the court implied a term that the buildings would be fit for habitation when completed.

The nature of the transaction may be such that the courts will imply a term as a matter of course. A tenancy agreement for example is automatically subject to a term that the landlord will do nothing to interfere with his tenant's quiet possession of the premises (*Kenny* v. *Preen* (1963)) and, in the case of a high rise block of flats, the landlord is under an obligation to take reasonable care with respect to the maintenance of the lifts and stairways (*Liverpool City Council* v. *Irwin* (1977)).

Terms may also be implied in a contract by statute. Contracts of sale of goods, for example, may be subject to the implied obligations contained in the Sale of Goods Act 1979 relating to the quality and fitness of the goods supplied. Similar provision is made in respect of hire-purchase agreements by the Supply of Goods (Implied Terms) Act 1973. The relevant parts of both these statutes are more fully discussed below.

The different categories of terms and their effect

The remedies available to the innocent party in the event of a breach of contract are dependent on the importance of the contractual obligation in dispute. A particular breach may be sufficiently serious or fundamental as to amount to a repudiation of the contract in which case the innocent party is given a right of termination. In *Poussard* v. *Spiers and Pond* (1876), an artiste contracted to take part in an opera but fell ill before the occasion of the first performance and was not available until some days afterwards. The court decided that the defendants were in the circumstances justified in terminating the contract and engaging a substitute.

In cases where the breach is not fundamental and does not affect the substance of the contract, the appropriate remedy is damages.

The importance to be attributed to an obligation may be decided in advance by the parties themselves, by statute (in the case of implied obligations), or by examining the consequences of the breach. Historically, the more important contractual obligations have been described as "conditions" and those of less significance as "warranties" (*Wallis, Son and Wells* v. *Pratt and Haynes* (1910)). This terminological approach is in fact adopted in the Sale of Goods Act 1979 which provides a right of repudiation for a breach of condition and a right to claim damages but no right to reject the goods and treat the contract as repudiated for a breach of warranty (ss.11(3) and 61).

It should be noted that the word, "condition", may also be used to describe a stipulation which must be complied with before a contract can come into effect. If therefore A agrees to purchase B's land subject to planning permission being obtained, the contract will be unenforceable if this *condition precedent* is not fulfilled. Similarly, the parties to a contract may provide for its termination on the occurrence of a certain event. For example, a tenancy agreement may be subject to automatic termination in the event of the tenant's bankruptcy (*condition subsequent*).

In the formation of their contract, the parties are quite free to stipulate that the breach of a particular obligation will be a sufficient act of repudiation to allow the party affected by the breach to terminate the contract irrespective of the consequences—the mere use of the word, "condition", in itself is not however conclusive as to such intention (*Schuler A.G.* v. *Wickman Machine Tool Sales Ltd.* (1974)). Further, the obligation in question may be widely accepted as having the status of a condition in which case the courts will tend to acknowledge this. In *The Mihalis Angelos* (1971), the Court of Appeal was required to consider whether the charterers of a ship were justified in terminating the charterparty, where the ship's owners were in breach of an undertaking that the vessel would be available for loading at a certain place and time. The court decided that the clause in question was in fact a condition, having regard to its general acceptance as such and the desirability of the parties being able to tell in advance what their rights following a breach would be.

There are many cases where the status of a particular obligation is not determinable in advance. Terms within this category are often described as "intermediate" (Lord Denning MR in *The Hansa Nord* (1976)). The approach adopted by the courts is to ascertain whether the effects of the breach of the obligation are sufficiently serious as to amount to a repudiation of the contract. The innocent party is allowed to accept the contract as discharged if he is deprived of substantially the entire benefit which he might have expected to obtain if the other party's obligations were satisfactorily performed. In *Federal Commerce and Navigation Ltd.* v. *Molena Alpha Inc.* (1979), a dispute arose between the charterers of three ships and the owners. It was a term of the charterparty that the captains of the ships should be under the authority of the charterers but the owners placed restrictions on the captains' authority thereby placing the charterers in considerable difficulty. The House of Lords had to decide whether the owners' conduct constituted a repudiation of the contract of hire. The term in contention was not drafted as a condition (it was an intermediate term) therefore it was necessary to examine its effects. The breach was found to go to the very root of the contract and, because of this repudiation, the charterers were justified in bringing the contract to an end.

The effect of termination is twofold in that:

(*a*) the as yet unperformed obligations of the innocent party are discharged, and

(*b*) there is substituted for the primary obligations of the party in breach a secondary obligation to pay damages to the innocent party,

in order to compensate him for the loss caused by the non-performance (Lord Diplock in *Photo Production Ltd.* v. *Securicor Transport Ltd.* (1980)). It must of course be emphasised that the innocent party has the option of keeping the contract in force (i.e. affirming the contract) in which case only damages are recoverable.

Note that where the innocent party does elect to terminate the contract, the operation of any term excluding or restricting liability for breach and which fulfils the requirement of reasonableness contained in the Unfair Contract Terms Act 1977 remains unaffected by such termination (s.9).

IMPLIED TERMS IN CONTRACTS FOR THE SALE AND SUPPLY OF GOODS

In this section we examine the various implied obligations affecting the supply of goods under contracts of sale and hire-purchase and contracts for work and materials.

Contracts of sale

Various obligations are implied in contracts for the sale of goods under the provisions of the Sale of Goods Act 1979. These implied terms are in principle subject to exclusion or variation by agreement, course of dealing or usage, subject however to the application of the Unfair Contract Terms Act 1977 (*see* p. 128).

The seller's title

There is an implied condition on the part of the seller that he has a right to sell the goods or will have such a right at the time when the property (ownership) is to pass (s.12). A clear breach of this obligation arises where the seller is not the lawful owner of the subject matter of the sale, in which case the innocent buyer may terminate the contract and recover the price he has paid. In *Rowland* v. *Divall* (1923), the purchaser of a motor vehicle was required to return it to the person from whom it had been stolen. Because there had been a total failure of consideration, the Court of Appeal allowed full recovery of the purchase price from the seller. It made no difference that the buyer had benefited from several months use of the vehicle. The simple fact was that he had not received that for which he had paid; namely, the right to possession.

This right of the innocent party to seek recovery of his purchase price after termination of the contract of sale remains unaffected by the subsequent acquisition of a good title by the seller, even though the buyer might still have possession of the goods. The breach of condition is the absence of a right to sell, at the time of sale if it is the parties' intention that the property in the goods should then pass (*Butterworth* v. *Kingsway Motors Ltd.* (1954)).

A breach of s.12 will arise where the seller's right to sell is subject to possible legal action by some third party. In *Niblett Ltd.* v. *Confectioners' Materials Co. Ltd.* (1921), the buyers of tins of condensed milk successfully established a breach by the seller where the labels on the tins constituted an infringement of another company's trade mark. Where, however, the seller does have a right to sell at the time of sale, there is no breach of the implied condition. Nevertheless, s.12 implies a warranty that the buyer will enjoy quiet possession of the goods and a breach of this particular obligation may occur both at the time of the sale and where the buyer's possession is subsequently disturbed. A case in point is *Microbeads A.G.* v. *Vinhurst Road Markings Ltd.* (1975), where a company purchased road marking machines to which the sellers were able to transfer a good title at the time of the transaction (unlike *Niblett's* case, above). Later, a third party acquired patent rights in respect of the machines and this event entitled the buyers to recover damages for disturbance of their possession.

It should be noted that s.12 also implies a warranty that the goods are free from any charge or encumbrance not disclosed or known to the buyer before the contract is made. Furthermore, there is nothing to prevent the transfer of a limited title to goods provided the necessary intention appears from the contract or can be inferred from the circumstances.

Sale by description
Where the contract contains words describing the goods being sold, there is an implied condition that they will correspond with that description (s.13). Quite clearly, a buyer will need to rely on a description of the goods where they are unascertained (*see* Chapter 7) or where they have yet to be manufactured or acquired by the seller. The application of this section is not however confined to such cases and includes situations where the buyer has sight of the goods before the sale, provided of course that some words of description are employed. In *Beale* v. *Taylor* (1967), a motor car was described in an advertisement as a "Herald . . . white, 1961". The buyer discovered subsequently that the vehicle comprised two parts joined together, one part being from a different type of vehicle. The fact that the vehicle had been examined before the sale did not prevent the buyer establishing non-compliance with the contractual description.

A sale by description can also occur where the buyer selects goods which have been exposed for sale or hire (e.g. in the case of self-service stores) (s.13(3)).

In sale of goods cases, the traditional approach of the courts has been that there should be strict observance by the seller with the contractual description. For instance, in *Arcos Ltd.* v. *Ronaasen and Son* (1933), the purchasers of a quantity of staves of timber were held by the House of Lords to be entitled to reject an entire consignment because of a slight deviation from the contractual stipulation that each stave should be $\frac{1}{2}$ inch thick. The staves were required for the manufacture of cement barrels, but the suitability for this purpose of the materials actually supplied did not affect the severity of the seller's breach. Where, on the other hand, the quality of the goods supplied is in some way unsatisfactory, it by no means follows that there is a breach of the implied condition as to description. Thus in a case concerning the sale of herring meal, the product actually supplied contained a toxic chemical. There was however no breach of s.13 because, although the *quality* of the product was affected, it could still be described as "herring meal" (*Ashington Piggeries Ltd.* v. *Christopher Hill Ltd.* (1972)).

Note that it is well established that the obligation contained in s.13 is not broken where the deviation from the contract description is so slight as to be of negligible significance (*Shipton, Anderson and Co.* v. *Weil Bros. and Co. Ltd.* (1912)).

Merchantable quality and fitness for purpose
Section 14 provides that goods supplied under a contract of sale are subject to implied conditions that they are of merchantable quality and are reasonably fit for the particular purpose for which they are purchased. It should be noted that, unlike the aforementioned obligations as to title and description, the implied conditions contained in s.14 operate only where the goods are sold in the course of a business, thereby excluding situations where goods are sold privately.

The definition of merchantable quality requires that the goods supplied must be fit for the purpose or purposes for which goods of that kind are commonly bought having regard to their description, the price and all the other relevant circumstances (s.14(6)). Goods described as "second hand" may therefore be imperfect yet merchantable if in a "usable" condition (*Bartlett* v. *Sidney Marcus Ltd.* (1965)). It is perhaps unreasonable to expect in such cases the same standard of quality as might be demanded if the goods were new. The plaintiff in *Bartlett's* case purchased a second-hand motor car knowing that it had a defective clutch. The defect was greater than at first realised and the plaintiff argued that the defendants were in breach of the conditions of fitness and merchantable quality. The action failed because the vehicle was not unroadworthy and the imperfection was not such as to render it unmerchantable (compare *Crowther's* case, below).

There is no implied condition of merchantable quality:

(*a*) as regards defects which are pointed out to the buyer before the contract is made, and
(*b*) where the buyer examines the goods before the sale,
in respect of any defects which that examination should reveal (s.14(2)).

The implied condition as to fitness for purpose operates where the particular purpose for which the goods are being bought is made known to the seller, whether expressly or by implication, and the circumstances are not such as to show that the buyer does not rely, or that it is unreasonable for him to rely, on the seller's skill or judgment. (Where the goods are being sold on credit, there will be a sufficient notification if the purpose for which the goods are required is communicated not to the seller directly but to a credit broker (as to which *see* Chapter 17).)

The particular purpose need not always be expressly notified to the seller since this will in many cases be implicit from the nature of the goods sold (*Grant* v. *Australian Knitting Mills Ltd.* (1935), a case concerning the sale of woollen underclothing). Nevertheless, even where the purpose is such an obvious one some express disclosure on the part of the buyer may be necessary. Thus, in *Griffiths* v. *Peter Conway Ltd.* (1939), the buyer of a tweed coat suffered from a skin complaint. The use of the coat led to dermatitis but an action for breach of the implied condition of fitness for purpose failed because of the buyer's failure at the time of purchase to inform the seller that the coat was required by a person with sensitive skin.

The buyer must rely on the seller's skill or judgment and this will normally be implied in the case of retail sales since the buyer is entitled to assume that the retailer has exercised skill in the selection of his stock (Lord Wright in *Grant* v. *Australian Knitting Mills Ltd.*).

Whether or not the goods are reasonably fit for their purpose is a question of fact. In *Crowther* v. *Shannon Motor Co.* (1975), the engine of a second-hand Jaguar motor car "seized" after covering only 2,000 miles from the time of purchase by the plaintiff. The Court of Appeal decided that a lot more mileage could reasonably have been expected by the buyer therefore the vehicle was not reasonably fit for the purpose of road use.

Liability for breach of the conditions implied by s.14 may be established despite the fact that the seller might have exercised reasonable care in performing his contractual obligations. In *Frost* v. *Aylesbury Dairy Co. Ltd.* (1905), the plaintiff's wife contracted typhoid after consuming infected milk supplied by the defendants. The defendants' breach could not be excused by the fact that all possible precautions had been taken in the preparation of the product.

Sale by sample

A sale by sample will occur where there is an express or implied provision in the contract to that effect (s.15). In such a case, conditions are implied that.

(*a*) the bulk will correspond with the sample in quality,

(*b*) the buyer will have a reasonable opportunity of comparing the bulk with the sample, and

(*c*) the goods will be free from any defect, rendering them unmerchantable, which would not be apparent on reasonable examination of the sample.

In the latter case, a purchaser is not expected to carry out every conceivable test in order to ascertain possible defects but only those which are reasonable in the circumstances (*Godley* v. *Perry* (1960)).

Hire-purchase agreements

(These are defined in Chapter 18.) Under the Supply of Goods (Implied Terms) Act 1973 (as amended), conditions and warranties similar to those operative with respect to contracts of sale of goods are implied in every hire-purchase agreement. Consequently, conditions are implied that the creditor (i.e. the person by whom the goods are bailed) will have a right to sell the goods at the time when the property is to pass; that the goods will correspond with the contract description; and that the goods are of merchantable quality and are reasonably fit for the purpose for which they are being bailed. In addition, there are implied warranties as to freedom from charges or encumbrances and the enjoyment of quiet possession (ss.8–10).

It should be noted further that, as conditional sale and credit sale agreements are contracts for the sale of goods (*see* Chapter 18), these are of course subject to the relevant provisions of the Sale of Goods Act 1979.

Contracts for work and materials and contracts for hire

Where a contract is concerned principally with the exercise of skill and labour by one of the parties, the provisions of the Sale of Goods Act 1979 are inapplicable, even though materials may be supplied under the terms of the agreement. Consequently, a contract to paint a portrait is not a contract of sale of goods (*Robinson* v. *Graves* (1935)). The courts are, however, prepared to regard such contracts as subject to obligations of quality and fitness similar to those operative under the statute. In *Young and Martin Ltd.* v. *McManus Childs Ltd.* (1969), tiles which were supplied in the course of the roofing of new houses were defective and had to be replaced. The contractors who had undertaken the work were held liable for breach of an implied warranty that the materials supplied would be of good quality. The view of the House of Lords was that the distinction between sale of goods contracts and those for the provision of work and materials should not affect the existence of this obligation.

In addition, note should now be made of the provisions of Part I of the Supply of Goods and Services Act 1982, which applies to:

(*a*) contracts under which the property in goods is transferred by one person to another (excluding contracts of sale of goods and hire-purchase contracts); and

(*b*) contracts of hire (other than hire-purchase).

In these cases, conditions relating to title (the right of the bailor to transfer possession in the case of contracts of hire), the contract description, merchantable quality and fitness for purpose of the goods etc. are implied (ss. 2–10). Thus, people who are given the ownership of goods in connection with the provision of a service (as in *Young and Martin's* case above) now have the same statutory protection with respect to the goods as those who acquire such ownership under contracts of sale of goods and hire-purchase.

EXCLUSION CLAUSES

This section is concerned with the nature and effect of exclusion and similar clauses in contracts having regard to the rules of common law and the provisions of the Unfair Contract Terms Act 1977.

Introduction

The provisions of a contract may include terms which purport to exclude or restrict the obligations of one of the contracting parties or his liability for breach of such obligations. For instance, a supplier of goods may seek to exclude the statutorily implied obligations of quality and fitness for purpose. Alternatively, a contract for the carriage of goods may contain a term limiting to a specified amount the carrier's liability in respect of damage to those goods (as in *Scruttons Ltd.* v. *Midland Silicones Ltd.* (1962)).

In many cases, such exclusion clauses are contained in "standard form" contracts which are presented to the other contracting party usually with no possibility of variation. This is a controversial function of the standard form of contract, in particular with respect to consumer transactions, but there are circumstances where the standard form does provide a useful mechanism for simplifying business since the necessity to negotiate a fresh bargain with each individual new customer in such cases as insurance, hire-purchase and holiday travel is avoided. The formulation of standard contracts may be regulated by statute, as in the case of hire-purchase and other credit agreements (see Chapter 18, and also Appendix II where standard hire purchase and credit sale agreement forms are reproduced), or businessmen operating within a particular area of activity may in this respect subject themselves to voluntary regulation (*see* Appendix III).

Whether or not exclusion or limitation clauses are effective in a given case is dependent upon rules developed by the courts and the provisions of statute law, in particular, the Unfair Contract Terms Act 1977.

The position at common law

A person who wishes to take advantage of an exclusion clause must establish that it is a term of the contract. Where therefore the exclusion is contained in a written document, it will be ineffective if it is not the parties' intention that the document should be contractually binding. In *Chapelton* v. *Barry Urban District Council* (1940), the plaintiff hired a deck chair from the defendants and was given a ticket on the back of which there was a clause purporting to exclude liability for loss or damage arising from the use of the chair. The chair collapsed and the plaintiff was injured but the defendants were prevented from relying on the exclusion clause because the ticket was nothing more than a receipt; it had no contractual significance.

Tickets or other documents containing exclusion clauses will however be effective at common law provided they form part of the contract and either the recipient is aware of the existence of the excluding term or reasonable steps have been taken to bring it to his attention (*Parker* v. *South Eastern Railway Co.* (1877)). Consequently, the Court of Appeal decided in *Thornton* v. *Shoe Lane Parking Ltd.* (1971) that a plaintiff injured in a multi-storey car park was not bound by the terms of a condition excluding the proprietors' liability, because the only reference to the excluding term was in a ticket issued by an unmanned machine at the entrance to the car park. In the view of the court, the defendants had not taken sufficient steps to notify the plaintiff of the existence of their terms.

An exclusion clause may be operative in a given case by virtue of past dealings between the same contracting parties. Accordingly, a person may be bound by the provisions of a document which has been issued to him on previous occasions even if, in the instant case, the document is not presented to him until after the conclusion of the agreement (*Spurling Ltd.* v. *Bradshaw* (1956)). Furthermore, fraud or misrepresentation apart, a person is automatically bound by an exclusion clause contained in a document which he has signed, even though he might not have read that document (*L'Estrange* v. *Graucob Ltd.* (1934)).

An exclusion clause which is properly incorporated in the contract is subject to the rule of construction that, if ambiguous, or uncertain in its scope, it will be interpreted against the person who seeks to take advantage of it (*contra proferentem* rule). A case in point is *Hollier* v. *Rambler Motors (AMC) Ltd.* (1972) where the plaintiff's motor car was damaged by a fire attributable to the negligence of the defendant garage proprietors. The defendants relied on a term in their usual invoice which excluded liability for "damage caused by fire to customers' cars on the premises". On the assumption that the invoice was a contractual document, the Court of Appeal decided that the exclusion clause was inoperative because, if the defendants wished to exclude liability for their negligence "they ought to have done so in far plainer language than the language here used" (Salmon LJ). Limitation of liability clauses are not however subject to so strict a rule (*Ailsa Craig Fishing Co. Ltd.* v. *Malvern Fishing Co. Ltd.* (1983)).

The effectiveness of exclusion clauses has been severely curtailed in recent times by the operation of the principle that no exclusion clause can protect a contract breaker in respect of "fundamental" breaches of contract (a case in point is *Farnworth Finance Facilities Ltd.* v. *Attryde* (1970)). In the *Suisse Atlantique* case (1967), however, the House of Lords adopted the view that the effectiveness of an exclusion clause was essentially a matter of construction and that a suitably worded clause might cover any breach, no matter how fundamental. This approach was reaffirmed by the House in *Photo Productions Ltd.* v. *Securicor Transport Ltd.* (1980) where their Lordships stated that there is no principle of English law that an exclusion clause loses all effect in cases of fundamental breach of contract. The facts were that an employee of Securicor caused the destruction by fire of the plaintiff's factory. The contract contained a provision excluding the defendants' liability and, because its wording was clear, it was held that the defendants could take advantage of it despite the serious nature of the consequences of their breach. In *George Mitchell (Chesterhall) Ltd.* v. *Finney Lock Seeds Ltd.* (1983) the House of Lords decided that the suppliers of defective cabbage seeds could not rely on a clause limiting their liability to pay damages for their breach because, although the wording of the clause was sufficiently clear to cover the breach, it was not a fair or reasonable one in the circumstances (see below).

Unfair Contract Terms Act 1977

The provisions of the Act with which we are concerned in this context apply in the main only to contractual or tortious liability arising in the course of a business or from the occupation of premises used for business purposes (s.1). The Act prohibits the exclusion by contract or notice of liability for death or personal injury resulting from negligence. In the case of other forms of loss or damage, however, the exclusion of liability for negligence is permitted but only in so far as the contractual term or notice satisfies the requirement of "reasonableness" (s.2). The test of reasonableness requires that the term shall have been a fair and reasonable one to be included having regard to the circumstances which were, or ought reasonably to have been, known to or in the contemplation of the parties when the contract was made (s.11).

Where one of the parties to a contract deals as a consumer or on the other party's written standard terms, then, subject to the provisions of ss.5, 6 and 7, the other party may use an exclusion clause to exclude or restrict his liability for breach (or to entitle him to perform his contract differently or render no performance) only to the extent that the excluding term satisfies the above test of reasonableness (s.3). A contracting party deals as a consumer where, unlike the other party, he does not make the contract in the course of a business and, if goods are supplied under the contract, they are of a type ordinarily supplied for private use or consumption (s.12).

It may be observed that certain contracts are excluded from the provisions of ss.2 and 3; examples are contracts of insurance and any contract in so far as it relates to the creation or transfer of an interest in land.

In relation to contracts for the supply of goods, s.6 prohibits the exclusion or restriction of liability for breach of the implied obligations as to title contained in s.12 of the Sale of Goods Act 1979 and s.8 of the Supply of Goods (Implied Terms) Act 1973. Similarly, as against a person dealing as a consumer (defined above), liability for breach of the implied obligations contained in ss.13, 14 and 15 of the Sale of Goods Act (and the corresponding provisions contained in the Supply of Goods (Implied Terms) Act) may not be excluded or restricted by the contract: except that, with respect to a person who does not deal as a consumer, such liability may be excluded or restricted provided the excluding term satisfies the test of reasonableness (s.6(3)). The application of s.6 is not of course confined to liabilities which arise in the course of business.

In those cases where the possession or ownership of goods is transferred under a contract which is not one for the sale of goods or hire-purchase (*see* pp. 124–5), as against a person dealing as consumer, the Act prevents the exclusion or restriction of liability for breach of the obligations of fitness for purpose and quality etc. which may arise by virtue of the common law or under the Supply of goods and Services Act 1982. Again, in non-consumer cases, the restriction or exclusion of such liability is allowed provided the requirement of reasonableness is met (s.7).

Finally, it should be noted that the Act prevents a manufacturer using a term in a guarantee in order to restrict or exclude his liability to a consumer in negligence in respect of loss or damage caused by defective goods (s.5). (A manufacturer's liability for defective products is discussed in Chapter 19.)

SUMMARY

On completion of this chapter you should be able to:

(*a*) Appreciate the difference between contractual terms and statements which are not intended to be contractually binding.

(*b*) Appreciate the circumstances in which the terms of a contract will arise by implication of law.

(*c*) Understand the importance of a contractual term with respect to remedies available for a breach of contract.

(*d*) Identify and outline the implied obligations affecting contracts under which goods are supplied.

(*e*) Explain the nature of an exclusion clause and the extent to which it can be relied on in English law.

SELF-ASSESSMENT QUESTIONS

(Relevant page numbers are given in brackets.)

1. How do the courts distinguish between the terms of a contract and other statements made by the contracting parties? (Page 116)

2. Why are the remedies available to a person following a breach of contract dependent on the nature of the term broken? (Page 117)

3. Describe the obligations which are implied by statute in contracts for the sale and supply of goods. (Pages 120–5)

4. Outline the provisions of the Unfair Contract Terms Act 1977 affecting the enforceability of exclusion clauses. (Page 128)

CHAPTER ELEVEN

Voidable, Void and Illegal Contracts

CHAPTER OBJECTIVES

After studying this chapter you should be able to:
* explain the main principles relating to misrepresentation, duress and undue influence, mistake and illegality; and
* understand the effect of each on the validity of a contract.

INTRODUCTION

A contract may become invalid and ineffective by the presence of one or more different factors. For example, a person who has been induced to enter into a contract, as the result of a false statement made by the other party, may be entitled to have the contract set aside (that is, rescinded); alternatively, he may choose to keep the contract in being (affirm) and seek damages (*see* p. 132). In such a case, the contract is said to be *voidable* in that it remains valid and enforceable by either party if no steps are taken to avoid it. Consequently, the ownership of goods may pass under such a contract and it is therefore possible for the transferee (albeit a wrongdoer) to pass a good title to a purchaser from him who acts in good faith (*Lewis* v. *Averay* (1971)). Alternatively, a contract will in certain cases be regarded by the courts as *void* in which case it may be completely ineffective with neither party having rights under it. A contract may for instance be void by virtue of a statute or because it infringes the common law rules concerning public policy (*see* p. 140). Finally, an *illegal* contract is one which the law prohibits or which is performed in an unlawful way. Nevertheless, even an illegal contract may not be entirely ineffectual as we shall see later (on p. 142).

MISREPRESENTATION

In this section we consider the circumstances in which a false statement made in the formation of a contract will amount to a misrepresentation and its effect.

The nature of a misrepresentation

We noted in Chapter 10 that the remedies for breach of contract do not apply in respect of a false statement which is not intended by the parties to be contractually binding (*see* p. 116). There are, however, other remedies which an aggrieved party may take advantage of provided the false statement about which he complains amounts to a misrepresentation. A misrepresentation is defined as a false statement of fact which induces a person to enter into a contract. The remedies which are available to some extent vary according to whether the untrue statement is made fraudulently, negligently or innocently (*see* p. 132).

It is clear from the above definition that a misrepresentation must be one of fact. Consequently, misstatements about the law or a person's intention and statements of opinion in themselves do not give rise to a misrepresentation. In *Bisset* v. *Wilkinson* (1927), the vendor of agricultural land informed the purchaser that he considered the land could carry two thousand sheep. As the fact that the land had not previously been used as a sheep farm was known to the purchaser, the vendor's statement was held to be one of opinion and did not constitute a misrepresentation. A statement of opinion may well be actionable, however, if it conveys a false impression and is based upon facts of which the other party is unaware (*Smith* v. *Land and House Property Corporation* (1884)). A statement of intention is in effect a promise and, provided adequate consideration can be shown, the appropriate remedies are those for a breach of contract.

The person to whom the false statement is made must show that it is at least one of the factors which induced him to enter into the contract and, further, that it was the other party's intention that he should be influenced by it (*Peek* v. *Gurney* (1873)). If therefore no reliance is placed on the false statement, there will be no cause of action (*Smith* v. *Chadwick* (1884)).

Silence

Normally, silence will not amount to a misrepresentation, but there are certain exceptions to this rule. It may be for example that a statement is true at the time when it is made but changed circumstances render it false before the contract is finalised. In such a case, there is an obligation to disclose the true position. Thus, in *With* v. *O'Flanagan* (1936), the defendant, who wished to sell his medical practice, told a potential purchaser that it was valued at £2,000 per annum. Before the contract was concluded some months later, the defendant became ill and the value of the practice became less. The Court of Appeal decided that the defendant's non-disclosure entitled the purchaser to rescind. An important category of contracts in respect of which there is an obligation to make full disclosure is that of contracts of utmost good faith (*uberrimae fidei*). For instance, a person who submits a proposal in respect of a contract of insurance must disclose to the insurers all facts which are material to the risk in respect of which insurance is sought; if he does not the contract is voidable. At common law, however, the proposer is under no obligation to disclose facts of which he is unaware (*Joel* v. *Law Union and Crown Insurance Company* (1908)). A duty of disclosure exists also in the case of certain confidential relationships such as that obtaining between partners (*see* Chapter 2). Similarly, company promoters are obliged to make certain disclosures to the company they have formed (Chapter 3). A contract of service is not a contract of utmost good faith, therefore an employee is not required to disclose to his employer past breaches of duty (*Bell* v. *Lever Bros. Ltd.* (1932)). Further, in relation to a separation agreement, a wife is under no obligation to inform her husband of an intention to remarry (*Wales* v. *Wadham* (1977)).

Remedies

A contract which is entered into on the basis of a misrepresentation is voidable, therefore the complaining party has a choice between affirming that contract or rescinding it. Rescission is effected either by notifying the other contracting party of an intention to terminate, or by commencing an action in the courts (for example, where it is necessary to recover property which has passed under the contract). In *Car and Universal Finance Company Ltd.* v. *Caldwell* (1965), X sold a car to Y in return for a cheque which was dishonoured when presented for payment. X was unable to locate Y in order to communicate the fact that he was rescinding the contract but he did report the matter to the police and the Automobile Association. Later, the car came into the possession of the plaintiffs who purchased it in good faith and without knowledge of the earlier wrongdoing. The Court of Appeal decided that X had effectively rescinded his contract with Y because he had done everything reasonably possible in the circumstances. This meant that the plaintiffs did not acquire a good title.

Note that the right to rescind will be lost in certain situations. Thus, if the innocent party, with knowledge of the misrepresentation, elects to affirm the contract, he cannot later change his mind (*Sharpley* v. *Louth and East Coast Railway Co.* (1876)). A failure to rescind over a period of time may normally be regarded as evidence of affirmation of the contract although in *Leaf* v. *International Galleries* (1950) a lapse of time in itself was sufficient to prevent rescission for an innocent misrepresentation. In that case, the plaintiff purchased from the defendants a painting, having been told by them that it was painted by Constable. The plaintiff discovered five years later that the painting was not in fact a Constable. The Court of Appeal held that there was no justification for rescission having regard to the period of time which had elapsed since the purchase.

Rescission is also impossible where the parties cannot be (substantially) restored to the position they enjoyed before the contract (*Clarke* v. *Dickson* (1858)) or where an innocent third party purchaser acquires rights in respect of any property which has been transferred under the voidable contract (*Lewis* v. *Averay* (1971)). Furthermore, by virtue of s.2(2) of the Misrepresentation Act 1967, in the case of a misrepresentation made without fraud, the court is empowered to declare the contract subsisting and award damages instead of the remedy of rescission if of the opinion that it would be equitable to do so.

There are circumstances where damages are available to an aggrieved party in addition to the right to rescind. Accordingly, if a misrepresentation is made fraudulently, damages may be recoverable in the tort of deceit. A fraudulent statement was defined in *Derry* v. *Peek* (1889) as one made "knowingly, or without belief in its truth, or recklessly, careless whether it be true or false" (Lord Herschell). Similarly, damages are available in tort in respect of a negligent misrepresentation provided the necessary duty of care can be established (*Hedley Byrne and Co. Ltd.* v. *Heller and Partners Ltd.* (1964)). In addition, a person who suffers loss following a misrepresentation made without fraud may recover damages under the Misrepresentation Act 1967 unless the maker of the false statement can prove that he had reasonable ground to believe and did believe up to the time the contract was made that the facts represented were true (s.2(1)). If the misrepresentor is able to discharge this burden of proof he will have made his statement completely innocently. In the past, the only remedy available for an innocent misrepresentation was rescission but, as we saw in the previous paragraph, the court now has the statutory power to award damages as an alternative to rescission in appropriate cases (assuming of course that the right to rescind has not been lost).

It may be noted that, if the person relying on the false statement is sued under the contract by the guilty party, he may plead the fact of the misrepresentation as a defence or counter claim in respect of it (*Laurence and Ano.* v. *Lexcourt Holdings Ltd.* (1978)).

Exclusion of liability for misrepresentation
Section 3 of the Misrepresentation Act 1967 (as substituted by the Unfair Contract Terms Act 1977) provides that a contractual term which purports to exclude or restrict liability for misrepresentation,

or the remedies available to the aggrieved party, shall be of no effect except in so far as it satisfies the test of reasonableness contained in the Unfair Contract Terms Act 1977 (for which *see* Chapter 10, p. 128). Thus, in *Walker* v. *Boyle* (1982), following an innocent misrepresentation, the vendor of a house was unable to rely on a clause providing that the validity of the contract of sale should not be affected by any misstatement because it could not be shown that the clause was a fair and reasonable one in the circumstances as required by s.11 of the 1977 Act. It appears that if the contractual term in question is one which merely limits the authority of an agent to make representations it will not amount to an exclusion or restriction of liability for a misrepresentation and s.3 will not therefore apply (*Overbrooke Estates Ltd.* v. *Glencombe Properties Ltd.* (1974)).

DURESS AND UNDUE INFLUENCE

In the following paragraphs we examine the effect of duress and less obvious forms of improper pressure on the validity of a contract.

Duress

As a contract is founded on agreement, a person who contracts following acts of violence or threatened violence is entitled to avoid the contract on the grounds of common law duress. Furthermore, a contract may be voidable for duress where the pressure on a party to enter into a contract is based not on violence but on threats of an economic nature. An example is a threat to break a contract. Thus, in *North Ocean Shipping Co. Ltd.* v. *Hyundi Construction Co. Ltd.* (1979), X agreed to construct an oil tanker for Y for a stated price. Subsequently, with no legal justification, X demanded an additional payment and threatened to terminate the contract if Y did not co-operate. Y had already contracted to charter the vessel to Z therefore they agreed to pay the required amount. In an action for the recovery of this sum, the court decided that the agreement to pay the additional money was binding (X had furnished consideration) but voidable by virtue of the economic pressure brought to bear on Y. Nevertheless, Y were deemed to have affirmed the contract having regard to such matters as their acceptance of the vessel and their delay in commencing their action.

Undue influence

Equity adopts a more comprehensive approach than the common law to the problem of contracts concluded without true consent. Relief was for instance granted by the House of Lords to a father who mortgaged property following threats to prosecute his son for forgery (*Williams* v. *Bayley* (1866)). Again, in *Lloyds Bank Ltd.*

v. *Bundy* (1975), a guarantee and charge effected by an elderly farmer in favour of his bank was set aside by the Court of Appeal because, given the relationship of trust and confidence existing between the parties, the bank had failed in their duty to ensure that their client obtained independent advice before committing himself. It is, in fact, in situations where one person places confidence in another, that the opportunity arises for the dominant party to abuse the relationship and obtain the benefit of a contract or gift. Consequently, the courts require that the person obtaining the benefit should prove that no unfair advantage was taken of the relationship and that the other party entered into the transaction or donated the gift with an independent mind. A case in point is *Lancashire Loans Ltd.* v. *Black* (1934) where an eighteen-year-old daughter was asked by her mother to sign a promissory note in order that the mother could borrow money from the plaintiffs. The daughter did receive advice with respect to the transaction but this was given by solicitors who were also acting for the mother and the plaintiffs. The relationship of parent and child created a presumption of undue influence which the mother was unable to rebut (the advice the daughter was given could not be said to have been independent). Further, as the plaintiffs were aware of the circumstances giving rise to the transaction, they were unable to enforce the promissory note against the daughter.

Other relationships raising a presumption of undue influence include those of solicitor and client, trustee and beneficiary and doctor and patient, but the categories are not necessarily exhaustive (*Re Craig* (1971)). In those cases where there is no relationship of confidence between the parties, the person who alleges undue influence must himself show that the disputed transaction resulted from the exercise of undue influence and that the necessary consent was lacking. Thus, apart from circumstances such as those which occurred in *Lloyds Bank Ltd.* v. *Bundy* the relationship between a bank and its customer is not one which gives rise to a presumption of undue influence (*National Westminster Bank p.l.c.* v. *Morgan* (1983)).

It has been suggested that the courts will intervene wherever there is "inequality of bargaining power" and that instances of undue influence and other forms of improper pressure (for example, as in *Williams* v. *Bayley*) are in fact based on such inequality (Lord Denning in *Lloyds Bank Ltd.* v. *Bundy*). Furthermore, it should be noted that the Consumer Credit Act 1974 empowers the courts to reopen a credit transaction which is extortionate (*see* Chapter 18). Such an agreement will be regarded as extortionate for example where it contravenes the ordinary principles of fair dealing.

Effect of undue influence
A contract which is made following the exercise of undue influence is voidable at the option of the complainant. It should however be noted that the right to rescind the transaction will be lost if the person unduly influenced can be taken to have affirmed it having regard to his conduct (*Allcard* v. *Skinner* (1887); *see also* the discussion of the right to rescind on p. 132). A contract may still be avoided against a third party who acquires an interest for value in the transaction provided that the third party has full knowledge of the facts (*Lancashire Loans Ltd.* v. *Black* (1934)).

MISTAKE

The following discussion is concerned with the circumstances in which a concluded agreement may be avoided for mistake.

Fundamental mistake
Readers may recall that, in certain cases, a mistake may be such that the parties do not reach agreement; in other words, there is no *consensus ad idem* and hence no contractual relationship (*Scriven Bros. & Co.* v. *Hindley & Co.* (1913); and *see* Chapter 9). Where however the parties have come to an agreement and there is a concluded contract, both the common law and equity recognise the possibility of a mistake that is sufficiently fundamental to affect the validity of that contract. Thus, in *Oscar Chess Ltd.* v. *Williams* (1957) (*see* Chapter 10, p. 116), Lord Denning stated that the mistake made by the defendant and the car dealer about the age of the motor car was of fundamental importance. Consequently, the car dealer might have had the contract set aside by the court on this ground but for his delay in seeking relief. The agreement in the Oscar Chess case was then *voidable* for mistake but the court went further in *Galloway* v. *Galloway* (1914) and held a separation deed between a husband and wife to be *void* where both parties entered into the agreement in the mistaken belief that they were lawfully married.

Where the parties contract on the assumption that the subject matter of their agreement is in existence, the fact that (unknown to them both) it does not exist may render the contract ineffective. In *Couturier* v. *Hastie* (1856), for example, both parties were unaware in a contract for the sale of goods that the subject of the sale, a cargo of corn, had become unfit and had already been sold off to a third person. Because the basis of the contract was the existence of the cargo at the time of sale, the purchaser was not obliged to pay the price. It may be that in such cases there is an implied condition precedent that the subject matter exists, failing which neither party can enforce the contract (*Solle* v. *Butcher* (1950); *see also* Chapter 10, p. 118). Nevertheless, the seller may be liable in damages for breach of contract if he has specifically promised that the subject matter of the contract is in existence (*McRae* v. *Commonwealth Disposals Commission* (1951)).

Provision with regard to contracts for the sale of goods is contained in the Sale of Goods Act 1979. Thus, in the case of a sale of specific goods (that is, goods identified and agreed on at the time the contract is made) and the goods without the knowledge of the seller have perished at the time when the contract is made, the contract is void (s.6).

It must be emphasised that the circumstances in which a mistake will affect the validity of a contract at common law are limited. Thus, in *Leaf* v. *International Galleries* (1950) (*see* p. 132) the mistake which the contracting parties made with respect to the origin of the painting was one of quality but not such as to avoid the contract. Similarly, in *Bell* v. *Lever Bros. Ltd.* (1932), Bell entered into an agreement with his employers for the termination of his contract of employment subject to a payment of £30,000 compensation. Levers discovered subsequently that Bell had committed various breaches of duty and that he could have been dismissed without compensation. The question for the courts was whether the money paid to Bell was recoverable having regard to the parties' common mistake as to the true position (at the time of making the agreement, Bell was unaware of the earlier breaches of his employment contract). The House of Lords held that the compensation agreement was not void for mistake because it had achieved its objective, that is, the termination of the contract of employment. It made no difference that the latter contract had been broken by Bell.

In their equitable jurisdiction on the other hand, the courts may be prepared to rescind an agreement founded on mistake although it might not be void at common law. A case in point is *Solle* v. *Butcher* (1950) where the parties to a lease of a flat were both of the opinion that the rent which could be charged was not controlled by statute. In actual fact the premises were subject to rent control and, in the tenant's action to recover the amount which he had overpaid, the landlord pleaded that the lease should be set aside because of the parties' mistake as to the status of the flat. The Court of Appeal decided that the lease was not void at common law yet it was voidable in equity. The relief granted to the landlord was however subject to the condition that he offer the tenant a new lease at the (higher) rent now recoverable under the statute.

Again, in *Magee* v. *Pennine Insurance Co. Ltd.* (1969), an insurance company entered into a binding agreement to pay one of its policyholders £385 in settlement of a claim for damage to his motor vehicle but discovered before actually paying the money that the policy itself could be avoided because certain material facts had not been disclosed in the original proposal form. On a claim by the policyholder, the court decided that the policy was voidable for non-disclosure and also that the settlement agreement could be set aside on account of the fundamental mistake made by both parties concerning the validity of the policy.

Note that where the parties have come to an agreement and a later written document which is intended to represent that agreement is by mistake incorrectly drafted, the courts may be prepared to award the equitable remedy of rectification in order to alter the document accordingly. It is not necessary that the prior agreement should itself be legally binding provided there is some external manifestation of it (*Joscelyne* v. *Nissen* (1970)).

Documents signed by mistake

In general, a person who signs a written document is bound by the transaction to which it may give rise, irrespective of whether he has read that document. Where the other party to the transaction has been fraudulent and has perhaps misrepresented the purpose of the document the transaction is of course voidable. Furthermore, the courts will in certain circumstances accept the signer's plea that he did not intend to sign the document in question, in which case the transaction based upon it will be void for want of consent. This plea of *non est factum* (it is not his act) has an obvious application where the signer is affected by some disability such as blindness but is not necessarily confined to such cases. For the plea to succeed, it must be shown that the document is radically or fundamentally different from that which the person signing it intended to sign. Furthermore, reasonable care must be taken to ascertain the purpose of the document.

In *Saunders* v. *Anglia Building Society* (1971), G, an elderly widow, signed a document assigning her interest in her house to L. She failed to read the document because she had mislaid her spectacles but she was told that the effect of the document was to transfer the interest to P, her nephew. L mortgaged the house to the defendants. The instalments were not paid and the defendants claimed possession of the house. G, relying on *non est factum*, asked the court to declare that the assignment was void. The House of Lords affirmed the Court of Appeal's decision that the plaintiff's plea should fail. The purpose of the document G had signed (an assignment of an interest in land) was not fundamentally different from that she intended.

Another illustration of the relevant principles is *United Dominions Trust* v. *Western* (1976). In this case, the defendant purchased a motor car from a dealer for £550. The purchase price was advanced on loan by the plaintiffs, whose standard form the defendant signed in blank at the dealer's premises, leaving the dealer to complete the basic particulars. The dealer wrongfully inserted a figure of £730 and the question was whether this sum was recoverable from the defendant. It was held that the defendant had assumed responsibility for the document even though the details were to be filled in later. Furthermore, there was no difference between the document signed and that intended.

ILLEGALITY

Under this heading, we note how a contract may be illegal or void by virtue of the provisions of a statute or the common law.

Illegal contracts

Both the common law and various statutes contain provisions rendering contracts illegal, whether in their formation or as regards their performance. Thus, the common law prohibits and invalidates agreements to commit crimes and other wrongs, agreements involving sexual immorality and agreements which are contrary to the interests of the state (dealing with an enemy alien is but one example in this latter category). In *Pearce* v. *Brooks* (1866), a contract for the supply of a carriage was held to be illegal because the carriage was to be used for the purposes of prostitution and a similar decision was reached in *Parkinson* v. *College of Ambulance Ltd.* (1925), a case involving the fraudulent sale of a knighthood.

An example of an agreement which is prohibited by statute is one between two or more suppliers to withhold supplies of goods from dealers who resell in breach of resale price stipulations (s. 1, Resale Prices Act 1976, and *see* Chapter 17). In this case, the agreement in question is expressly declared to be unlawful but the position is not always so clear. For instance, in *Archbold's (Freightage) Ltd.* v. *S. Spanglett Ltd.* (1961) the question for the court was whether the defendant carriers' failure to obtain the proper licence for the carriage by road of other people's goods rendered illegal the contract of carriage between themselves and the plaintiffs. The Court of Appeal decided that the object of the relevant statute was to promote the efficiency of carriers and not to make illegal the performance of the contract. Consequently, the plaintiffs could recover in respect of the loss of their goods whilst in the defendants' charge. On the other hand, in *Ashmore, Benson, Pearce and Co. Ltd.* v. *Dawson Ltd.* (1973), a case concerning a contract for the carriage of heavy machinery, the weight of the defendants' lorry when loaded was in excess of that permitted by statute. The machinery was damaged during the course of the journey and again the question was whether the owners (the plaintiffs) were entitled to recover damages from the defendants. The decision of the court was that the contract was illegally performed therefore the plaintiffs' claim should fail because, as their transport manager was aware of the circumstances, they were deemed to have participated in the illegality.

Void agreements
The agreements which the courts in the interests of public policy regard as void are:

(*a*) those under which the contracting parties are prevented from referring questions of law to the ordinary courts (*Lee* v. *Showmen's Guild of Great Britain* (1952));

(*b*) agreements which are harmful to the institution of marriage (for example, an agreement never to marry); and

(*c*) agreements in restraint of trade.

The last category is an important one and, subject to certain exceptions, includes any contract which imposes restrictions on the freedom of a person to pursue his trade, business or profession. In those cases to which the doctrine of restraint of trade applies, the courts regard such restrictions as being in the first instance contrary to public policy but are never the less prepared to accept a particular restriction as valid provided it can be shown to be reasonable and is justified in the circumstances of the case. Accordingly, a provision in the contract of employment of a glass blower, by which he undertook not to work anywhere in the United Kingdom for five years after the expiration of his present employment, was held to be reasonable and hence lawful, given that the employer wished to protect various trade secrets (*Forster and Sons Ltd.* v. *Suggett* (1918)). It should be noted that if a restriction is to operate during the continuance of the contract—for example an undertaking by one person to give his services exclusively to another over a specified period of time—and the restriction is found to be unreasonable, the contract is not void but unenforceable in so far as it has not been fully performed (*O'Sullivan* v. *Management Agency and Music Ltd.* (1984)).

Not all trading restrictions are subject to the doctrine, notable exceptions being restrictive covenants in leases and conveyances of freeholds and covenants by which the occupiers of public houses agree to take all their supplies of liquor from one brewery. The reason is that such covenants have become "accepted as part of the structure of a trading society" (Lord Wilberforce in *Esso Petroleum Co. Ltd.* v. *Harper's Garage (Stourport) Ltd.* (1968)).

Where the restraint of trade doctrine is applicable, no restriction will be accepted as valid if it is wider than is necessary for the protection of the interest of the person seeking to enforce it. Thus, in the *Esso Petroleum* case (above), a covenant in a mortgage agreement, whereby a garage proprietor promised to purchase and sell only Esso's motor fuels for a period of twenty-one years, was held to be unreasonable since the period of commitment was well in excess of that justified by the suppliers' distribution requirements (a covenant limited to a period of four years and five months in respect of another garage owned by the same proprietor was held to be valid).

Again, in *Greer* v. *Sketchley Ltd.* (1979), the defendant dry cleaners operated their business in London and the Midlands, with the plaintiff being their employee responsible for the Midlands area. The plaintiff's contract of employment contained a provision preventing him from working anywhere in the United Kingdom, for twelve months after the termination of his employment, in any business which might benefit from the trade secrets and processes which he had learnt. The Court of Appeal held that the restraint was too wide because it was not confined to those parts of the country where the defendants' business was carried on.

Apart from contracts of employment and exclusive dealing agreements (as in the *Esso Petroleum* case), other categories of contracts where the restraint of trade doctrine has traditionally been applied are those between the vendors and purchasers of businesses and contracts regulating the membership of trade associations. The categories are not however confined to these cases. Thus, in *Greig* v. *Insole* (1978), a rule of the International Cricket Conference by which a cricketer who played for a competing organisation could be disqualified from taking part in test matches was declared unreasonable and void.

Contracts void by statute
Gaming and wagering contracts
Under the provisions of the Gaming Act 1845 all contracts of gaming or wagering are null and void, and no action may be brought or maintained for recovering any sum of money or valuable thing alleged to be won upon any wager (s.18). A wagering contract displays the following characteristics.

(*a*) two persons (or groups of persons) only;

(*b*) each side having the chance of winning or losing on the outcome of a particular (uncertain) event; and

(*c*) neither side having any interest in the contract apart from the sum at risk (*Carlill* v. *Carbolic Smoke Ball Co.* (1892)).

Consequently, contracts made with football pools companies are clearly not wagers, nor are contracts of insurance (since normally the proposer has an interest in the well-being of the life or property subject to the insurance). Further, in *Tote Investors Ltd.* v. *Smoker* (1968), it was decided that betting through the Horseracing Totalisator Board did not amount to wagering because the Board did not stand to lose on the outcome of a race.

Because a wagering contract is void, the winner is unable to claim the agreed sum, but money which has actually been paid to the winner is irrecoverable (Bowen LJ in *Bridger* v. *Savage* (1885)). It should be noted that s.18 not only renders void the wagering contract itself but any secondary contract is also unenforceable if its object is the recovery of an earlier unpaid sum of money (*Hill* v. *William Hill (Park Lane) Ltd.* (1949)). The Act also provides that where the parties have deposited their bets with a stakeholder pending the outcome of the particular event, neither party may sue to recover the winnings. Nevertheless, either party may claim back his own individual stake provided it has not already been transferred to the winner (*Diggle* v. *Higgs* (1877)).

Restrictive trading agreements

This topic is considered in Chapter 17 but it may be noted at this stage that, under the Restrictive Trade Practices Act 1976, where the Restrictive Practices Court finds that restrictions contained in a registrable agreement are contrary to the public interest, they are void and the parties to the agreement may be restrained from giving effect to or enforcing the agreement (s.2). In addition, it is necessary to consider in this context the relevant provisions of European Community Law (*see* in particular Articles 85 and 86 of the EEC Treaty which are discussed in Chapter 17).

Effect of illegal and void contracts

An agreement which is illegal upon formation (for example, an agreement to commit a crime) is void and may not be enforced by either party. In *Parkinson* v. *College of Ambulance Ltd.* (1925), an action for breach of contract in respect of a promised knighthood failed because of the illegal nature of the transaction. An additional consequence is that a collateral or subsequent agreement may also be declared void where it is in some way affected by the illegality of the original contract. A case in point is *Spector* v. *Ageda* (1973). The facts were that a loan of money made by X to Y was illegal because the transaction infringed the statutory requirements relating to moneylending (*see* Chapter 18). In an effort to correct matters, Z, X's sister, lent a further sum of money to Y out of which the advance made by X was repaid. It was held that Z's loan was also irrecoverable because of her knowledge of the earlier illegality. Nevertheless, recovery may be possible under a collateral agreement where the plaintiff is not personally at fault (*Strongman (1945) Ltd.* v. *Sincock* (1955)).

The transfer of money or other property under an illegal contract has the effect of passing a good title to the transferee if this is the parties' intention (*Belvoir Finance Co. Ltd.* v. *Stapleton* (1971)) and the general rule is that such money or property is irrecoverable by the transferor (*Parkinson* v. *College of Ambulance Ltd.* (1925)). The exceptions to this rule are as follows.

(*a*) Firstly, a person who has not parted with complete ownership may establish rights over the property transferred provided reliance on the illegal agreement is not necessary for the furtherance of the claim. In *Bowmakers* v. *Barnett Instruments Ltd.* (1945), the defendants had possession of the plaintiffs' machine tools under a hire-purchase agreement which contravened wartime regulations. Some of the tools were wrongfully sold to a third party and the plaintiffs' action for damages in the tort of conversion was successful, despite the illegality of the contract under which the goods had been supplied.

(*b*) Secondly, property may be recovered where the plaintiff's claim is made before the illegal agreement is put into effect. The parties are in fact given an opportunity in which to change their minds but the "repentance" must be genuine and not the result of a failure on the plaintiff's part to secure performance of the contract (*Bigos* v. *Bousted* (1951)).

(*c*) Thirdly, a statute rendering a particular contract illegal may be intended to protect a certain class of individuals to which one of the contracting parties belongs. Thus, in *Bonnard* v. *Dott* (1906), securities given by the borrower to an unlicensed moneylender were held to be recoverable because the object of the relevant legislation was the protection of borrowers generally.

We have seen that contracts may be lawfully created yet illegally performed. In such cases, if one of the parties is unaware of the illegality, he may enforce the contract and pursue any other remedies which may be available to him. (Where on the other hand the plaintiff is aware of the illegal performance, his claim will fall

(*Ashmore, Benson, Pearce and Co. Ltd. v. Dawson Ltd.* (1973).)
   Where a contract is void at common law it is not necessarily void in its entirety since it may be possible for the court to "sever" that part of it which contravenes public policy. In *Goldsoll* v. *Goldman* (1915), the vendor of a jewellery business agreed that he would not deal in jewellery in the United Kingdom and in certain places overseas. In an action commenced by the purchaser to enforce the restriction, the court decided that that part of it which referred to places overseas was too wide but that it could be severed leaving thereby a valid and enforceable agreement.

SUMMARY

On completion of this chapter you should be able to:

   (*a*) Describe the effect of misrepresentation, duress and undue influence and other factors on the validity of a contract.
   (*b*) Appreciate the distinction between voidable, void and illegal contracts.
   (*c*) Be aware of the rights of the parties to an invalid contract.
   (*d*) Understand the various perspectives of illegality in the law of contract.

SELF-ASSESSMENT QUESTIONS

(Relevant page numbers are given in brackets.)

   1. What is meant by misrepresentation in the law of contract? (Page 131)
   2. What options are available to the innocent party where a contract is voidable? (Page 132)
   3. Distinguish between duress and undue influence. (Pages 134–5)
   4. To what extent, if at all, is a person bound by what he has signed? (Page 138)
   5. What is a promise in restraint of trade? (Page 140)

CHAPTER TWELVE

Performance and Discharge of the Contractual Obligations

CHAPTER OBJECTIVES
After studying this chapter you should be able to:
* explain the meaning of performance in relation to a contract; and
* understand generally the circumstances in which the parties to a contract are discharged from their obligations.

INTRODUCTION

A basic requirement of the law of contract is that the parties' promises must be carried out exactly, although there are exceptions to this strict rule (*see* p. 147). Once the obligations have been satisfactorily performed, they are said to be discharged. There are in addition other circumstances where a discharge will arise without performance or where performance is incomplete. For instance, as we discussed in Chapter 10 (*see* p. 117), a breach of contract may in some cases be so serious that the innocent party is permitted to bring the contract to an end and, in so doing, refuse further performance. The position is covered further in this chapter.

PERFORMANCE

In this section we examine the meaning of performance and note the circumstances in which performance exactly in accordance with contractual requirements is not necessary.

Introduction
A contract will be terminated and the obligations contained therein discharged provided they are performed by the parties in accordance with the contractual terms. Performance may be effected of course by simply carrying out what the contract requires, yet action in this respect by one party is sometimes dependent upon the co-operation of the other. If such co-operation is not forthcoming (for instance, a refusal by the buyer to accept delivery

under a contract of sale of goods), an offer to perform (i.e. tender) constitutes a valid performance (*Startup* v. *Macdonald* (1843)).

Where the contract requires that money should be paid, the amount tendered must be for the exact sum and be in legal tender (for example, not £100 in coin). Further, if a cheque or bill of exchange is offered and accepted in payment of the debt, it is only effective as a conditional payment. Thus, if it is ultimately dishonoured, the creditor may treat the document as worthless and claim the original sum (Cockburn CJ in *Bottomley* v. *Nuttall* (1858)).

Frequently, the performance of a contractual obligation is required within a specified period of time. The approach of the common law in such cases was to treat any provision as to time as a condition precedent (i.e. "of the essence") and demand strict compliance. Various exceptions to this rule evolved, however, and one of these is now to be found in s.10 of the Sale of Goods Act 1979 which provides that stipulations as to the time of payment are not of the essence of a contract of sale of goods, unless the contract provides otherwise. On the other hand, a stipulation as to the time of delivery in a commercial contract for the sale of goods (as opposed to a consumer sale) is of the essence and, if not adhered to strictly, the buyer is entitled to treat the contract as ended. This was held to be the position in *Hartley* v. *Hymans* (1920) where the court attached importance to the nature of the contract and the character of the goods (in this case cotton yarn) which constituted its subject matter.

In contrast to the above, the position in equity was that time was never of the essence unless:

(*a*) the contracting parties stipulated that it should be so; or
(*b*) the nature of the subject matter of the contract and the surrounding circumstances made it inequitable that time should not be important (Lord Diplock in *United Scientific Holdings* v. *Burnley Borough Council* (1978)).

In addition, the aggrieved party could always notify the party in breach of a time stipulation that time was to be henceforth of the essence and thereby impose a reasonable period in which compliance with the contract would be expected (*Charles Rickards Ltd.* v. *Oppenheim* (1950)). In all cases where a contract contains a provision governing the time for performance, the rule now is that the above-mentioned principles of equity apply (s.41, Law of Property Act 1925).

It should be emphasised that the breach of a time stipulation that is not of the essence does not enable the other party to terminate the contract, but he is of course entitled to claim damages for the breach in the normal way.

Complete performance

In considering performance, a distinction must be made between entire contracts and those containing obligations which are divisible or severable (*see* p. 148). In the former case, a strict rule of law applies in that precise performance by one of the contracting parties is required as a condition precedent to the performance by the other of his obligations. For example, in *Cutter* v. *P Powell* (1795), a seaman died during a voyage in respect of which he was to have received 30 guineas. His widow claimed a part of this sum for the work actually put in, but the court held that nothing was recoverable because payment was conditional on complete performance. Similarly, in *Sumpter* v. *Hedges* (1898), the plaintiff builder abandoned a contract when the buildings he was constructing were still unfinished. Because he had agreed to receive a lump sum on completion of the work, the builder's claim to be paid a reasonable sum for the work he had done failed.

Exceptions to the complete performance rule

This strict approach of the courts with respect to the performance of an entire contract is subject to a number of qualifications. In the first place, if a contractual obligation is substantially performed, the partial performer is allowed to recover the agreed contract price, although subject to a deduction by the other party of a sum in respect of any loss caused by the breach.

In *Hoenig* v. *Isaacs* (1952), the plaintiff decorator agreed to carry out work for the defendant in return for a lump sum payment of £750. On completion, there were various defects in the work the cost of remedying which amounted to £60. The defendant withheld a final payment of £350, pleading the plaintiff's failure to perform an entire contract in justification. The Court of Appeal decided that the plaintiff was entitled to the full contract price less an amount to cover the defects. Nothing at all was recoverable, however, by the contractor in *Bolton* v. *Mahadeva* (1972), because the defects in the central heating system he had installed at the defendant's home for £560 were such that the contract could not be said to be substantially performed.

A second exception arises where the person for whom the work is being done agrees to accept the partial performance as the basis of a new contract, in which case he becomes liable to pay on a *quantum meruit* (i.e. a reasonable sum) for the benefit thereby received. This benefit must however be the product of a true option. Thus in *Sumpter* v. *Hedges* (above), the defendant took possession of building materials left behind by the plaintiff and used them to complete the buildings. The plaintiff was able to recover the value of these materials but he was not entitled to any payment for his partial performance because, in taking possession of the partly completed buildings, the defendant was merely claiming what belonged to him (i.e. the land on which they stood).

Another case in which the right to recover a reasonable sum can be asserted exists where the partial performance is the fault of the person for whom the work is being done (*Planché* v. *Colburn* (1831)).

Finally, it may be noted that, where the failure to perform a contractual obligation is caused by a frustrating event a person who receives a valuable benefit before the time of discharge (i.e. the time when the contract is frustrated) may be required to pay the partial performer whatever sum the court considers just in the circumstances (s.1(3), Law Reform (Frustrated Contracts) Act 1943). The event giving rise to incomplete performance in *Sumpter* v. *Hedges* (i.e. abandonment of the contract by the plaintiff) was not a frustrating event therefore the statutory provision would have had no application in those circumstances.

Divisible contracts

The obligations comprised in a contract may in some circumstances be regarded as divisible (or severable) in which case a claim to be paid in respect of a partial performance is not conditional on complete performance of the contract. As an illustration, the parties to a contract of sale of goods may provide for delivery by instalments, with each instalment to be paid for separately. Consequently, once the seller makes one or two deliveries under the contract he is entitled to some payment although, if he fails to complete the contract, he is liable to be sued for breach by the buyer. (It is perhaps convenient to note at this stage that, in the absence of agreement a buyer of goods is under no obligation to accept delivery by instalments (s.31(1), Sale of Goods Act 1979).)

An alternative way of looking at the obligations in a contract is in terms of whether they are dependent on or independent of each other. Thus, in *Taylor* v. *Webb* (1937), a landlord sued his tenant in respect of non-payment of rent and, in the same action, the tenant claimed damages from the landlord on account of the latter's failure to observe a repair obligation. The court held that perform- ance by the landlord of his repairing covenant was not conditional on the prior payment of rent by the tenant (i.e. the covenants were independent) therefore the tenant's counterclaim could succeed.

Conversely, an employer cannot justifiably insist that an employee continues to observe a promise in restraint of trade (*see* Chapter 11) if the employer has wrongfully terminated the contract of service. In such a case, the termination of the employee's con- tract takes with it the obligations which it contains (*General Billposting Co. Ltd.* v. *Atkinson* (1909)).

Performance under the Sale of Goods Act 1979

In a contract for the sale of goods, there are two basic obligations to consider in deciding whether or not there has been satisfactory performance. A duty to deliver the goods to the buyer is imposed on the seller and the buyer is, in his turn, required to accept the goods and pay the price (s.27).

"Delivery" is defined in s.61 of the Act to mean the voluntary transfer of possession from one person to another and clearly this can be achieved in several ways. Thus, a seller who is in actual possession of the goods, discharges his duty to deliver by trans- ferring possession to the buyer at his (the seller's) place of busi- ness. This is of course the usual method of delivery in many consumer sales (as, for example, in the case of self-service stores) but there is nothing to prevent the contracting parties making other arrangements. If the goods at the time of sale are in the possession of some third party (e.g. a warehouseman), delivery to the buyer is effected by the third party acknowledging that he holds the goods for the buyer (s.29). Furthermore, if by the contract the seller is obliged to send the goods to the buyer, delivery to a carrier for this purpose is prima facia a good delivery (s.32), but the goods must be despatched within a reasonable time if none is otherwise specified (s.29).

As will be seen in Chapter 13, the delivery to a buyer of a bill of lading is equivalent to the actual delivery of the goods and, further- more, there is a valid tender of performance in such a case even though the goods which are the subject matter of the sale have been lost (*Golodetz and Co.* v. *Czarnikow-Rionda* (1980)).

In our discussion of s.13 of the Act (*see* Chapter 10, p. 121), we noted that the goods delivered under the contract must comply exactly with their description. Following on from this, s.30 of the Act confers on the buyer the right to reject the goods if:

(*a*) the quantity delivered is less or larger than that contracted for, or

(*b*) where the correct goods are delivered but are mixed with goods of a different description.

Thus, in *Re Moore and Co. Ltd. and Landauer and Co.* (1921), the seller agreed to deliver canned fruit in cases containing thirty tins but part of the consignment comprised cases containing twenty-four tins only. The value of the goods overall was not affected yet the buyers were allowed to reject all the cases under (*b*) above because of the failure by the seller to adhere to the contract description.

It should be noted that, unless agreed to the contrary, a buyer is under no obligation to return to the seller the goods he has rejected; it is sufficient for him to advise the seller of the fact of rejection (s.36).

Acceptance is deemed to occur:

(*a*) where the buyer informs the seller that he has accepted the goods or, without stating that he has rejected them, by the buyer keeping the goods for an unreasonable period of time, and

(*b*) after delivery, where the buyer acts in a way which is not consistent with the seller's ownership (e.g. by consuming the goods) (s.35).

This latter provision is subject, however, to s.34 which confers on the buyer a reasonable opportunity for examination of the goods supplied in order to ensure that they are in accordance with the terms of the contract.

Performance under the Supply of Goods and Services Act 1982

In the case of a contract to provide a service in the course of a business (excluding contracts of service or apprenticeship—*see* page 237), Part II of the Act provides for the implication of terms:

(*a*) that the supplier will carry out the service with reasonable care and skill, and

(*b*), in the absence of express provision, that the supplier will carry out the service within a reasonable time (ss. 12–14).

If no provision is made in the contract with respect to the price payable for the service, the other contracting party need only pay a reasonable charge (s.15).

DISCHARGE OF THE CONTRACTUAL OBLIGATIONS BY BREACH

This section considers the cases where a breach of contract is sufficiently serious to justify termination of the contract.

Termination of the contract

There are instances where a breach of contract is so serious in its effect that it amounts to an act of repudiation by the contract breaker thereby entitling the aggrieved party to terminate the contract if he so wishes (*see* the discussion on p. 118). Other breaches of contract (e.g. a breach of warranty under the Sale of Goods Act 1979) do not go to the root of the contract in which case the remedy of the innocent party is in the main confined to damages.

It is important to emphasise at this point that a breach which does constitute a repudiatory act does not itself terminate the contract. Termination is a consequence of the innocent party accepting the repudiation with this in mind. Essentially, therefore, the participation of both parties is necessary for the contract to be ended (*Decro-Wall International S.A.* v. *Practitioners in Marketing Ltd.* (1971)).

The effect of termination is that the various obligations of the contracting parties are discharged and there is imposed on the contract breaker a secondary obligation to pay damages in respect of his breach (Lord Diplock in *Photo Production Ltd.* v. *Securicor Transport Ltd.* (1980)).

As we have already seen (Chapter 10), the importance of a term in a contract of sale of goods depends upon whether it amounts to a condition or a warranty. In this connection, it should be noted that, if the contract is non-severable (i.e. entire) and the whole or some part of the goods have already been accepted by the buyer (within the meaning of s.35 of the Act), a breach of condition by the seller may only be treated as a breach of warranty (s.11(4), Sale of Goods Act 1979). Consequently, the buyer has no right in such a case to reject the goods and treat the contract as repudiated. On the other hand, if the goods under the contract are deliverable by instalments, each one to be separately paid for, the buyer may be entitled to reject all the goods if there are several defective deliveries and they are such as to amount to a repudiation of the contract by the seller (s.31(2), Sale of Goods Act 1979, and *R. A. Munro and Co. Ltd.* v. *Meyer* (1930)). In one case, a seller contracted to supply sixty-two suits, deliverable by instalments, but one delivery was one suit short. The court decided that this defective delivery did not justify the buyer's refusal to accept further instalments (*Regent OHG Aisenstadt und Barig* v. *Francesco of Jermyn Street Ltd.* (1981)).

Finally, it may be noted that a clear distinction should be made between an act which amounts to a repudiation of contractual obligations and the situation in which a contracting party is seeking termination in accordance with a provision of the contract. In *Woodar Investment Development Ltd.* v. *Wimpey Construction U.K. Ltd.* (1980), purchasers of land had the right under the contract of sale to terminate the agreement if, for example, compulsory purchase proceedings were instituted before completion of the transaction. Subsequently, the purchasers purported to terminate in accordance with this provision although it later transpired that they had no justification for doing so. In an action brought by the vendors, the House of Lords decided that the purchasers had not demonstrated an intention to abandon or repudiate the contract merely because they sought termination in accordance with its provisions.

Anticipatory breach

It is possible for a breach of contract to arise by the repudiation of contractual obligations in advance of performance. For instance, if in January A agrees to employ B with effect from May, but in April notifies B that the arrangement is cancelled, the breach may be described as anticipatory. In these circumstances, the aggrieved party is permitted to pursue his remedies for breach of contract immediately: he is not obliged to await the agreed time for performance (*Frost* v. *Knight* (1872)).

Again, it must be emphasised that an anticipatory breach does not itself discharge the contractual obligations. The innocent party has an election and, if he so wishes, can choose to keep the contract in force until the time for performance. Further, in *White and Carter (Councils) Ltd.* v. *McGregor* (1962), the House of Lords decided that the innocent party can in such cases fulfil his own commitments under the contract and (with some exceptions) claim the full contract price. Such a course of action would not however be possible where, for example, it is dependent upon the co-operation of the contract breaker.

DISCHARGE BY FRUSTRATION

In some circumstances, the parties may be unable to achieve the purpose of the contract and the cases in which this will lead to discharge by frustration are discussed below.

Nature of frustration
The duties of the parties to comply with the terms of their contract may in exceptional circumstances be discharged on the ground that the contract is frustrated.

This situation may come about in several different ways but, essentially, in all cases the circumstances are such that either:

(*a*) the contracting parties' objectives can no longer be achieved, or

(*b*) the contract can only be performed in a way that is radically different from that originally contemplated.

In *Taylor* v. *Caldwell* (1863), a contract for the hire of a music hall became impossible to perform when the hall was destroyed by fire. In the view of the court, the continued existence of the building was an implied condition of the contract and its failure excused both parties from further performance. Another illustration is *Krell* v. *Henry* (1903). This case involved a contract for the hire of a room overlooking the route to be followed by the King during his coronation procession. The occasion was in fact cancelled because the King became ill and, although the room could clearly still be used, the court held that the contract was frustrated given the fundamental change in the circumstances. Similarly, in *B.P. Exploration Co. (Libya) Ltd.* v. *Hunt* (1982), a contract for the development of an oil concession was frustrated when the contract became impossible to perform after the interests in the concession of both contracting parties were taken over by the Libyan government.

A contract can be frustrated on the ground of illegality, for example, further dealings in timber become illegal by virtue of a wartime regulation (*Denny, Moth and Dickson Ltd.* v. *Fraser and Co. Ltd.* (1944)).

There are other cases where the courts are not prepared to recognise the existence of a frustrating event. In *Davis Contractors Ltd.* v. *Fareham Urban District Council* (1956), because of a shortage of skilled labour and materials, the plaintiff builders incurred expenditure in excess of that allowed for in their contract with the defendants. The plaintiffs argued that the contract itself was frustrated (hence, the contract price would cease to apply) and that they were entitled to a reasonable sum (*quantum meruit*) to cover their actual costs. The House of Lords held that there was no frustration because the actual performance of the contract (albeit more onerous than anticipated) was not radically different from that orginally expected.

Effect of frustration

The rule at common law is that a frustrating event automatically terminates the obligations of the contracting parties, with effect from the time of frustration, not before. One consequence of this rule is that money paid under a contract, prior to the moment of frustration, cannot be recovered unless there has been a total failure of consideration (in this context, total non-performance by the person who receives the payment) (*Fibrosa* case, (1943)). The position with respect to many contracts is however now regulated by the Law Reform (Frustrated Contracts) Act 1943. Thus:

(*a*) money paid before the time of discharge can be recovered (whether non-performance by the other party is total or partial);

(*b*) money payable under the contract before its discharge need not be paid; and

(*c*) if the person to whom the money was paid or payable incurred expenses in performing his obligations before the time of discharge, the court has a discretion to allow him to retain this money or recover his expenses up to the amount so paid or payable.

It should be noted that nothing at all is recoverable in respect of expenses incurred if no money is paid or payable before the moment of frustration.

The provisions of the Act do not apply to:

(*a*) charterparties (with the exception of time charterparties and charterparties by demise), and other contracts for the carriage of goods by sea;

(*b*) contracts of insurance; and

(*c*) contracts to which s.7 of the Sale of Goods Act 1979 applies, and other contracts for the sale of specific goods (*see* Chapter 7) which are frustrated by the perishing (i.e. destruction) of the goods.

Section 7 of the Sale of Goods Act provides that an agreement for the sale of specific goods is avoided where the goods perish before the risk of loss or damage has passed to the buyer.

The 1943 Act does apply to contracts for the sale of specific goods which are frustrated by some occurrence other than the perishing of the goods (for example, illegality).

DISCHARGE BY AGREEMENT AND WAIVER

Both contracting parties may be released from their respective obligations by mutual agreement and, furthermore, one party may agree to vary or waive strict compliance by the other.

Agreement

Where the obligations of the contracting parties have yet to be performed, they may agree to simply terminate their contract or replace it with a completely new transaction (the latter alternative being described as "novation"). The substituted contract may be confined to the original parties or additional parties may be introduced. Thus, to take the example of a partnership, a retiring partner may be discharged from responsibility for the debts of the existing firm by an agreement under which the members of the new firm become responsible (*see* Chapter 2).

If, on the other hand, one of the contracting parties has already performed his obligations, he may release the other from liability for non-performance of an obligation stipulated for in the contract by agreeing to accept some alternative performance or consideration (for example, by accepting some article of value instead of the payment of cash). An arrangement of this nature is described as "accord and satisfaction". Alternatively, the release may be effected by deed in which case no alternative consideration (i.e. satisfaction) is necessary.

The contract itself may expressly provide for its own automatic termination on the occurrence of a specified event (condition subsequent) or at the option of one or both contracting parties (as in *Woodar Investment Development Ltd.* v. *Wimpey Construction U.K. Ltd.* (1980); *see* p. 151).

Waiver

A person will be prevented by the courts from asserting his contractual rights where he has waived the need for strict compliance with the contract and leads the other contracting party to understand that these rights will not be enforced. It is not necessary that consideration be furnished by the other party in return for the waiver but an essential requirement is that it would be inequitable to allow the person conferring the privilege to subsequently reverse the situation and insist on the letter of the contract being observed (Lord Denning MR in *W. J. Alan and Co. Ltd.* v. *El Nasr Export and Import Co.* (1972)). An illustration of the application of this principle is to be found in *Brikom Investments* v. *Carr and Others* (1979) where (as we saw in Chapter 10, p. 116) the landlords of various flats promised to carry the cost of certain repairs notwithstanding a provision in each lease that repairs should be borne by the tenants. One aspect of the Court of Appeal's decision was that the original tenants could take advantage of a collateral promise, the consideration for which was their agreement to enter into the 99 year leases. Further, it was held that assignees of the original tenants could rely on the landlords' waiver of their right to claim the cost of repairs from each tenant because (as was pointed out by Roskill LJ) they had been assigned leases from which the repair obligation had been removed by the act of waiver.

SUMMARY

On completion of this chapter you should be able to:

(*a*) Explain the meaning of performance in relation to the discharge of contractual obligations.

(*b*) State the exceptions to the strict performance rule.

(*c*) Outline the rules under the Sale of Goods Act 1979 relating to delivery and acceptance.

(*d*) Indicate the circumstances where a breach of contract will give rise to a right to terminate the contract.

(*e*) Explain the meaning and effect of frustration.

SELF-ASSESSMENT QUESTIONS

(Relevant page numbers are given in brackets.)

1. Is it necessary to perform a contractual obligation within the time stipulated? (Page 146)

2. What is meant by substantial performance? (Page 147)

3. Explain the meaning of "delivery" in relation to contracts of sale of goods. (Page 149)

4. Is an innocent party entitled to terminate a contract following its breach? (Page 150)

5. Indicate the circumstances in which a contract will be discharged by frustration. (Page 152)

CHAPTER THIRTEEN

The Carriage of Goods

CHAPTER OBJECTIVES

After studying this chapter you should be able to:
* understand some important aspects of the law relating to the carriage of goods; and
* explain some principal terms associated with this area of business law.

INTRODUCTION

The law relating to contracts for the carriage of goods is quite wide-ranging and embraces carriage by land, air and sea. Consequently, any consideration of this topic cannot be confined to domestic carriage but must take into account the international context also. In the latter respect, English law gives effect in several cases to the provisions of international conventions in accordance with which the rights and obligations of the parties to a contract of carriage must be determined (*see*, for example, p. 161).

We begin the chapter with a discussion of the law relating to common carriers and then consider (in outline) some other features of carriage by land (p. 161) together with the Warsaw Convention relating to carriage by air (p. 162). The final section is concerned with carriage by sea where some attention is given to various subsidiary topics such as bills of lading (p. 164), freight (p. 168) and general average (p. 169).

COMMON CARRIERS

In this section we consider the characteristics of the common carrier and the extent of his liability for loss or damage.

Definition

A common carrier is one who declares to the public that he is prepared for reward to carry from one place to another the goods of any person who wishes to use his services. This function must be in the nature of a business as opposed to a casual occupation and whether or not a carrier is a common carrier depends very much on the facts of each case (*Belfast Ropework Co. Ltd.* v. *Bushell* (1918)). The term "common carrier" may be applied to both carriage by sea and carriage by land.

A person is not a common carrier where his willingness to enter into a particular transaction varies according to the circumstances. Thus, in *Belfast Ropework Co.* v. *Bushell*, it was decided that the defendant lorry owner was not a common carrier where, in inviting offers for carriage, he reserved the right to reject those which he considered to be unattractive. The point is that a common carrier is one who is ready to carry for anybody, without discrimination, provided the goods are of a kind he professes to carry and the route is one he normally follows.

Liability

The significance of identifying a carrier of goods as a common carrier lies in the fact that, unlike a private carrier (for which, *see* p. 161), the common carrier is deemed to be an "insurer" of the goods in his charge; that is, subject to certain exceptions, he is liable at common law for loss of or damage to the goods irrespective of negligence. The liability of the common carrier is in fact twofold since his strict liability as an insurer is supplemented by the normal liability of a bailee for negligence (*Joseph Travers and Son Ltd.* v. *Cooper* (1915)). In the absence of a special contract regulating his position (*see* below), the common carrier's strict liability is removed only where the loss or damage is caused by one or more of the following:

(*a*) act of God;
(*b*) Queen's enemies;
(*c*) an inherent defect in the goods themselves; and
(*d*) in the case of carriage by sea, general average sacrifice (*see* p. 169).

The defence of act of God includes such events as violent storms and earthquakes and can be pleaded by the common carrier provided that he does all that can be expected of him to avoid the loss or damage that occurs.

In *Nugent* v. *Smith* (1876), a mare was fatally injured during a stormy sea journey. There was no evidence of negligence on the defendant shipowner's part but, as he was a common carrier, the question was whether liability for the loss should be imposed upon him as a matter of course. The Court of Appeal decided that the defendant was not responsible because the death was caused by the mare becoming frightened and injuring herself during extraordinary weather. Nothing the carrier could reasonably have done would have prevented this.

Given the conduct of the mare during the storm, Nugent's case was also concerned with the exception of inherent defect in the nature of the goods carried. In a similar connection, it may be noted that a common carrier is not to be held responsible where damage occurring during transit is the result of the goods being improperly packed (*Gould* v. *South Eastern and Chatham Railway Co.* (1920)).

The common carrier is under a common law duty to carry the goods offered for carriage unless they are of a kind which he does not usually carry or his vehicle is full (*Johnson* v. *Midland Railway Co.* (1849)). Further he must deliver the goods to their destination within a reasonable time.

Limitation of liability

Subject to the provisions of the Unfair Contract Terms Act 1977 a common carrier is free to enter into a special contract restricting his liability for loss or damage. In addition, he may stipulate expressly that goods are accepted for carriage on the understanding that he is not to be regarded as a common carrier. In this event, he is not liable as an insurer of the goods.

Even if there is no such stipulation, the terms of the contract may be so far reaching in their effect that the carrier ceases to be a common carrier anyway (*Great Northern Railway Co.* v. *L.E.P. Transport and Depository Ltd.* (1922)).

Special contracts apart, the liability of common carriers by land is limited to some extent by the Carriers Act 1830. The Act provides that, in relation to specified articles, the common carrier is not liable for loss of or damage to an article exceeding £10 in value, unless its owner has declared its value and nature and paid an additional charge if so requested by the carrier. The articles to which the Act applies are those which are normally of some value and include items made of gold and silver, jewellery, watches, paintings, stamps and silks (s.1). A case concerning the Carriers Act is *Rosenthal* v. *London County Council* (1924). Here a parcel belonging to the plaintiff and valued at more than £80 was lost whilst in the custody of the driver of one of the defendant's tram-cars. The driver had clearly been negligent but the defendants argued that, as common carriers, they were protected by the Carriers Act 1830 because the value of the parcel had not been declared before commencement of the journey. For several reasons, however, the court decided that the defendants were not common carriers and could not therefore take advantage of the Act. On the one hand, the defendants were under no obligation to carry the parcel and this, as we have seen, is a feature inconsistent with the status of common carrier. Secondly, the charges imposed by a common carrier must be reasonable but the defendants were not restricted in this way since they could charge whatever sum they considered appropriate.

THE CARRIAGE OF GOODS BY LAND AND AIR

We are here concerned (in outline) with the liability of the private carrier as bailee and the carrier's position with regard to international carriage.

Private carriers

This category represents any carrier of goods by land who is not a common carrier (*Belfast Ropework Co. Ltd.* v. *Bushell*). Of the two, the private carrier is the more significant category nowadays. For instance, neither the British Railways Board nor the National Freight Company are to be regarded as common carriers (Transport Acts 1962–1980).

As a custodian of goods, the liability of the private carrier for loss or damage is that of a bailee for negligence (*see* Chapter 8), although, in practice, a carrier commonly operates under special conditions by which his liability is limited (*see also* p. 160).

Where loss or damage is established, it is for the private carrier to show that there was no negligence on his part. A case in point is *James Buchanan and Co.* v. *Hay's Transport Services* (1972). A trailer containing a consignment of whisky was stolen from the defendants' compound where it had been placed by the carriers. The security arrangements at the compound were unsatisfactory and both the defendants and the carriers were held liable for the loss because, as bailees, it was for them to disprove negligence and this they could not do.

International carriage by road

Where goods are transported by road vehicle between the United Kingdom and a foreign country, the liability of the carrier for loss or damage is in most cases governed by the Convention on the Contract for the International Carriage of Goods by Road (C.M.R.). This Convention was signed at Geneva in 1956 and given the force of law by the Carriage of Goods by Road Act 1965. The Convention applies to the whole of a journey, provided the goods are not unloaded from the vehicle, even though the journey may be partly by sea, rail, inland waterways or air (Article 2). Further, any stipulation in the contract of carriage which purports to exclude the application of the Convention is null and void (Article 41).

The carrier is made liable for loss of or damage to the goods and for delay in delivery except where such loss, damage or delay is caused by:

(*a*) the fault of the claimant,
(*b*) inherent defect, or
(*c*) unavoidable circumstances (Article 17).

It should be noted that liability under Article 17 cannot be avoided simply by establishing that there was no negligence. The carrier must show that the loss, damage or delay could not have been avoided. For instance, in *Michael Galley Footwear Ltd.* v. *Iabini* (1982), a lorry containing shoes was stolen while its drivers were a short distance away having a meal. Although in the circumstances there was no evidence of negligence, the court found that the loss could have been avoided by the drivers eating separately and taking it in turns to remain with the vehicle.

There are provisions limiting the compensation which the carrier may be liable to pay although the amount payable may be higher in those cases where the sender has declared the value of the goods in the consignment note and paid the agreed surcharge (Article 23).

The carrier's right to limit his liability is lost where the damage is caused by his wilful misconduct or that of his servants or agents.

Carriage by air
In international carriage, the carrier's position is regulated by the Warsaw Convention (as amended and revised) which is scheduled to the Carriage by Air Act 1961. The Convention applies to all international carriage of persons, baggage or cargo performed by aircraft for reward (Article 1).

Under the Convention, the carrier is liable for loss of or damage to the cargo during the time that it is in his charge. The carrier can however avoid liability if he can prove that the loss or damage was caused by:

(*a*) inherent defect,
(*b*) defective packing,
(*c*) act of war, or
(*d*) act of public authority (Article 18).

In addition, the carrier is not liable if he and his servants or agents have taken all necessary measures to avoid the damage or that it was impossible for such measures to be taken (Article 20). The carrier's liability is limited to the amounts specified in the Convention except where the consignor has made a special declaration of interest and paid a supplementary sum if so required (Article 22A).

Note that any provision in the contract of carriage which seeks to relieve the carrier of liability or establish a lower limit than that specified in the Convention shall be null and void (Article 23).

With regard to non-international carriage by air, the position is governed by the Carriage by Air Acts (Application of Provisions) Order 1967 made under s.10 of the 1961 Act and which applies in the main the provisions of the Warsaw Convention.

CARRIAGE BY SEA

The contract of carriage

Contracts for the carriage of goods by sea (contracts of affreightment) are of two types. On the one hand, an exporter of goods (the shipper) may enter into a written *charterparty* by which a complete ship is chartered or hired from its owner (the carrier) for the purpose of transporting the goods to the buyer (the consignee) in accordance with the contract of sale. Alternatively, the exporter may arrange for his goods to be carried with those of other shippers and the different contracts of carriage are then evidenced in each case by a *bill of lading* issued on the shipowner's behalf. A charterparty may provide for the charter of a ship for a specified period of time or the contract may relate only to a particular voyage (or several voyages); thus, in *Federal Commerce and Navigation Ltd.* v. *Molena Alpha Inc.* (1979) (Chapter 10, p. 119), the charterparties were for six year periods.

Charterparties

It should be noted that, under an ordinary charterparty, the ship's master and crew normally remain in the direct employment of the shipowner, even where the charterer uses the vessel to transport the goods of other shippers. In such a case, it is the shipowner, not the charterer who is responsible at common law for the safety of the cargo. In *Sandeman* v. *Scurr* (1867), for example, the plaintiff shipped a quantity of wine unaware that the vessel in question was under charter to a third party. Part of the consignment was lost and the defendant shipowner was held liable because the ship's master was deemed to be acting under the shipowner's authority when he assumed responsibility for the goods: the charterer had merely the use of the vessel together with the services of the crew. Where, on the other hand, the arrangement is such that the possession and control of the ship is vested in the charterer (albeit temporarily), there is said to be a charter "by demise" with responsibility for the safety of the goods carried devolving on the charterer. This situation arose in *Baumwoll* v. *Furness* (1893) where the court decided that the charterer had become owner for the purposes of the adventure, because he had appointed and paid the master of the ship and most of its crew. Where there is no "demise" of the vessel, the mere fact that the charterparty provides that the ship's master and crew should be the charterers' servants does not prevent the shipper holding the shipowner responsible under the bill of lading for loss or damage to the cargo (*Manchester Trust* v. *Furness* (1895)). Consequently, a charterparty will often require the charterer to indemnify the shipowner in respect of liability he may incur resulting from the crew complying with the charterer's instructions.

The bill of lading

This is a document issued to the shipper and signed on behalf of the shipowner by the master or some other authorised person. The bill of lading normally has three basic functions:

(*a*) it is a receipt for the goods accepted by the carrier for shipment;

(*b*) it operates as a document of title; and

(*c*) where the shipper does not charter the vessel, the bill of lading evidences the contract of carriage made with the shipowner.

If the sale to the consignee is being financed by means of a documentary credit (for which *see* Chapter 15, p. 193), the bill of lading is one of the shipping documents which must be given to the bank in the exporter's country before payment of the price is made (the other usual shipping documents are a policy of insurance and an invoice). These documents are then forwarded through the banking system to the consignee who becomes entitled to the possession of the goods upon their arrival at the agreed destination.

It is a breach of the contract of carriage for the carrier to transfer the goods to the consignee without taking the bill of lading in return. Thus, in *Sze Hai Tong Bank Ltd.* v. *Rambler Cycle Co. Ltd.* (1959), the carrier was held liable to the shipper where the consignee was able to obtain possession of the contract goods without producing the bill of lading (this document was still with the shipper's bank pending payment of the purchase price).

A bill of lading is a *document of title*, in that it represents or symbolises the goods which are the subject matter of the contract of sale and, in the case of *c.i.f.* contracts (*see* below), is the vehicle by which the ownership and possession of goods may be transferred from one party to another. In *Clemens Horst Co.* v. *Biddell Bros.* (1912), a *c.i.f.* contract for the sale of hops made no provision with respect to the time and payment of the purchase price. The buyer argued that the appropriate time was when the goods, still in transit, were actually delivered (*see*, for example, s.28 of the Sale of Goods Act 1979, which provides that payment and delivery are concurrent conditions unless otherwise agreed). The House of Lords decided however that the seller was entitled to payment when he tendered the bill of lading, since this was equivalent to delivery of the goods themselves.

Note that in those cases where a bill of lading is transferable, it is possible for the named consignee to effect a further sale of the goods whilst they are in transit, simply by indorsing the bill of lading and delivering it to the new buyers. Unlike the position with negotiable instruments, however, the person to whom the goods are transferred in this way can never obtain a better title than that held by the transferor (*Kum* v. *Wah Tat Bank Ltd.* (1971)). In addition, where it is intended that the property in the goods should pass to a consignee named in the bill of lading or an indorsee, the latter acquire the rights and become subject to the obligations contained in the contract of carriage as if they were themselves originally party to it (s.1, Bills of Lading Act 1855).

It must be emphasised that a bill of lading is not the contract of carriage but is merely evidence of a pre-existing agreement. If therefore a bill of lading contains a term not previously agreed to by the shipper, that term will be ineffective (*Crooks & Co.* v. *Allan* (1879)). Furthermore, although a bill of lading must evidence an enforceable contract of carriage, it is not necessary that the purpose of the contract should be fulfilled. Thus, in *Golodetz & Co.* v. *Czarnikow-Rionda* (1980), a bill of lading was issued in respect of 200 tons of sugar which had already been totally lost following a fire on the carrying vessel. The court decided that the bill could nevertheless be lawfully tendered to the consignees who then become liable to pay the sale price.

The consignee's remedy in such a case is to seek redress from the carrier under the provisions of the bill of lading or institute a claim under the policy of insurance (*see also* the *Manbre Saccharine* case, below).

Note that a shipper is entitled by the Carriage of Goods by Sea Act 1971 (considered below, p. 168), to demand from the carrier a bill of lading showing specified particulars as to the identification and quantity of the goods exported and indicating their apparent order and condition.

C.i.f. contracts

Where goods are sold on *c.i.f.* terms (that is, cost, insurance and freight) the seller must arrange for the goods to be carried to the agreed destination, pay the freight charged by the carrier, effect a contract of insurance and ultimately present the insurance policy, together with the bill of lading and invoice to the buyer. Under this form of contract, the property in the goods normally passes upon delivery of the shipping documents to the buyer but the goods are at the latter's risk from the time they are shipped (*Golodetz & Co. v. Czarnikow-Rionda* (1980)), hence the importance of the policy of insurance from his standpoint. The buyer is not therefore justified in refusing to accept the shipping documents, when tendered by the seller, on the grounds that the vessel carrying the goods has been lost (*Manbre Saccharine Co. Ltd* v. *Corn Products Co. Ltd.* (1919)). Because the goods are at the buyer's risk from the moment of shipment, the carrier may be liable to the buyer for loss of or damage to the goods in the tort of negligence. This is of particular significance from the buyer's standpoint if for some reason he never becomes holder of the bill of lading and is therefore unable to sue the carrier in contract (*Schiffahrt und Kohlen G.m.b.H.* v. *Chelsea Maritime Ltd.* (1982)).

F.o.b. contracts

In this case, the goods are sold "free on board": that is, the seller undertakes to have the goods loaded on board the carrying vessel at his own expense with the buyer being responsible for the contract of carriage and the provision of insurance cover. In practice, however, it may be agreed between the parties that the contracts of carriage and insurance should be arranged by the seller on the buyer's behalf. Normally, both the property in the goods and the risk of their being lost or damaged pass to the buyer from the time of loading (*Stock* v. *Inglis* (1884)), but, if the seller fails to give sufficient notice to the buyer to enable him to effect insurance cover, the goods travel at the seller's risk (s.32(3), Sale of Goods Act 1979).

In the absence of special provision in the contract of sale, it is the buyer's duty to nominate the ship on which the goods are to be loaded (*N.V. Handel* v. *English Exporters (London) Ltd.* (1957)).

The shipowner's liability for loss or damage

The obligations of the parties to the contract of carriage may arise expressly, or by implication of law. Furthermore, liability for loss of or damage to the goods in his charge may devolve on the shipowner as a common carrier (*see Nugent* v. *Smith* (1876), p. 159) or in negligence. In the case of a contract of carriage contained in a charterparty, it is possible for the shipowner to make provision for the modification or exclusion of the obligations implied by the common law and to limit and similarly exclude any other liability which he may incur in respect of loss of or damage to the cargo. The shipowner's position is affected also by statute. The Merchant Shipping Act 1979 enables both shipowners and charterers to limit their liability for loss or damage to property occuring either on board the vessel or in direct connection with its operation (s.17 and Sched.4). In addition, the owner or charterer of a British ship is immune from liability:

(*a*) where any property is lost or damaged by reason of fire on board, or

(*b*) where valuables (for example, gold, silver and jewellery) on board the vessel are lost or damaged by reason of theft, robbery or other dishonest conduct and their nature and value were not declared at the time of shipment to the ship's master (s.18).

No immunity from or limitation of liability is conferred where the loss is the result of the defendant's personal act or omission, committed recklessly or with intent to cause such loss.

Where the goods are covered by a bill of lading, the exclusion or limitation of liability arising under the contract of carriage is also regulated by the Carriage of Goods by Sea Act 1971 (*see* below), and from the provisions of which there can be no contracting out.

The obligations implied by the common law include the following. In the first place, the shipowner is required to provide a ship that is seaworthy: that is, at the time of sailing, it must be fit for the performance of the voyage. In *Kopitoff* v. *Wilson* (1876), a consignment of armour plates was badly stowed and broke loose during a storm, holing the defendant's ship and causing it to sink. In an action brought by the shipper, the court held that the ship was unseaworthy because the method of stowage of the plates rendered it unfit.

Seaworthiness is an absolute obligation at common law, therefore a shipowner may not evade liability for its breach by pleading that he has done his best to make the vessel fit (*McFadden* v. *Blue Star Line* (1905)). It should be noted though that, where the Carriage of Goods by Sea Act 1971 applies, the obligation to provide a seaworthy ship is not an absolute one.

Another common law requirement is that there must be no deviation from the usual or agreed route unless such deviation is necessary for the safety of the ship, its cargo and crew and, otherwise, in order to save human life. There was held to be a justified deviation in *Kish* v. *Taylor* (1912), for instance, where the master put his ship into the nearest port, in order to save the ship and crew following the shifting of the cargo, despite that the danger was caused by the master overloading his vessel in the first place.

The Carriage of Goods by Sea Act 1971 gives effect in English law to the provisions of an international convention regulating bills of lading and known as the Hague Rules. For the Rules to apply, the contract of carriage must provide for the issue of a bill of lading or any similar document of title (s.1(4)). The Rules do not apply to charterparties (Article V) and the definition of goods excludes live animals and cargo carried on deck in accordance with the contract of carriage (Article I).

The effect of the Rules is that the carrier (whether shipowner or charterer) is subjected to various obligations with regard to the shippers' goods and, conversely, has the benefit of certain rights and immunities (Article II). For instance, the carrier must make the ship seaworthy and ensure that it is properly manned, equipped and, supplied (Article III(i)). The position in this respect is different from that obtaining at common law (*see* above) since liability for breach of this obligation is not absolute and is dependent on the absence of due diligence that is, reasonable care (Article IV(i)). The Rules go further than the common law in permitting deviation in order to save property as well as life and, in fact, any reasonable deviation will not constitute a breach of the contract of carriage (Article IV(4)).

In some circumstances, examples are default in the navigation or management of the ship, fire (unless caused by the carrier's actual fault or privity), act of war and insufficiency of packing, the carrier is not responsible for loss of or damage to the shipper's goods at all (Article IV (2)). In other cases, any liability which the carrier does incur is limited (£471.96 per package or £1.42 per kilo of gross weight of the goods lost or damaged); unless the nature and value of the goods were declared before shipment and inserted in the bill of lading. The right of the carrier to limit his liability is however removed where the damage results from an act or omission of the carrier done with intent to cause damage, or recklessly and with knowledge that damage would probably result.

Freight

The remuneration payable to the shipowner for carrying the goods to their destination is known as freight. This is, in the first instance, payable by the shipper of the goods as the original contracting party, yet the obligation to pay freight may devolve on the consignee named in the bill of lading or an indorsee, by virtue of s.1 of the Bills of Lading Act 1855 (*see* p. 165). A principal requirement of the section is that the property in the goods must pass to the other party by reason of the consignment or indorsement. Consequently, where the bill of lading is indorsed and transferred by way of security for a loan, the creditor does not become liable to pay freight under the Act because the property in the goods remains with the shipper (*Sewell* v. *Burdick* (1884)).

It should be noted that, subject to special provision to the contrary, a carrier is not entitled to his freight where he fails to deliver the cargo to the agreed destination. Nevertheless, the fact that the goods arrive in a damaged condition does not invalidate a claim to be paid freight (*Montedison* v. *Icroma* (1980)). Furthermore, where there is damage, it is a well established principle of English law that, in contrast to the position obtaining with respect to contracts of sale of goods and contracts for services, the shipper is not entitled to deduct from the freight payable an amount in respect of the loss (Lord Wilberforce in *Aries Tanker Corporation* v. *Total Transport Ltd.* (1977)). In such a case, the aggrieved party must pay the whole freight and, if he can, institute a separate claim for damages.

No freight is payable though where the damage is such that the goods become transformed and what actually arrives at the port of destination can in no way be described as the original cargo. The reason is that, in this situation, the shipowner cannot be said to have performed his contract. Thus, in *Asfar* v. *Blundell* (1896), no freight was payable in respect of a cargo of dates because, having become seriously contaminated by sewage and seawater during the voyage, it could be said that the nature of the dates had changed and they had become something else.

The parties to the contract of carriage may provide that freight should be paid in advance of the voyage in which case the obligation to pay will remain despite the loss of the goods and their non-delivery (*Byrne* v. *Schiller* (1871)).

Finally, it may be observed that a charterer is often required by the terms of the charterparty to load a full and complete cargo. If he fails to do this, the charterer becomes liable to pay damages to the shipowner; such damages are known as "dead freight" (*Kish* v. *Taylor* (1912)).

General average

If, during the voyage, damage is sustained by the ship or its cargo, this loss will normally fall on the person to whom the property in question belongs. Thus, the ship may be damaged as the result of a fire or storm and it is the shipowner who must bear what is described in this case as a particular average loss. Alternatively, the loss or damage may be caused by a general average act, that is, any extraordinary sacrifice or expenditure voluntarily and reasonably made or incurred in time of peril for the purpose of preserving the property imperilled in the common adventure (s.66(2), Marine Insurance Act 1906). For instance, it may become necessary to throw some of the ship's cargo overboard in order to save the ship and the remaining cargo. In this event, maritime law demands that the persons who are interested in the ship and freight and the other cargo owners must make some contribution towards the loss, rather than it should be entirely borne by the owner of the property affected.

In *Harrison v. Bank of Australasia* (1872), a ship's supply of coal became exhausted during bad weather and it became necessary to employ some of the ship's stores as fuel for an engine used for pumping. The court held that the shipowner could recover a general average contribution from the owners of the cargo on board, because the sacrifice of the stores was made to prevent the vessel from sinking. Similarly, in *Pirie v. Middle Dock Co.* (1881), a shipowner was unable to recover freight because the cargo in respect of which it would have been payable had been dampened down to prevent a fire on board from spreading and then sold off at a port other than the port of destination. The court decided, nevertheless, that the shipowner could demand a general average contribution from the owner of the cargo given that there had in effect been a sacrifice of freight for the latter's benefit.

In the above case, the court listed the requirements which must be met for a general average loss to occur and these are as follows:

(*a*) a danger common to the interests of all those concerned in the adventure;

(*b*) the sacrifice or expenditure must be necessary and voluntarily made;

(*c*) the sacrifice must be real and not the discarding of something already worthless; and

(*d*) all interests must benefit.

Furthermore, a claim in general average will fail if the person who has endured the loss was himself responsible for the danger (*Diestelskamp v. Baynes (Reading) Ltd.* (1968)).

It is usual for the parties to effect a policy of insurance covering both the risk of a general average sacrifice expenditure and the liability to make a general average contribution. Thus, in the case of a general average sacrifice, the policy-holder may recover his whole loss in full from the insurer, without needing to pursue individual claims against the other persons who are liable to contribute (s.66(4), Marine Insurance Act 1906).

Finally, it should be noted that the settlement of a general average claim may be subject to the provisions of an international agreement known as the York-Antwerp Rules, last revised in 1974. These are in many cases expressly incorporated in bills of lading and charterparties and are therefore enforced by the courts in accordance with the wishes of the contracting parties.

SUMMARY

On completion of this chapter you should be able to:

(*a*) Distinguish between common carriers and private carriers and indicate in each case the extent of responsibility for goods carried.

(*b*) Define: (*i*) charterparty, (*ii*) bill of lading, (*iii*) c.i.f. and f.o.b. contracts.

(*c*) Understand the difference between the passing of the property and the transfer of risk in relation to the carriage of goods by sea.

(*d*) Outline the liability of a shipowner for loss of or damage to goods.

SELF-ASSESSMENT QUESTIONS

(Relevant page numbers are given in brackets.)

1. State the characteristics of a common carrier. (Page 158)
2. Consider the purpose and principal provisions of the C.M.R. (Page 161)
3. What are the functions of a bill of lading? (Page 164)
4. What are the differences between c.i.f. and f.o.b. contracts? (Pages 165–6)
5. State the requirements for a general average loss to arise. (Page 169)

Agency

INTRODUCTION

An agency relationship will arise where one person (the agent) is authorised to make contracts with third parties on behalf of another (the principal). The agency function is not necessarily confined to the making of contracts however, since an agent may be concerned with some other activity such as the transfer of property. An estate agent for instance may be employed by a vendor of land simply to secure an offer (*see* p. 175).

The principal/agent relationship may be brought about by express agreement or it may be inferred from the surrounding circumstances (i.e. agreement will be implied). Readers will recall for instance that a partnership (and, hence, an agency relationship) was deemed to exist on the basis of the parties' conduct in *Davis* v. *Davis* (*see* Chapter 2, p. 9). The agreement may be made informally although, where an agent is employed to execute a deed (e.g. a deed of conveyance), the necessary authority must be conferred by deed (described as a power of attorney).

Even in the absence of a contract of agency, a person may in certain circumstances ratify an earlier unauthorised act of another and thereby acquire rights and obligations as a result. We have seen for example that the members of a company in general meeting may in this way validate retrospectively the unauthorised acts of the company's directors (*see* Chapter 4, p. 44). Ratification is discussed on p. 178 below.

In addition, an agency relationship may arise by common law estoppel. Where therefore one person by his words or conduct represents to a third party that another person has the authority to act on his behalf, he will be prevented from disputing that authority if the third party proceeds on the basis of the representation. Thus, in *Spiro* v. *Lintern* (1973) a husband was bound by an agreement entered into by his wife to sell their house, despite her lack of authority to make such a contract, because, by his subsequent conduct, he led the third party purchaser to believe that the necessary actual authority had been conferred.

A particular type of agent is a mercantile agent who is defined as one having in the customary course of his business as such agent authority either to sell goods, or to consign goods for the purpose of sale, or to buy goods, or to raise money on the security of goods (s.1, Factors Act 1889).

DUTIES OF THE AGENT

Performance

Where the relationship between principal and agent is founded in contract, the agent has a duty to perform what he has undertaken and, furthermore, this duty must be discharged in accordance with the terms of the agency agreement. In *The Hermione* (1922), for instance, a ship's agents were held to be in breach of duty for failing to settle a salvage claim for the sum stipulated by their principal.

Performance must be carried out with a certain degree of care and skill. Thus, in *Lee* v. *Walker* (1872) the defendant patent agent was held liable to the plaintiff for not bringing "reasonable and ordinary care and knowledge to the performance of his duty as a skilled agent" (Brett J). He had not for example kept himself abreast of the latest legal developments. It should be noted that the duty of care and skill applies whether or not the agency is contractual.

Because of the confidence and trust implicit in the agency relationship, an agent must perform his duties personally since, without his principal's express or implied authority, he may not delegate performance to another. The authority to delegate will be implied for example with respect to ministerial tasks (such as typing) not involving the exercise of discretion (*Allam and Co. Ltd.* v. *Europa Poster Services Ltd.* (1968)).

An agent is under no obligation to perform an illegal or void contract such as one unenforceable under the Gaming Act 1845 (*Cohen* v. *Kittell* (1889)).

Duty to account

An agent is liable to account to his principal for any money received on the principal's behalf and, in this respect, it is immaterial that the transaction giving rise to the payment is void (*De Mattos* v.

Benjamin (1894)—a case involving the winnings received from a horse-race). In addition, the agent is required to maintain proper accounts of his agency work and ensure that his own money is kept quite separate from that belonging to his principal. In fact, under the Estate Agents Act 1979 a person involved in estate agency work must pay his principal's money (e.g. a pre-contract deposit) into a "client account". This is defined as a current or deposit account with an authorised institution (e.g. a recognised bank or licenced institution within the meaning of the Banking Act 1979), is in the name of the person engaged in estate agency work and which contains the word "client" in its title (s.14).

Duty of good faith

The agency relationship is essentially a fiduciary one therefore no agent may permit his own interests to conflict with the duty of good faith owed to his principal, unless the latter is made fully aware of all the circumstances and gives his consent to the transaction (for a discussion of this principle in connection with partners and company directors, *see* Chapter 2, p. 12, and Chapter 4, p. 39).

In *McPherson* v. *Watt* (1877), a principal was justified in avoiding a contract for the sale of land because the purchaser was in fact his agent acting through a nominee. Similarly, a contract for the purchase of shares could be avoided in *Armstrong* v. *Jackson* (1917) where the stockbroker who was employed to effect the transaction sold his own shares to the principal. In such cases, it is sufficient for a breach of duty that the occasion for a conflict of interest arises; it is not necessary to establish that the agent has acted fraudulently.

It may be noted that an estate agent now has a statutory obligation to disclose the nature and extent of any interest he may have in any land which he is employed to acquire or sell for his principal (s.21, Estate Agents Act 1979).

Another circumstance in which an agent commits a breach of his duty to exercise good faith is where he obtains a commission, from both his principal and the third party, without disclosing this fact (*Fullwood* v. *Hurley* (1928)). Furthermore, an agent is precluded from taking advantage of his position as agent in order to obtain some personal benefit (*Boardman* v. *Phipps* (1967)). If he does, he must account to the principal for the benefit derived. The position is similar to that obtaining in the case of company directors who, as we have seen, must account to their company for any advantage obtained in the course of their duties (see the discussion of *Regal (Hastings) Ltd.* v. *Gulliver* in Chapter 4, p. 40).

An agent is also accountable for any profit resulting from his use of his principal's property: for instance, by using information belonging to the principal in order to benefit a competitor after the termination of the agency contract (*Lamb* v. *Evans* (1893)).

If the third party pays a bribe or secret commission to the agent (i.e. the payment is made with the knowledge of the agency relationship), the principal can recover the amount of the bribe (*Reading* v. *Attorney-General* (1951)), deny the agent his commission and repudiate the contract made with the third party. Further, an agent who accepts a bribe is liable to be dismissed without notice (*Boston Deep Sea Fishing & Ice Co.* v. *Ansell* (1888)).

THE AGENT'S RIGHTS

Remuneration

Whether or not an agent is entitled to be paid for his services depends upon the terms of the agency contract. Thus, the advertising of a vendor's property by an estate agent might be deemed to be a condition precedent (for which *see* page 118) which will first have to be fulfilled before commission can be claimed (*Spiers* v. *Taylor* (1984)). An estate agent for instance must inform his client (the principal) of the circumstances in which remuneration will be required and the amount (s.18, Estate Agents Act 1979).

Where nothing is specifically agreed on the question of payment, yet it is clear from the circumstances of the case that the agent is entitled to be paid something, his claim will be for a reasonable sum.

If payment is conditional on the agent bringing about a particular transaction, it must be shown that the agent's efforts are the effective cause of the transaction which actually materialises and in relation to which a payment is claimed. Thus, in *Toulmin* v. *Millar* (1887), an agent who was employed to find a tenant for his principal, could not recover a commission on a subsequent transaction by which the tenant purchased the principal's interest. Again, in *Hodges and Sons* v. *Hackbridge Park Residential Hotel Ltd.* (1939), agents who undertook to find a purchaser for their principal's hotel, introduced a person who represented the War Office. A sale on a voluntary basis did not take place, but the War Office compulsorily acquired the property at a price less than that originally sought by the principal. The Court of Appeal decided that the agents were not entitled to their commission because what had been contemplated as giving rise to its payment was a voluntary sale.

In addition to the above, the agent must establish that the event brought about by him is precisely that in respect of which it was agreed a payment would be made. Consequently, if it is agreed that commission will be payable on the agent's "securing an offer", an offer which is made subject to contract (i.e. unenforceable) will not be sufficient (*Bennett, Walden and Co.* v. *Wood* (1950)).

An agent's entitlement to commission will normally cease on the termination of the agency contract but the parties may make provision to the contrary. Remuneration in the form of damages was therefore payable to an agent in such circumstances where it had been agreed that he should be paid a commission on orders received from customers he had introduced to his principal during the currency of the agency relationship (*Roberts* v. *Elwells Engineers Ltd.* (1972)).

Indemnity

The principal is under an obligation to indemnify his agent in respect of any loss or liability which may be incurred in the performance of the agency function. In *Anglo Overseas Transport Ltd.* v. *Titan Industrial Corporation (United Kingdom) Ltd.* (1959), agents who were employed to obtain space on a certain ship for their principal's goods were, under a custom of the port, obliged to pay damages to the shipowners when the goods did not arrive. The agents were entitled to an indemnity.

No indemnity is recoverable where the agent exceeds his authority, where the loss is occasioned by the agent's own wrongdoing and in respect of any illegal transaction. In the latter instance, however, the agent may recover if he is unaware of the illegality (*Adamson* v. *Jarvis* (1827)).

Lien

Provided an agent is lawfully in possession of his principal's goods or other property, he may retain such property until the principal discharges any obligations with respect to remuneration or indemnity owed to the agent. This right of lien may be particular or general. In the former case, the lien is limited to obligations owed by the principal with respect to the property retained whereas, in the case of a general lien, the agent's right to retain possession may relate to a wider range of claims against the principal. "The law of England does not favour general liens" (Campbell LC in *Bock* v. *Gorrissen* (1861)) therefore the situations in which these are met are limited. Nevertheless, certain agents, such as bankers and solicitors, have a general lien by virtue of custom.

An agent's lien will be lost where, for instance, he voluntarily parts with possession of the goods or other property affected. (Other aspects of the law relating to liens are considered in Chapter 8.)

THE AGENT'S AUTHORITY

In considering whether a legal relationship exists between a principal and a third party, it is necessary to ascertain whether the agent had authority to bring such a relationship about.

Actual and apparent authority

Actual authority is that which is conferred on the agent with the agreement of the principal. Such agreement may be express, or it may be implied from the circumstances of the particular case. For instance, the managing director of a company is impliedly authorised to do those things which usually come within the scope of that office (Lord Denning in *Hely-Hutchinson* v. *Brayhead Ltd.* (1968)).

Whereas actual authority is founded on an agreement between the principal and his agent, apparent or ostensible authority may exist independently of agreement but is, nevertheless, effective to bind the principal in law to the third party with whom the agent deals. Essentially, apparent authority may arise following a representation by the principal that the agent is empowered to enter into a particular transaction, despite that this transaction may not come within the agent's actual authority. The representation may be effected by words or conduct and, provided it is relied on by the third party, the principal will be estopped by the court from asserting the absence of authority.

A case in point is *Panorama Developments (Guildford) Ltd.* v. *Fidelis Furnishing Fabrics Ltd.* (1971) where a company secretary exceeded his actual authority in hiring motor vehicles from the plaintiffs. Despite this, the defendant company was held liable for its employee's act because, in appointing a company secretary, it was representing that he had the authority to enter into those transactions with which company secretaries were usually concerned (the hiring of vehicles being regarded in this case as an aspect of company administration).

Clearly, therefore, the mere fact of engaging a person in a particular capacity may be sufficient to give rise to an apparent agency. Thus, an agent who is employed to sell property, has the additional authority to describe the property and make other relevant statements to the purchaser (Bacon VC in *Mullens* v. *Miller* (1882)). On the other hand, it has been held that an estate agent has no apparent authority to receive on his vendor's behalf a pre-contract deposit from the purchaser (*Sorrel* v. *Finch* (1977)).

A further example of apparent authority is contained in s.2 of the Factors Act, 1889. If therefore a mercantile agent (defined above, p. 173) is in possession of goods (or of the documents of title) with their owner's consent, an unauthorised sale, pledge, or other disposition by him in the ordinary course of his business to a person who takes the goods in good faith without notice of the absence of authority to sell, is as valid and effective as if he had the express authorisation of the owner to enter into that transaction. An illustration of the operation of the provision is *Weiner* v. *Harris* (1910), where the plaintiff manufacturer sent jewellery to a retailer, subject to the stipulation that the jewellery should remain within the plaintiff's ownership until finally sold and paid for. The retailer's agreed remuneration was a percentage of the profit derived from each sale. Without authority, the retailer pledged the jewellery to the defendant moneylender. The court decided that the retailer was the plaintiff's agent and, as such, had authority to pledge by virtue of the Factors Act. Consequently, the plaintiff's claim to recover the goods from the defendant failed.

It should be noted that any limitations which a principal purports to place on his agent's apparent authority will have no effect as against the third party unless, before entering into the transaction, the third party becomes aware of such limitations (as in *Overbrook Estates* v. *Glencombe Properties Ltd.* (1974) where an auction catalogue contained a clause restricting the apparent authority of a firm of auctioneers).

Ratification

As indicated in the introductory part of this chapter, it is open to a principal to ratify or adopt a transaction entered into on his behalf by an agent acting without prior authority. The effect of such ratification if validly made is to create a contractual relationship (albeit retrospectively) between the principal and the third party. In *Bolton Partners* v. *Lambert* (1889), the third party made an offer with respect to property to the plaintiffs' agent which, without authority, the latter accepted. Subsequently, the third party withdrew his offer but, afterwards, the plaintiffs ratified the transaction. The Court of Appeal decided that a binding contract had come into being since the ratification dated back to the time of the agent's act and the purported revocation by the third party was therefore of no effect.

On the other hand, the revocation of an offer prior to ratification by the principal was effective in *Watson* v. *Davies* (1931) where the agreement between the agent and the third party was made "subject to ratification". Further, the ratification of an agent's unauthorised notice of stoppage in transit (*see* Chapter 16) was not binding on a trustee in bankruptcy who had already acquired possession of the goods in question before such ratification (*Bird* v. *Brown* (1850)).

For an act of ratification to be validly exercised, certain requirements must be met. Thus, the principal must be in existence at the time of the agent's act. We have already seen for instance (*see* Chapter 3, p. 24) that a registered company is precluded from ratifying a transaction brought about on its behalf before incorporation (*Kelner* v. *Baxter* (1866)). In addition to this, a principal must have the capacity to enter into the particular transaction both at the time of its creation and at the moment of ratification. Consequently, there can be no ratification where, at the time of the unauthorised act, the principal was an alien enemy and hence unable to contract (*Boston Deep Sea Fishing and Ice Co.* v. *Farnham* (1957)). Another requirement is that the agent must disclose to the third party that he is contracting on behalf of an indentifiable principal, since a person whose existence is not disclosed may not be a party to the earlier contract. In *Keighley Maxted and Co.* v. *Durant* (1901), an agent exceeded his authority in purchasing wheat at a certain price and conducted the transaction in his own name. The principal subsequently ratified and the question was whether he was liable to the third party for the price. The House of Lords decided that he was not, since the ratification was ineffective.

Finally, it may be noted that a contract must be ratified within a reasonable time. In any event, the principal must ratify before the time at which performance of the contract is to commence (*Metropolitan Asylums Board* v. *Kingham* (1890)).

Agency of necessity

In a situation of emergency, a person may sometimes have the authority to act as another's agent by operation of law. Thus, in *Great Northern Railway* v. *Swaffield* (1874), the plaintiff carriers were held entitled to recover from the owner of a horse certain unforeseen stabling costs, which were necessitated by a failure to take delivery of the animal.

The requirements for this category of agency to exist are as follows:

(*a*) the agent must be unable to communicate with the principal for the purpose of obtaining his instructions,

(*b*) the act in question must be necessary in the circumstances, and

(*c*) the agent must act in good faith (*Prager* v. *Blatspiel, Stamp and Heacock Ltd.* (1924)).

Where, therefore, a person was in possession of another's furniture and for his own reasons wanted to return it, but was unable to contact the owner, a sale of the furniture was not justified on the grounds of necessity and constituted a wrongful interference with goods (*Sachs* v. *Miklos* (1948)).

(It may be noted however that a bailee may have a statutory power to sell uncollected goods by virtue of s.12 of the Torts (Interference with Goods) Act 1977 (*see* Chapter 8).)

RELATIONS BETWEEN THE PARTIES

In this section we consider the rights and obligations which may arise with respect to the contract made between the principal and the third party.

The position of the agent

An agent does not in general become a party to the contract he effects with the third party on his principal's behalf. Consequently, he may not normally sue or be sued under that contract. Nevertheless, in the following circumstances, this general rule is displaced.

The agent may accept a personal liability under the principal/third party contract. The question is essentially one of ascertaining the necessary intention (*The Swan* (1968)). Thus, if the principal/third party contract is in writing, the agent will be taken to have contracted on a personal basis if he simply signs the written document without indicating that he is acting on his principal's behalf. On the other hand, where he signs "as agent", the agent is not liable under the contract even though he may be contracting for an unnamed principal (*Universal Steam Navigation Co.* v. *McKelvie* (1923)). An exception to this however is *Pike* v. *Ongley* (1887) where an agent, clearly signing as such, was held liable under his principal's contract because of a custom in the hop trade that an agent undertook personal liability where he acted for an unnamed principal.

A personal liability may also arise where the agent seeks to contract on behalf of a company in the course of formation (*Kelner* v. *Baxter* (1866)). In fact, liability now devolves in such cases by virtue of s.9(2) of the European Communities Act 1972 (*see* Chapter 3, p. 24).

Another situation in which the agent is liable under the principal/third party contract is where the agent acts for an undisclosed principal (*see* below).

In those cases where the agent contracts on behalf of an unnamed principal, he will acquire the right to sue the third party under the contract, where it was his intention throughout to become principal himself. This was, in fact, the position in *Schmalz* v. *Avery* (1851) where the plaintiff purported to act as agent in a contract made with the defendant shipowner. The latter refused to accept a cargo for shipment and the court allowed the plaintiff to bring an action as principal because it made no difference to the defendant who the other contracting party was.

Again, depending on the terms of the principal/third party contract, an agent will normally have a personal right of action where he would have been personally liable.

Breach of warranty of authority

Where an agent represents to the third party (whether innocently or otherwise) that he is acting with the authority of his principal, but this is not in fact the case, he becomes liable to the third party for breach of an implied warranty that he had the required authority. Thus, in *Collen* v. *Wright* (1857) a third party was able to recover damages from an agent who purported (wrongfully) to act for a landowner with respect to the grant of a lease. Again, in *Yonge* v. *Toynbee* (1910), the defendant solicitors were held liable for legal costs incurred by a third party, where they continued with an action unaware that their authority had been terminated by reason of their principal's insanity. (It should also be noted that an agent who fraudulently misrepresents his authority will be liable in the tort of deceit.)

The principal

The basic rule is that a disclosed principal (whether named or unnamed by the agent) is entitled to sue or be sued under the contract made on his behalf (*Schmalz* v. *Avery* (1851)). Similarly, yet subject to certain limitations, a principal whose existence is not disclosed to the third party may become a party to the contract despite the fact that, at the time of contracting, the third party's intention is clearly to transact with the agent as principal. This doctrine of undisclosed principal is an exception to the general rule that only the contracting parties may sue or be sued (*see* the discussion of privity of contract in Chapter 9). An illustration of the application of the principle in *Watteau* v. *Fenwick* (1893). In this case, the defendant owner of an hotel employed a manager but forbade him to purchase cigars and other goods. The manager disobeyed this instruction and ordered these goods from the plaintiff, who was unaware that the hotel belonged to the defendant and that the purchaser was in fact transacting as agent. Despite the limitation imposed upon the manager, the plaintiff was allowed to recover the price of the goods he had supplied from the defendant owner because the latter was, in reality, the other contracting party and the goods in question were those which persons in the agent's position usually purchased.

Certain limitations affect the operation of the doctrine of undisclosed principal. Thus, the contract between the agent and third party may expressly or by implication exclude the possibility of an undisclosed principal (*Humble* v. *Hunter* (1842)). Further, an undisclosed principal may not ratify an unauthorised transaction (*see* p. 179) nor can he sue where the personality of a contracting party is important to the third party. In *Said* v. *Butt* (1921), the plaintiff purchased a theatre ticket through the agency of a friend, knowing that if he had applied for the ticket personally it would have been refused him. The plaintiff was nevertheless denied admission and, in an action against the manager of the theatre, the court decided that no contract had come into being having regard to the personal element in the case.

The third party

In those cases where both principal and agent are liable under the contract, the third party can, in the event of a breach of contract, elect to sue either party but he is precluded from recovering from both. Thus, whereas the commencement of legal proceedings is not conclusive in the matter (*Clarkson, Booker Ltd.* v. *Andjel* (1964)), if the third party sues either the principal or the agent to judgment, he may not institute fresh proceedings against the other (*Priestley* v. *Fernie* (1865)).

If the third party is owed money by the principal, the fact that the latter has paid this to his agent does not normally discharge him from liability and the principal may be required to make a second payment if the agent defaults (*Heald* v. *Kenworthy* (1855)). The principal will be discharged from the debt, however, where the third party has stipulated that payment should be made through the agent or conveys the impression that the agent has already settled the debt (by, for example, giving the agent a receipt as in *Wyatt* v. *Hertford* (1802)).

In the converse situation, where the third party owes money to the principal, a payment through the agent will only give rise to a valid discharge where the agent is authorised to receive payment on his principal's behalf. Thus, it does not necessarily follow that a person who is employed to sell goods also has the authority to receive payment (*Butwick* v. *Grant* (1924)).

SUMMARY

On completion of this chapter you should be able to:

(*a*) Understand the circumstances in which the relationship of principal and agent will arise.

(*b*) Describe the rights and duties of the parties to a contract of agency.

(*c*) Appreciate the different forms of agency authority.

(*d*) Show an understanding of the different relationships between principal, agent and third party.

SELF-ASSESSMENT QUESTIONS

(Relevant page numbers are given in brackets.)

1. Explain the nature of the agent's duty to exercise good faith. (Page 174)

2. In what circumstances is an agent entitled to be remunerated for his services? (Page 175)

3. Distinguish between actual and apparent agency authority. (Page 177)

4. What are the requirements for a valid ratification? (Page 178)

5. Explain the doctrine of undisclosed principal. (Page 181)

CHAPTER FIFTEEN

Banking Transactions

CHAPTER OBJECTIVES

After studying this chapter you should be able to:
* outline the principal rules affecting the banker/customer relationship;
* explain further the law relating to cheques, and in particular to describe the statutory provisions protecting bankers in the collection and payment of cheques; and
* understand other matters relevant to banking transactions.

INTRODUCTION

The meaning of "banker"

There is no satisfactory statutory definition of the term "banker". For instance, for the purposes of the Bills of Exchange Act 1882 and the Cheques Act 1957 (considered below), a banker is defined merely as including a body of persons whether incorporated or not (s.2, Bills of Exchange Act). Further, the Banking Act 1979 contains no formal definition of a banker, although it does specify criteria which must be fulfilled before an institution will be recognised as such (*see* below). In *United Dominions Trust* v. *Kirkwood* (1966), the usual characteristics displayed by bankers were stated to be:

(*a*) the acceptance of money from and collection of cheques for customers;

(*b*) the honouring of cheques drawn by customers; and

(*c*) the keeping of current accounts and the entering of debits and credits.

The question for decision in the case was whether the plaintiff finance company was exempt from the registration provisions of the Moneylenders Acts 1900 and 1927 (now replaced by the provisions of the Consumer Credit Act 1974) as a person bona fide carrying on the business of banking. The Court of Appeal found in the plaintiff's favour on the basis of the reputation it enjoyed as a banker amongst the mercantile community.

It is now an offence for an institution to describe itself as a bank or banker, or to indicate that a banking business is being carried on, unless it is specifically exempted from the prohibition (as are, for instance, the Bank of England, trustee savings banks and the

Post Office) or it is a recognised bank (s.36, Banking Act 1979). Recognition as a bank may be granted by the Bank of England provided the applicant institution:

(a) enjoys a high reputation and standing in the financial community;

(b) provides in the United Kingdom either a wide range of banking services or a specialised banking service (in the former case it must provide current or deposit account facilities, overdraft or loan facilities, foreign exchange services etc.); and

(c) carries on its business with integrity and prudence and with appropriate professional skills.

In addition, the business of the institution must be directed by at least two individuals and its net assets (i.e. paid up capital and reserves) must meet specified minimum requirements. No recognition may be granted to an unincorporated institution where the whole of its assets are owned by a single individual (s.3 and Sched. 2, Banking Act 1979).

The customer

Whereas a person with an account at a particular bank will clearly be a customer of that bank, a banker/customer relationship may exist between two parties although at the time the customer has no account. Thus, in *Woods* v. *Martins Bank Ltd.* (1959), such a relationship was deemed to arise between the plaintiff and the defendant bank from the time the bank agreed to manage the plaintiff's financial affairs, albeit several weeks before an account was actually opened. Again, in *Ladbroke and Co.* v. *Todd* (1914), the banker/customer relationship was held to be established where the customer simply opened an account and deposited a cheque: the fact that it was the customer's first transaction was irrelevant. It was decided in *Importers Co. Ltd.* v. *Westminster Bank Ltd.* (1927) that one bank could be the customer of another bank. Whether or not a particular person is a customer is of importance to the collecting banker (*see* p. 191) since the statutory protection which is available to him is only applicable where, *inter alia*, he receives payment "for a customer" (s.4, Cheques Act 1957).

THE BANKER/CUSTOMER RELATIONSHIP

Introduction

The relationship between a banker and his customer is essentially contractual, with obligations devolving on both parties (*Joachimson* v. *Swiss Bank Corporation* (1921), and see below).

A banker is the customer's debtor with respect to any credit balance in the customer's account (*Foley* v. *Hill* (1848)) except that the customer has no claim to his money until he has first demanded payment in writing at the branch where his account is kept (*Joachimson*). For his part, the banker impliedly undertakes to give reasonable notice before terminating the relationship.

It should be noted that the banker is normally under no obligation to account for the use to which he puts his customer's money (in contrast to the duty which an agent has to account to his principal: *see* Chapter 14, p. 173). Nevertheless, if money which is deposited with a banker is earmarked for a particular purpose, it may be subject to a trust and be incapable of use for any other purpose (*Quistclose Investments Ltd.* v. *Rolls Razor Ltd. and Another* (1968)—money lent by plaintiff to first defendant for the purpose of paying a dividend could not be retained and set off by the banker (second defendant) against money owed to the banker by the first defendant).

The customer's duty of care

A customer is under a contractual obligation to take reasonable care in drawing cheques in order to minimise the risk of fraud. In *London Joint Stock Bank Ltd.* v. *Macmillan and Arthur* (1918), the respondents signed a cheque for £2 which contained no sum in words and sufficient space between the digits to make it possible for their clerk to fraudulently alter the amount to £120. The clerk presented the cheque to the appellant bankers (it was payable to bearer) and received payment of the money. The House of Lords decided that the loss should be borne not by the bank but by the respondents, because it was a direct consequence of their carelessness in the drawing of the cheque. In a later case (*Slingsby and Others* v. *District Bank Ltd.* (1932)), it was decided that a customer was not careless in omitting to draw a line after the payee's name and before the words "or order" but the court emphasised that it could well become a usual precaution to draw such lines in the future.

If a customer discovers that his signature to a cheque has been forged, he is under an obligation to notify the banker in order that the necessary corrective action may be taken. A customer who fails in this respect cannot prevent the banker debiting his account by the amount of the cheque (*Greenwood* v. *Martins Bank Ltd.* (1933)).

The banker's duties

(*a*) Provided the customer's account is in credit, the banker has an obligation to honour the customer's cheques. Each cheque is in effect a mandate to the banker to pay the amount specified (Lord

Finley in *London Joint Stock Bank Ltd.* v. *Macmillan and Arthur* (1918)). In this particular respect, the relationship between the parties is that of principal and agent (Ungoed-Thomas J in *Selangor United Rubber Estates Ltd.* v. *Cradock* (*No. 3*) (1968)).

A banker may only dishonour a cheque where he has sufficient justification (e.g. insufficient funds in the customer's account to meet the cheque). Payment on a cheque cannot therefore be refused where for instance the banker has agreed to provide the customer with overdraft facilities (*Rouse* v. *Bradford Banking Co.* (1894)).

The remedy available to an aggrieved customer following the banker's breach is nominal damages (*see* Chapter 16, p. 196), unless some special loss can be shown, or the customer is a trader (*Gibbons* v. *Westminster Bank Ltd.* (1939)—cheque dishonoured because money paid in by the plaintiff, which was sufficient to cover it, had in error been credited to another person's account). Apart from liability for breach of contract, however, a banker who wrongfully dishonours a cheque may be guilty of libel if, in the process, he writes on the cheque words which are likely to injure the customer's reputation. Thus, the words "not sufficient" were held to be defamatory in *Davidson* v. *Barclays Bank Ltd.* (1940).

A banker has no mandate to honour a cheque the drawer's signature on which is forged and he may not therefore debit his customer's account by the amount (*National Westminster Bank Ltd.* v. *Barclays Bank International Ltd.* (1975). (*See also* s.24, Bills of Exchange Act 1882, which renders a forged or unauthorised signature on a bill of exchange wholly inoperative.) Nevertheless, a customer may by his conduct be estopped from relying on the forgery as against the banker (*Greenwood* v. *Martins Bank Ltd.* (1933)—customer did not advise the bank that his wife had forged his signature to various cheques).

If a banker has reason to suspect that his customer's funds are being misapplied, he must not pay a cheque even though it is properly signed. Thus, in *Karak Rubber Co. Ltd.* v. *Burden and Others* (*No. 2*) (1972), the funds of a registered company (the customer) were used to purchase the company's own shares (an illegal act at the time). The court decided that a reasonable banker would have realised what the authorised signatories were up to and refuse payment. Consequently, the defendant bank was in breach of a contractual duty of care and hence liable for the loss.

The banker's duty and authority to pay a cheque is terminated where the customer countermands payment (s.75, Bills of Exchange Act 1882) and also by notice to the banker of the customer's death (s.75, 1882 Act) or mental incapacity (*Drew* v. *Nunn* (1879)) and (in the case of a registered company) the commencement of winding up proceedings (*see also* the discussion of the Mareva injunction and garnishee proceedings (p. 192) below).

(*b*) In addition to his obligation to honour cheques, a banker, undertakes to act as agent for the collection of cheques paid in by the customer; that is, by receiving payment from the bankers on whom the cheques are drawn (the paying bankers) and crediting the various amounts to the customer's account. At the same time, on receiving a cheque, a banker may become a holder for value (defined in Chapter 7, p. 85). This will arise where the banker has for instance given value, by permitting the customer to draw against the cheque before it has been cleared. Furthermore, if the banker takes the cheque in good faith and without notice of any defect in the previous holder's title, he becomes a holder in due course (defined in Chapter 7) and can therefore assert title to the cheque in his own right (*Barclays Bank Ltd.* v. *Astley Industrial Trust Ltd.* (1970)).

(*c*) It is an implied term of the banker/customer relationship that the banker will not disclose confidential information concerning his customer (for example, the state of the customer's account) without approval (*Tournier* v. *National Provincial and Union Bank of England* (1924)). There are, however, some exceptions to this duty to maintain secrecy. Thus there may be a public duty or some particular legal requirement compelling the banker to disclose.

(*d*) There may be a special or confidential relationship between the banker and his customer which imposes additional obligations on the banker. In *Lloyds Bank Ltd.* v. *Bundy* (1975), a guarantee and mortgage, taken from an elderly farmer to secure an advance made by the plaintiffs to the farmer's son, were set aside on the ground of undue influence where the only advice received by the defendant with respect to the transaction was furnished by the bank's local assistant manager. The Court of Appeal considered that the relationship in this case imposed upon the bank a fiduciary duty to ensure the provision of independent advice and this the plaintiffs had failed to discharge (*see also* Chapter 11, p. 135).

In another case, *Rowlandson and Others* v. *National Westminster Bank Ltd.* (1978), money was deposited with the defendants in what was described as a "trust account". One of the trustees wrongfully drew a cheque on the account and this was paid by the defendants. The court held that the plaintiffs could recover their loss from the defendants because, given the nature of the account, the bank was under a fiduciary obligation to prevent a withdrawal of the money in this way (*see also* the *Karak Rubber case* discussed on p. 187).

CROSSED CHEQUES

The Bills of Exchange Act 1882

The Act provides that a cheque may be crossed generally or specially (s.77). A cheque is crossed generally where it carries across its face an addition of either:

(*a*) two parallel lines with or without the words "not negotiable" (for which, *see* below); or

(*b*) the words "and company" (or an abbreviation) between two parallel lines with or without the words "not negotiable".

A special crossing exists where the cheque carries an addition of the name of a banker with or without the words "not negotiable" (s.76).

The effect of crossing a cheque by one of these methods is that the banker on whom the cheque is drawn (the paying banker) must pay the proceeds only to another banker (in the case of a special crossing, the banker to whom the cheque is crossed), failing which he may become liable to the true owner for any loss the latter may suffer (where for instance the proceeds are paid across the counter to a person without lawful possession of the instrument). The banker will however not incur liability where the cheque which is presented to him for payment does not appear to have been crossed, or to have a crossing which has been obliterated, or to have been added to or altered in an unauthorised manner, provided he pays the cheque in good faith and without negligence (s.79).

The significance of the use of the words "not negotiable" on a crossed cheque is that a person to whom the cheque is transferred does not acquire, and is not capable of giving, a better title to the instrument than that held by the person from whom he received it (s.81). It must however be emphasised that a cheque which is crossed in this way continues to be negotiable to the extent that a transferee may acquire rights under it as a holder for value (*see* Chapter 7, p. 87) but the words effectively prevent the transferee becoming a holder in due course and he consequently takes the cheque subject to possible defects in the title of the transferor.

"Account payee"

These words when added to a cheque refer to the original payee and are a direction to the collecting banker (*see* p. 191) to pay the proceeds of the cheque to the payee's account. If the banker does not do this, he may be unable to rely on the statutory protection in an action for conversion (*see* below). The words "account payee" do not prevent the negotiation of the cheque but the onus is on the collecting banker to make proper inquiry before paying the proceeds into an account other than that of the named payee (*Universal Guarantee Property Ltd.* v. *National Bank of Australasia Ltd.* (1965)).

STATUTORY PROVISIONS PROTECTING BANKERS

References are to the Bills of Exchange Act 1882 and the Cheques Act 1957.

The paying banker

If a cheque payable to order carries a forged indorsement, the common law position is that the banker on whom the cheque is drawn cannot pay the holder and debit his customer's (the drawer's) account. Further, if the banker does pay, he may become liable in the tort of conversion to the true owner of the cheque (that is, the payee or subsequent indorsee whose indorsement has been forged).

Protection for the paying banker in these circumstances is afforded by statute. Thus, provided the banker pays an order cheque in good faith and in the ordinary course of business, he is deemed to have paid it in due course (that is, he is discharged from further liability) and can debit the customer's account despite the fact that an indorsement on the cheque has been forged or made without authority (s.60, 1882 Act). This particular provision operates whether the cheque is crossed or uncrossed. In addition, the banker on whom is drawn a crossed cheque carrying a forged indorsement is also protected if he pays the instrument to another banker, provided he acts in good faith and without negligence. The position here, in fact, is as if payment had been made to the true owner therefore the customer's account can be debited by the amount of the cheque (s.80, 1882 Act).

The application of s.60 (above) presupposes the existence of a forged indorsement. Nevertheless, if a banker in good faith and in the ordinary course of business pays a cheque which is not indorsed or is irregularly indorsed (for example, the indorsement does not correspond exactly with the payee's name as in *Arab Bank Ltd.* v. *Ross* (1952)), he incurs no liability by reason only of the absence of an indorsement, or the fact an indorsement is irregular, and he is deemed to have paid the cheque in due course (s.1, 1957 Act).

The effect of this latter provision is that, if a person with no title to a cheque (for example, a crook claiming to be the payee) pays it into a bank for collection, the fact that the collecting bank does not require the cheque to be indorsed does not prejudice the right of the paying banker to protection provided the latter acts in good faith and pays the proceeds in the ordinary course of business.

The collecting banker

In the collection of a cheque (*see* p. 188), a banker may become liable in conversion to the true owner where he collects for a customer who has no title or whose title to the cheque is defective. In *Midland Bank Ltd.* v. *Reckitt* (1933) for example, an agent who was empowered to draw cheques on his clients' behalf wrongfully drew cheques which he paid into his own account with the appellants. The latter were held to be liable in conversion in collecting the cheques because their customer had no authority to use his power in this way.

Nevertheless, if the collecting banker can establish that he received payment for his customer in good faith and without negligence (or having credited the customer's account with the amount of the cheque, he received payment in good faith and without negligence for himself), he will incur no liability to the true owner by reason only of such payment if his customer either lacks title or has one which is defective (s.4, 1957 Act, replacing s.82, 1882 Act).

In seeking to take advantage of this provision, it is clearly important for the banker to prove the absence of negligence. Thus, in *Motor Traders Guarantee Corporation Ltd.* v. *Midland Bank Ltd.* (1937) (a case on s.82, 1882 Act) the banker's customer, a car dealer, paid in a cheque on which he had forged the indorsement of the payee. The dealer had a history of dishonoured cheques and although the cashier did ask him how the cheque had come into his possession, the court considered that, in view of the dealer's record, the bankers had failed to discharge the burden of the statute in not making further inquiry. Similarly, in *Midland Bank Ltd.* v. *Reckitt* (above), the bankers were not protected by the statute because of their carelessness in failing to inquire why the agent was paying cheques drawn on his clients' account into his own account with themselves.

A case illustrating the successful application of the statutory protection is *Marfani and Co. Ltd.* v. *Midland Bank Ltd.* (1968). Here, a person opened an account with a cheque for £3,000 and untruthfully represented himself to the defendant bankers as the person to whom the cheque was payable. The bankers relied on a reference from one of their other customers and, in due course, the crook was allowed to withdraw the entire sum. In an action brought by the true owner for conversion of the cheque, the Court of Appeal held that the bankers could rely on s.4 because they had acted reasonably in the circumstances.

THE MAREVA INJUNCTION AND GARNISHEE PROCEEDINGS

We saw on p. 187 that the banker's duty to honour his customer's mandate may terminate by reason of such matters as death and mental incapacity. Another factor which may affect a banker's obligation to act in accordance with his customer's instructions is the existence of a court order relating to the customer's account.

The Mareva injunction

This is a remedy which is granted to a plaintiff pending a final judgment (that is, it is interlocutory) and which derives its name from the case, *Mareva Compania Naviera S.A.* v. *International Bulkcarriers S.A.* (1975). If A is claiming a sum of money which is owed to him by B, but it is possible that B may dispose of his assets in such a way as to frustrate an eventual judgment against him (for example, by removing his assets out of the country), A may be granted an injunction to prevent this happening. Consequently, if the assets in question are deposited with a banker, the latter will be in contempt of court if he chooses to ignore the fact that his customer's funds are now subject to restriction (*Rahman (Prince Abdul)* v. *Abu-Taha* (1980)). Any money which is in excess of the amount specified in the order can however be dealt with in the usual way.

A Mareva injunction may be granted whether the defendant is resident in this country or not (s.37(3), Supreme Court Act 1981).

Garnishee proceedings

These proceedings are governed by the Rules of the Supreme Court and are one particular method whereby a judgment debt may be enforced. Thus, in the illustration used above, if A is finally successful in his action against B and is awarded a sum of money, the judgment in A's favour may be enforced by the court ordering B's banker (the garnishee), as a person indebted to the judgment debtor (B), to pay to the judgment creditor (A) the funds which are in B's account, or such part of them as is sufficient to satisfy the judgment debt. The banker is obliged to comply with the order and, in this respect, he may disobey his customer's mandate and incur no liability in so doing.

DOCUMENTARY CREDITS

A method of financing international trade is for the parties to the contract of sale of goods to arrange for a documentary credit to be opened in the exporter's favour. This is effected by the buyer instructing his banker to issue a credit for the price of the goods to be made available to the exporter after the goods have been shipped and on production of the shipping documents (for which, *see* Chapter 13, p. 163). To this end, the services of a banker in the exporter's own country are employed (the correspondent bank) with the credit taking the form of a direct cash payment to the exporter, or the credit arrangement may require that he draw a bill of exchange which the correspondent bank may accept or negotiate.

If the credit is irrevocable, the issuing banker is bound by it. Furthermore, if the correspondent banker confirms the irrevocable nature of the credit to the exporter, he also becomes liable provided the exporter complies fully with the terms on which the credit is opened. A banker is in fact obliged to pay under a confirmed credit irrespective of any dispute there may be between the parties under the contract of sale (*Hamzeh Malas and Sons* v. *British Imex Industries Ltd.* (1958)).

Nevertheless, the banker is justified in refusing to honour the credit where, for example, the description of the goods in the shipping documents differs from that contained in the buyer's instructions to the issuing bank (*J. H. Rayner and Co. Ltd.* v. *Hambros Bank Ltd.* (1942)).

DEPOSIT-TAKING

Control

Subject to important exceptions, the acceptance of a deposit of money in the course of carrying on a deposit-taking business is prohibited (s.1, Banking Act 1979). A deposit-taking business is defined as one in the course of which money received from depositors is either lent to others or is used to finance any other activity of the business. A business does not fall within the definition if it does not accept deposits on a day-to-day basis and, in fact, accepts deposits only on particular occasions.

Institutions which are exempted from the prohibition on deposit-taking are the Bank of England, a recognised bank (defined on p. 185) and certain other bodies such as the National Savings Bank, the Post Office and building societies (s.2, Sched. 1) In addition, an institution may be given a licence to carry on such a business by the Bank of England provided the following criteria are met:

(a) its directors, controllers and managers must be fit and proper persons;

(b) at least two individuals must effectively direct the institutions business;

(c) the institution's net assets (i.e. paid up capital and reserves in the case of a body corporate) must satisfy specified requirement; and

(d) the business of the institution must be conducted in a prudent manner (s.3, Sched. 2).

No licence will be granted to an unincorporated institution if the whole of its assets are owned by a single individual (s.3(4)).

The protection of depositors

In the interests of depositors, the Act provides for the setting up of the Deposit Protection Board whose function is to administer the Deposit Protection Fund (s.21). This Fund is financed partly by a levy imposed on all recognised banks and licensed institutions (collectively termed contributory institutions) (ss.22 and 23). In the event of a recognised bank or licensed institution becoming insolvent (for the purposes of the Act, this will be on the making of a winding up order in the case of a body corporate and on the making of a receiving order in the case of a partnership), the Board is required to pay to a depositor three-quarters of his protected deposit (s.28). A protected deposit is broadly the total liability of the insolvent institution to the depositor but limited to a maximum of £10,000 or such larger sum as may be specified by the Treasury (s.29).

SUMMARY

On completion of this chapter you should be able to:

(a) Explain the meaning of "banker".

(b) Understand the principal characteristics of the banker/customer relationship.

(c) Know the rules relating to (a) crossed cheques, and (b) the protection of bankers.

(d) Outline the provisions of the Banking Act 1979 relating to the recognition of banks and the licensing of deposit-taking institutions.

SELF-ASSESSMENT QUESTIONS

(Relevant page numbers are given in brackets.)

1. What criteria must be fulfilled before an institution will be recognised as a bank? (Page 185)

2. Indicate the duties which a customer owes to his banker. (Page 186)

3. What is the effect of a cheque on which the drawer's signature is forged? (Page 187)

4. Describe the statutory protection which is available to a paying banker. (Page 190)

5. Indicate the circumstances in which a banker need not honour his customer's mandate. (Page 187)

CHAPTER SIXTEEN

Remedies for Breach of Contract

CHAPTER OBJECTIVE

After studying this chapter you should be able to:
* discuss the principal remedies available to an innocent party
  following a breach of the contractual obligations, with
  particular reference to the remedy of damages.

INTRODUCTION

As we have already seen (Chapter 12), one possible course of
action open to an innocent party following a breach is to terminate
the contract and refuse further performance. This option is only
available however if the breach goes to the root of the contract and,
where it does not, the innocent party is confined to damages
(money compensation) or one of the other remedies which the law
provides. These include an order of specific performance and an
injunction which are both awarded in accordance with equitable
principles (*see* p. 201).

It may also be noted that money paid in advance by the guilty
party (e.g. under a contract for the sale of land) may be irrecoverable if the contract so provides or where the amount paid is a
"deposit"; that is, is in the nature of a guarantee that the contract
will be performed (*Howe* v. *Smith* (1884)). Where, on the other
hand, the money pre-paid is intended simply as a part payment, it
cannot be forfeited in this way and must be returned to the
wrongdoer (*Harrison* v. *Holland* (1921)).

DAMAGES

The nature and object of damages

Damages may be nominal or compensatory (substantial). Whereas
nominal damages (possibly a few pounds) are awarded to a person
who suffers no loss or damage following a breach of contract,
compensatory damages are given when such a loss is incurred, with
the object of placing the innocent party (in so far as it is possible by
a monetary award) in the situation which would have existed if the
contract had been performed in accordance with its terms (*Robinson* v. *Harman* (1848)). An illustration of the application of this
principle is *Jarvis* v. *Swans Tours Ltd.* (1973). In this case, a holi-
daymaker was awarded damages to compensate for the fact that

the type of holiday and facilities he had been promised during a stay in Switzerland did not materialise.

In some circumstances it may be difficult to ascertain the appropriate amount of damages but this should not impede a successful claim. Thus, in *Chaplin* v. *Hicks* (1911), the plaintiff was awarded £100 damages in respect of a lost possibility of employment where, having been shortlisted for a position as an actress, she was not given proper notification of the interview by the defendant theatre manager.

In the above cases, the damages awarded were *unliquidated* (i.e. assessed by the court) but, at the time of contracting, the parties may expressly provide that, in the event of a breach of contract, a specific sum of money should be payable as compensation. The amount fixed in this way is recoverable as *liquidated* damages provided it represents a reasonable attempt by the contracting parties to estimate in financial terms the actual loss or damage (Lord Dunedin in *Dunlop Pneumatic Tyre Co. Ltd.* v. *New Garage and Motor Co. Ltd.* (1915)). The courts will uphold an action to recover *liquidated* damages even though the sum in question is in excess of the (*unliquidated*) damages to which the claimant would otherwise be entitled. On the other hand, if the pre-arranged sum is greatly in excess of the loss which could reasonably be anticipated and is nothing more than a device to compel performance of the contract, it will be treated as a penalty and be unenforceable. In the *Dunlop* case (above), dealers in the appellants' products agreed to pay £5 in respect of every article sold in breach of a price maintenance agreement. The House of Lords held that the amount specified was the result of a genuine attempt to assess possible loss and was therefore recoverable as a liquidated sum. In another case involving the maintenance of resale prices however, a car dealer undertook to pay £250 for every breach and this amount the Court of Appeal held to be a penalty (*Ford Motor Co. Ltd.* v. *Armstrong* (1915)).

One further point should be made at this stage. An aggrieved party may sometimes be able to recover from the wrongdoer the exact amount which it has been agreed should be paid under the contract and is not limited therefore to a claim in damages. Thus, under the Sale of Goods Act 1979 the seller may sue the buyer for the price of the goods sold, provided the property in the goods (ownership) has passed to the buyer and the latter wrongfully neglects or refuses to pay as required by the terms of the contract (s.49). Clearly, the contract (whatever its nature) must still be in force and the person claiming the agreed sum must have performed his own obligations under it. The full contract price was for instance recoverable in *White and Carter (Councils) Ltd.* v. *Mc*

Gregor (1962) and also in *Hoenig* v. *Isaacs* (1952), although in the latter case a sum was deducted in respect of defective workmanship (both cases are referred to in Chapter 12). In circumstances such as these, problems with regard to the assessment of damages and remoteness of loss (*see* below) do not arise.

Mitigation of loss

The plaintiff is under an obligation to minimise as far as possible the incidence of loss caused by the other party's breach of contract in so far as it is reasonable to expect him to do this. For example, in *Payzu Ltd.* v. *Saunders* (1919), a contract for the sale of goods by instalments provided that payment should be made one month after each delivery. The buyers failed to pay for the first delivery on time, whereupon the sellers (unjustifiably) refused to make further deliveries except on the basis of cash with order. The buyers rejected this offer and claimed as damages the difference between the contract price of the goods and the higher market price. The court held that the buyers were under a duty to mitigate their loss by accepting the sellers' offer. In *Brace* v. *Calder* (1895), the plaintiff employee was dismissed following the dissolution of a partnership but was offered re-employment by another firm, which he refused. In an action for wrongful dismissal against the original employers, the plaintiff received only nominal damages by reason of his failure to mitigate the loss.

Remoteness of loss

A person who is in breach of contract is not required to compensate the innocent party in respect of all the loss or damage resulting from the breach: certain losses may be considered by the court to be too remote and hence unactionable, even though they may well be foreseeable. Instead, the wrongdoer is responsible only for that loss which occurs in the usual course of things or which, at the time of entering into the contract, he ought reasonably to have contemplated would be a probable result of the breach (*Hadley* v. *Baxendale* (1854)). The party in breach is not responsible then for loss or damage which, albeit foreseeable, is likely to occur only in a small number of cases. The loss or damage contemplated must be such that it is "not unlikely" (or liable) to occur as a result of the breach (*Koufos* v. *Czarnikow Ltd.* (*The Heron II* (1969))).

In *Hadley* v. *Baxendale*, the defendant carriers were employed by the plaintiff mill owners to deliver a broken shaft for repair. The carriers unreasonably delayed delivery for several days with the result that work at the mill stopped for longer than necessary, because the plaintiffs did not possess a spare shaft. Despite the defendants' breach, the plaintiffs' claim for damages for loss of profits failed, because the loss was not such as the defendants ought reasonably to have contemplated would be a probable consequence of their breach. The defendants could not have been expected to anticipate that all work at the mill would stop if they delayed delivery. Nevertheless, knowledge of special circumstances can affect liability and, if the importance of delivering the shaft on time had been impressed on the defendants by the plaintiffs, the decision of the court might well have been otherwise.

A case in which the innocent party's action was successful is *Koufos* v. *Czarnikow Ltd.* Here, shipowners contracted to transport a large cargo of sugar for the respondent charterers. The shipowners'knew that there was a market for sugar at the port of arrival yet they were unaware that it was the charterers' intention to sell the sugar immediately. Delivery of the sugar was delayed by nine days and, in the meantime, the price of sugar fell. The House of Lords decided that the charterers could recover as damages the difference between the price they actually obtained for the commodity and the price which they would have received if there had been no delay. The shipowners ought to have appreciated the likelihood of the sugar being sold on the arrival at the prevailing market price and, given market fluctuations in price, that any delay on their part would be likely to lead to loss.

REMEDIES UNDER THE SALE OF GOODS ACT 1979

Contracts for the sale of goods are subject to the rules considered above but there are additional provisions in the Act which are considered in this section.

The seller's remedies

These comprise an action to recover the price of the goods under s.49 (*see* p. 197); damages for non-acceptance, provided the buyer's refusal to accept and pay for the goods is unjustified (s.50 (1)); and, in addition, an unpaid seller has various rights or remedies in respect of the goods themselves. A seller of goods is an "unpaid seller" if the whole price has not been paid or tendered or a negotiable instrument (e.g. a cheque) has been dishonoured. The remedies in respect of the goods are as follows.

(*a*) The unpaid seller has in certain circumstances a lien on the goods, thereby entitling him to retain possession until the price is paid or tendered. This right of lien will only arise, however, where there is no stipulation as to credit in the contract of sale, or there is such a stipulation but the credit term has expired, or the buyer becomes insolvent (ss.39 and 41).

(b) However only where the buyer does in fact become insolvent (i.e. has either ceased to pay his debts in the ordinary course of business or cannot pay his debts as they become due—s.61(4)), the unpaid seller has the right to resume possession of the goods whilst they are in the course of transit (s.44).

(c) The Act confers on the seller in the above cases the right to resell the goods to another buyer where they are of a perishable nature or where he has informed the original buyer of his intention to resell and the latter fails within a reasonable time to pay or tender the price. It may be noted that the resale is effective to convey to the second buyer a good title to the goods as against the original buyer (s.48).

The measure of damages for non-acceptance of the contract goods by the buyer is the estimated loss directly and naturally resulting, in the ordinary course of events, from the breach (s.50(2)). This is in effect the common law rule relating to remoteness of loss which we considered on p. 198. Thus, in *Lazenby Garages Ltd.* v. *Wright* (1976) the defendant agreed to purchase from the plaintiff dealers a second-hand motor car for £1,670 but subsequently repudiated the transaction. The plaintiffs claimed as damages £345 loss of profit, the difference between the contract price and that which they had earlier paid themselves, despite the fact that they were able to resell the vehicle for the higher price of £1,770. In applying s.50(2), the Court of Appeal decided against the plaintiffs because the only likely consequence of their breach which the defendants would reasonably have contemplated was that the plaintiffs might suffer loss by having to resell the vehicle at a price lower than that agreed with them.

In those situations where the goods with which the seller is left can be readily disposed of to other purchasers (i.e. there is an "available market"), the measure of damages for non-acceptance is prima facie to be ascertained by the difference between the contract price and the market or current price of the goods, at the time when the goods ought to have been accepted, or at the time of the refusal to accept (s.50(3)). On the other hand, where the supply of goods exceeds the demand for them, there cannot be said to be an available market, therefore the aggrieved seller is entitled to the profit lost on the particular transaction (*Thompson* v. *Robinson (Gunmakers) Ltd.* (1955)). Further, if demand exceeds supply and the seller's financial position following the breach of contract is unaffected because of the ease with which all his goods can be sold, he will be entitled to nominal damages only.

Section 50(3) was not the appropriate measure of damages in the *Lazenby Garages* case (above) because the court considered that there was no available market for second-hand cars.

The buyer's remedies

We may summarise the buyer's remedies for breach of a contract of sale of goods as follows. In the first place, he is in certain circumstances entitled to reject the goods (*see* the discussion in Chapter 12, pp. 149 and 150). Secondly, the buyer may institute an action for damages:

(*a*) where the seller wrongfully refuses to deliver the contract goods (s.51); and

(*b*) where the seller is guilty of other breaches; for instance, with respect to the quality and fitness of the goods supplied (s.53).

Thirdly, the buyer may be entitled to recover the exact price he has paid for the goods where there has been a total failure of consideration (s.54; and *see Rowland* v. *Divall* (1923), Chapter 10, p. 120). Fourthly, in a case of non-delivery by the seller, the court may be willing to order that the contract be specifically performed provided the contract goods are specific or ascertained (s.52). The remedy of specific performance is considered further below.

As is the case where the buyer refuses to accept the goods, the measure of damages under both ss.51 and 53 is the estimated loss directly and naturally resulting, in the ordinary course of events, from the seller's breach (ss.51(2) and 53(2)). Where, however, the buyer seeks to obtain undelivered goods from some other market source, the measure of damages is prima facie to be ascertained by the difference between the contract price and the market or current price at the time when the goods should have been delivered (s.51(3)). Moreover, if the breach relates to the quality of the goods, the buyer's loss is prima facie the difference between the value of the goods at the time of delivery to the buyer and the value they would have had if the seller had complied with his contractual obligation (s.53(3)). It should be noted that, as an alternative to a claim for damages under s.53, the buyer may rely on the seller's breach in diminution or extinction of the price of the goods (s.53(1)(*a*)).

EQUITABLE REMEDIES

Specific performance

This is a discretionary remedy whereby a contracting party may be compelled to perform the obligations he has undertaken. Specific performance is not available to the aggrieved party in every case, since the common law remedy of damages is normally adequate. Consequently, this remedy will only be awarded in sale of goods cases for instance where the subject matter of the contract is unique (e.g. an antique) or is not readily obtainable elsewhere. Thus, specific performance of a contract for the sale of a ship was ordered in *Behnke* v. *Bede Shipping Co. Ltd.* (1927) because the vessel in question was particularly attractive to the buyer and no suitable alternative could be found.

The remedy of specific performance is usually appropriate with respect to contracts for the sale of an interest in land (e.g. to compel conveyance by the vendor) but even in this area there are limitations. In *Warmington* v. *Miller* (1973), for example, the court refused specific performance of a contract for a sublease of land because the defendant lessee would otherwise have been in breach of a provision of the head lease prohibiting sub-letting.

Certain contracts will not be specifically enforced. Examples are, contracts for personal services and those in which the award of specific performance will necessitate constant supervision by the court. For instance, in *Ryan* v. *Mutual Tontine Association* (1893), only damages were ordered for breach of a covenant in a lease requiring the lessors to provide a resident porter for cleaning and other duties.

Injunction
This remedy, like that of specific performance is discretionary. It is awarded to prevent the breach of a negative provision in a contract and examples of its application are to be found in the cases concerning restraint of trade (*see* Chapter 11, p. 140). We saw above that a contract for personal services will never be specifically enforced and, in accordance with this principle, an injunction will be refused where it would have this effect. Consequently, in *Whitwood Chemical Co.* v. *Hardman* (1891), the court refused to award an injunction to prevent an employee breaking a commitment to give all his time to the business of his employers (i.e. not to work for anybody else) because to do so would be to specifically enforce the contract. Nevertheless an injunction will be awarded in such cases where its effect would only be to encourage the defendant employee to work for the employer in a particular capacity. For example, in *Warner Bros. Picture Inc.* v. *Nelson* (1937), the defendant was in breach of an agreement not to work as a motion picture and stage actress for any person other than the plaintiffs. The court granted the plaintiffs an injunction because the defendant remained free to seek employment elsewhere in some other capacity; she was not

confronted with the choice of either working for the plaintiffs or not working at all.

LIMITATION OF ACTIONS

Under the Limitation Act 1980, an action for damages for breach of a simple contract may not normally be brought once more than six years have passed from the date of the breach. A twelve year limitation period applies if the contract is incorporated in a deed and the relevant period is only three years where the plaintiff's claim includes damages for personal injury.

If the person to whom a right of action accrues is under some disability (e.g. an minor), the limitation period does not begin to run until that disability has ceased. Furthermore, if the defendant has acted fraudulently or the plaintiff's claim is for relief from the consequences of a mistake, the limitation period does not begin until the fraud or mistake is discovered.

The provisions of the Act do not operate with respect to a claim for an equitable remedy. Nevertheless, such an action will be barred in accordance with equitable principles if the plaintiff's delay is unreasonable (*see*, for instance, the discussion of *Leaf* v. *International Galleries* (1950), Chapter 11, p. 132).

SUMMARY

On completion of this chapter you should be able to:

(*a*) Indicate the nature and object of damages.

(*b*) Distinguish between liquidated and unliquidated damages.

(*c*) Appreciate the circumstances in which a particular loss may be unactionable.

(*d*) Understand the purpose of equitable remedies.

SELF-ASSESSMENT QUESTIONS

(Relevant page numbers are given in brackets.)

1. Distinguish between liquidated damages and a penalty. (Page 197)

2. What is the test for establishing an obligation to pay damages for loss suffered by an aggrieved party following a breach of contract? (Page 198)

3. In relation to a breach of a contract of sale of goods, indicate the remedies of (*a*) the seller, and (*b*) the buyer. (Page 199)

4. In what circumstances will the remedy of specific performance be awarded to compel the performance of a contract? (Page 201)

CHAPTER SEVENTEEN

Fair Trading

CHAPTER OBJECTIVE

After studying this chapter you should be able to:
* explain the principal statutory provisions regulating consumer trade practices, restrictive trade practices and anti-competitive practices, and monopolies and mergers.

INTRODUCTION

The statutes which are relevant to the discussion in this chapter are the Fair Trading Act 1973, the Restrictive Trade Practices and Resale Prices Acts 1976, and the Competition Act 1980. Furthermore, with reference to restrictive practices in particular, it is necessary to take into account the provisions of European Community law which operate in parallel with the relevant United Kingdom domestic law (s.5, Restrictive Trade Practices Act 1976, and *Wilhelm and Others* v. *Bundeskartellamt* (1969)).

This wide-ranging body of rules constitutes a serious constraint on the freedom of suppliers of goods and services to take advantage of the competitive process to the detriment of the private consumer.

An office which figures prominently in the administration of this area of the law is that held by the Director-General of Fair Trading. The Director is appointed under the Fair Trading Act 1973 and his functions include:

(*a*) keeping under review commercial activities relating to the supply of goods and services in order to identify practices adverse to the economic interests of consumers,

(*b*) the detection of monopoly situations or practices which prevent, restrict or distort competition,

(*c*) informing, assisting and making appropriate recommendations to the Secretary of State in connection with such practices, and

(*d*) recommending suitable legislation for the elimination of adverse consumer trade practices (ss.2 and 17).

In addition, the Director has responsibilities with respect to the regulation of monopoly situations and uncompetitive practices under Part IV of the Fair Trading Act 1973; he is charged with taking proceedings before the Restrictive Practices Court in relation to restrictive agreements (s.1(2), Restrictive Trade Practices Act 1976); and, under the Competition Act 1980, he may refer anti-competitive practices to the Monopolies and Mergers Commission (s.5).

CONSUMER TRADE PRACTICES

Definition
These are governed by the Fair Trading Act 1973. A consumer trade practice is one which is carried on in connection with the supply of goods and services and which relates to one or more of the following:

(*a*) the terms and conditions of supply;

(*b*) the manner in which such terms and conditions are communicated to the persons supplied;

(*c*) the promotion of the goods and services and methods of salesmanship employed;

(*d*) the method of packing; and

(*e*) methods of demanding or securing payment (s.13).

References
Whether or not a particular consumer trade practice is adverse to the economic interests of consumers is an issue which may be referred by the Secretary of State or any other Minister or the Director-General of Fair Trading to the Consumer Protection Advisory Committee (established under s.3 of the Act) which must then consider the matter and ultimately produce a report (s.14). Legal, medical, dental and various other professional services are excluded from the reference procedure (s.15 and Sched. 4) and, furthermore, ministerial consent is necessary before the Director can refer to the Advisory Committee practices connected with the supply of goods and services by public corporations (e.g. gas and electricity undertakings) (s.16, and Sched. 5).

In certain circumstances, the Director may include in a reference made by him proposals that the Advisory Committee recommend to the Secretary of State that subordinate legislation be enacted, providing for the modification or discontinuance of the consumer trade practice specified in the reference (ss.17 and 19). Such proposals may be made where it appears to the Director that the practice in question is likely to mislead consumers (for example, as to their rights and obligations), or subject consumers to undue pressure to enter into transactions, or cause terms and conditions under which consumers transact to be so adverse to them as to be inequitable (s.17(2)).

Where the proposals do result in legislation, it becomes an offence to contravene any prohibition imposed thereby (s.23) although such contravention does not of itself invalidate any contract for the supply of goods and services (s.26).

Implementation

Following reports of the Consumer Protection Advisory Committee, the following are two of the orders which have been made.

The Consumer Transactions (Restrictions on Statements) Order 1976 (as amended)
This order makes it unlawful for a person supplying goods in the course of a business to seek to introduce into a consumer transaction, whether by notice displayed at his premises or by advertisement or on the goods themselves, a term which would be void by virtue of s.6 of the Unfair Contract Terms Act 1977 (this section it will be recalled prohibits the exclusion or restriction of the supplier's liability for breach of the various implied obligations which are contained in the Sale of Goods Act 1979 and the Supply of Goods (Implied Terms) Act 1973: *see* Chapter 10, p. 128). In *Cavendish-Woodhouse Ltd.* v. *Manley* (1984), it was held that the words "bought as seen" in an invoice relating to the sale of specific goods did not amount to a void term for the purposes of this order. The same order also makes it unlawful for sellers and manufacturers to supply goods bearing a statement of rights the consumer has in respect of the goods (for example, under the provisions of a guarantee) unless such a statement is accompanied by another statement to the effect that the consumers' statutory rights are unaffected.

The Business Advertisements (Disclosure) Order 1977
Where goods are being sold in the course of a business, the seller must, in any advertisement relating to those goods, make it reasonably clear that the goods are being sold in the course of a business in order that consumers may not be misled as to his true status.

CONDUCT DETRIMENTAL TO THE INTERESTS OF CONSUMERS

The Director-General of Fair Trading has additional responsibilities and powers under the Fair Trading Act 1973 where it appears to him (whether on the basis of his own information or complaints received) that a businessman is persisting in a course of conduct which:

(a) is detrimental to the interests of consumers, and
(b) is unfair to consumers (s.34).

Conduct will be regarded as unfair where, for instance, it involves breaches of contract or contraventions of enactments which impose duties, prohibitions or restrictions enforceable by criminal proceedings.

In these circumstances, the Director is required to obtain assurances from the person concerned that he will discontinue the course of conduct, failing which the matter may be brought before the Restrictive Practices Court (s.34 and 35). The court may then order discontinuance if the conduct is established (s.27).

RESTRICTIVE TRADE PRACTICES

In this section, we consider the regulation of agreements which contain provisions restrictive of competition.

Agreements which are subject to regulation

The principal provisions are contained in the Restrictive Trade Practices Act 1976 which consolidates the provisions of earlier enactments relating to this topic. The Act requires that certain restrictive agreements relating to the provision of goods and services be registered with the Director-General of Fair Trading (s.1). The persons who are party to the agreements specified must furnish the Director with their names and addresses and details of all the terms of their agreement (s.24). If an agreement is not registered as required by the Act, it is void in respect of the restrictions contained within it and, furthermore, it becomes unlawful for the contracting parties to give effect to or enforce such restrictions (s.35).

The agreements which must be registered in respect of goods are those between two or more persons carrying on the business of producing or supplying goods and under which restrictions are accepted by two or more parties with respect to any of such matters as:

(a) the prices to be charged for the goods or those which are to apply on their resale,
(b) the terms or conditions on which the goods are to be supplied or acquired,
(c) quantities or descriptions of the goods to be produced, supplied or acquired,

(*d*) the processes of manufacture to be applied, and

(*e*) the persons to whom the goods are to be supplied and from whom they are to be acquired (s.6).

Agreements relating to the provision of services are subject to registration also provided the restrictions accepted by the parties relate to "designated" services (s.11 and Restrictive Trade Practices (Services) Order 1976). Designated services do not include legal, medical, dental and various other professional services (s.13 and Sched. 1). The Act may also be made to apply (by statutory instrument) to information agreements. That is to say, an agreement whereby the parties exchange information with respect to such matters as the prices they charge for their goods and services (ss.7 and 12).

Certain agreements are specifically exempted from regulation by the Act. These include agreements authorised by statute, agreements between two persons only under which one party agrees to resell only goods supplied by the other (for an example of this "exclusive dealing" arrangement *see Esso Petroleum Co. Ltd.* v. *Harper's Garage (Stourport) Ltd.*, Chapter 11, p. 141) and various agreements and arrangements relating to trade marks, patents and copyright (s.28 and Sched. 3 as amended).

It should be noted that an agreement may be subject to the registration provisions of the Act irrespective of whether it is legally enforceable (s.43).

References

Registered agreements may be referred by the Director-General of Fair Trading to the Restrictive Practices Court which may declare whether or not the restrictions contained in the agreements are contrary to the public interest (s.1(3)). Agreements which are found to be contrary to the public interest become void in respect of the restrictions (or information provisions) and the parties may be restrained from giving effect to the restrictions or from making any other agreement to the like effect (s.2).

In examining an agreement, the court presumes that in the first instance a restriction is contrary to the public interest (ss.10 and 19). Nevertheless, this presumption may be rebutted where the Court is satisfied that the restriction (or information provision) fulfils one or more of the following:

(*a*) it is reasonably necessary to protect the public against injury,

(*b*) its removal would deny to the public as purchasers, consumers or users other specific and substantial benefits,

(c) it is reasonably necessary in order to counteract anti-competitive measures taken by some person not party to the agreement,

(d) it is reasonably necessary to enable the parties to the agreement to negotiate fair terms with an important supplier or purchaser,

(e) its removal would be likely to affect adversely the general level of unemployment,

(f) to remove the restriction would have a substantial adverse effect on export earnings,

(g) it is reasonably required for the maintenance of another restriction which the court has found not to be contrary to the public interest, and

(h) the restriction does not restrict or discourage competition to any material degree.

In addition, the court must be satisfied that the restriction is not unreasonable having regard to the balance between the above matters and any detriment to the public which may result from the operation of the restriction (ss.10 and 19).

In *Re Tyre Trade Register Agreement* (1963) the manufacturers of new tyres in this country sought to establish a register of tyre traders to which only those traders fulfilling specified criteria would be admitted. The effect of non-registration would be that a trader would not be supplied with new tyres. The court held that the restriction could not be justified under (a) above, because there was no evidence that the abolition of the scheme would lead to a greater risk of injury to the public than already existed.

On the other hand, in *Re Net Book Agreement* (1962), an agreement between publishers that certain books should not be sold at less than a "net" or fixed price was upheld under paragraph (b) because it was likely that the abolition of the restriction would lead to price-cutting, a reduction in the number of stockholding booksellers and ultimately higher prices for books generally.

Resale Prices Act 1976

The regulation of resale price maintenance is in fact now provided for by this statute (again, a consolidating enactment). Thus, the collective enforcement of resale price maintenance is prohibited, in that it is unlawful for two or more suppliers of goods to make or carry out any agreement or arrangement whereby, for instance, they refuse to deliver goods to dealers who have resold goods in breach of a price-maintenance condition or they supply goods to such dealers on terms less favourable than those applied to other dealers (s.1).

Any attempt by an individual supplier to enforce minimum resale prices by the withholding of supplies of goods is also prohibited and any term or condition of a contract which provides for minimum prices on the resale of goods is deemed to be void (ss.9 and 11).

Individual resale price maintenance may be permitted, however, by the Restrictive Practices Court making an order granting exemption with respect to a given class of goods (s.14). To this end, application to the court may be made by the Director-General of Fair Trading, a supplier of the goods, or any association of such suppliers (s.15).

Exemption may be granted where it appears to the court that without the system of resale price maintenance applicable to the goods in question, one or more of the following would result:

(*a*) a substantial reduction in the quality of the goods on sale,

(*b*) a substantial reduction in the number of retail outlets for the goods,

(*c*) an increase in retail prices in the longer term,

(*d*) the retailing of the goods under conditions likely to cause a danger to health, and

(*e*) a cessation of or reduction in after-sales service.

In each case, it must further be established that the resulting detriment to the public as consumers or users of the goods would outweigh any detriment resulting from the continuance of resale price maintenance (s.14).

In *Re Medicaments Reference (No.2)* (1971) (decided under the Resale Prices Act 1964), the court permitted the continued existence of resale price maintenance with respect to proprietary medicines because it was considered that its removal would lead to an accelerated reduction in the number of retail chemists (by, for instance, such goods being sold more cheaply in other outlets, such as supermarkets).

Finally, as we noted in Chapter 9, at common law a term of a contract may be enforced only against a contracting party (*Dunlop Pneumatic Tyre Co. Ltd.* v. *Selfridge and Co. Ltd.* (1915)). Apart from any statutory prohibition then, the effect of this rule is that a manufacturer may not normally enforce a price maintenance condition in his contract with a wholesaler against, say, the retailer. However, under the Act, a supplier of goods is permitted to enforce a lawful (i.e.exempted) price maintenance condition against any person who is not party to the contract under which the goods are supplied provided that person subsequently acquires the goods with notice of the condition (s.26).

European Community Law

Under the competition provisions of the E.E.C. Treaty, certain agreements are regarded as being prima facie incompatible with the Common Market and are automatically void. The agreements in question are those which (*a*) may affect trade between member states and (*b*) have as their object or effect the prevention, restriction or distortion of competition within the Common Market (Article 85).

An agreement which was held by the European Court of Justice to infringe this provision was that between the parties in *Consten and Grundig* v. *Commission* (1966). Grundigs appointed Consten to be the sole distributor of their goods in France and, to this end, assigned to Consten the exclusive right to use the trade mark relating to the goods in that country. Constens undertook not to re-export the goods from France to other Common Market countries and a similar undertaking was obtained by Grundigs from their exclusive dealers in Germany and other member states.

The Court of Justice decided that both the restriction imposed on Consten, and the use to which the trade mark was put, infringed Article 85 because other traders were prevented from dealing in Grundig's products in France.

The parties to a restrictive agreement may therefore be subject to two sets of rules: those of European Community law and their own domestic legislation (in the case of the United Kingdom, the Restrictive Trade Practices Act 1976). In point of fact, apart from any sanction which may operate under domestic provisions, the European Commission is empowered to impose financial penalties for breach of the treaty provisions and the secondary legislation made thereunder (Articles 15 and 16 of Regulation 17). The Commission can, however, exempt a particular agreement or category of agreements from the above prohibition provided certain requirements are fulfilled (Article 85(3) and Regulation 17).

ANTI-COMPETITIVE PRACTICES

These are defined and controlled by the Competition Act 1980. An anti-competitive practice arises where, in the course of a business, a person pursues a course of conduct (whether alone or in conjunction with others) which has the effect of "restricting, distorting or preventing competition in connection with the production, supply or acquisition of goods in the United Kingdom or any part of it or the supply or securing of services . . ." (s.2(1)). This definition does not include any course of conduct which is caught by the provisions of the Restrictive Trade Practices Act 1976 (s.2(2)).

The Competition Act provides for an investigation to be conducted by the Director-General of Fair Trading into those practices which may be anti-competitive. On completion of his investigation, the Director must publish a report stating whether, in his opinion, the course of conduct investigated does amount to an anti-competitive practice (s.3). If the Director considers that it does, he may either:

(a) accept an undertaking from the person or persons engaged in the practice that it will be discontinued, or

(b) refer the matter to the Monopolies and Mergers Commission who, in their turn, are then required to report to the Secretary of State (ss.4, 5 and 8).

If the conclusion is that there does exist an anti-competitive practice which operates against the public interest, the persons engaged in it may be asked (through the Director) to give suitable undertakings (s.9). Alternatively, the Secretary of State may make an order prohibiting a named person from taking part in any anti-competitive practice specified in the Commission's report and/or, with a view to dealing with particular adverse effects, he may declare certain forms of conduct to be unlawful (for instance, the withholding of supplies and services) (s.10).

MONOPOLIES AND MERGERS

References are to the Fair Trading Act 1973 unless otherwise specified.

Monopolies

Where it appears to the Director-General of Fair Trading that a monopoly situation may exist with respect to:

(a) the supply of goods or services or

(b) the exporting of goods from the United Kingdom, he may make a monopoly reference to the Monopolies and Mergers Commission (s.50).

A monopoly situation may be taken to exist in relation to the supply of goods where at least one-quarter of goods of a particular description are supplied by or to the same person (or are supplied by or to members of one and the same group of interconnected bodies corporate) (s.6). Similar provision is made with regard to the existence of monopoly situations in relation to services and exports (ss.7 and 8). References to the Commission may also be made by the Secretary of State (s.51).

The supply of gas, electricity, water and various other goods and services such as sugar beet and the carriage of passengers by road and rail may not be the subject of a monopoly reference (s.50 and Scheds. 5 and 7).

The reference may require the Commission to investigate and report not only on whether a monopoly situation exists on the facts of the case but may further require the Commission to decide whether the facts found operate against the public interest (s.49). In this event, the Commission are required:

(a) to specify in their report the particular effects adverse to the public interest which the facts found may have, and

(b) to consider and recommend appropriate remedial action (s.54).

For the purpose of removing or preventing the adverse effects specified, the Secretary of State may by order then declare certain forms of conduct to be unlawful (s.56). Furthermore, the Director may seek to obtain undertakings from the parties involved in the monopoly situation with respect to future remedial action (s.88).

Mergers

A reference may be made to the Monopolies and Mergers Commission by the Secretary of State where it appears to him that two or more enterprises may cease (or have ceased) to exist as distinct enterprises and either

(a) a monopoly situation (as defined earlier) will come about or prevail to a greater extent or

(b) the value of the assets acquired exceeds £30 million (s.64).

The Director-General of Fair Trading is under a duty to recommend to the Secretary of State appropriate action with respect to possible merger situations (s.76).

Where the Commission find that a merger situation will operate against the public interest they may consider what steps should be taken to remedy or prevent the adverse effects resulting from that situation and make the necessary recommendations (s.72). Again, the Secretary of State is given power to declare particular forms of conduct unlawful. He may for instance prohibit a proposed merger in its entirety (s.73 and Sched. 8).

The Fair Trading Act contains special provisions with respect to newspaper mergers. Thus, the Secretary of State must give his consent to the transfer of a newspaper or of newspaper assets to a proprietor whose newspapers (with the newspaper concerned in the transfer) have an average circulation per day of publication of

500,000 or more copies. If the Secretary of State's consent is not obtained, the transfer is unlawful and void (s.58). With certain exceptions, the consent may not be given until the matter has been referred to the Monopolies and Mergers Commission and a report obtained (s.58(2)).

Competition Act 1980
This statute adds further to the circumstances in which a reference can be made to the Monopolies and Mergers Commission. Thus, the Secretary of State may refer to the Commission any question relating to

(a) the efficiency and costs of,
(b) the service provided by, or
(c) possible abuse of a monopoly situation by public corporations and other persons (s.11).

Included in the reference may be the question whether there is being pursued a course of conduct which is adverse to the public interest. If the Commission find this to be the case, the person specified in the reference may be ordered by the Secretary of State (or relevant Minister) to prepare a plan for remedying or preventing the adverse effects resulting from such conduct. The plan must then be laid before Parliament (s.12).

Also available to the Secretary of State if he chooses to take advantage of them are powers to declare specific forms of conduct unlawful (s.12(5)).

European Community Law
It should be noted that the E.E.C. Treaty prohibits any abuse by one or more undertakings of a dominant position in the Common Market if trade between member states is affected (Article 86). Consequently, in any discussion of monopolistic situations, this provision must be taken into account.

The Treaty does not define the meaning of "dominant position" but this would appear to be reflected in a position of economic strength of such a degree that the undertaking concerned has the power to operate independently of its competitors, its customers and consumers (*United Brands Co.* v. *Commission* (1978)). In ascertaining whether or not there is a dominant position, importance will be attached to the share of the market held by the undertaking concerned. Thus, one of the factors taken into account by the European Court of Justice in deciding, in the above case, that United Brands held a dominant position in the market relating to bananas, was its market share of between 40 and 45 per cent. On the other hand, a market share of as little as 10 per cent may rule out any question of a dominant position unless there are other compelling factors to take into account (*Metro* v. *Commission and Saba* (1978)).

An abuse of a dominant position will arise where for instance the undertaking in the dominant situation refuses to supply products of which it holds a monopoly to a customer with whom it has decided to compete (*Commercial Solvents Corporation* v. *Commission* (1974)). Again, an abuse may arise where an undertaking which is already in a dominant position in the market further strengthens and reinforces that position by merging with another undertaking (*Europemballage Corporation and Continental Can Co. Inc.* v. *Commission* (1972)).

SUMMARY

On completion of this chapter you should be able to:

(*a*) Indicate the principal statutory and other rules relating to consumer trade practices, restrictive trade practices, anti-competitive practices and monopolies and mergers.

(*b*) Outline specifically the rules relating to the registration and referring of restrictive agreements and those providing for resale price maintenance.

(*c*) Appreciate the relevance of European Community law in this context.

SELF-ASSESSMENT QUESTIONS

(Relevant page numbers are given in brackets.)

1. Outline the functions of the Director-General of Fair Trading. (Page 204)

2. Define what is meant by a consumer trade practice. (Page 205)

3. What presumption is adopted with respect to registered agreements under the Restrictive Trade Practices Act 1976? (Page 208)

4. Why was the price maintenance agreement in *Re Net Book Agreement* (1962) upheld? (Page 209)

5. What is a "monopoly situation"? (Page 212)

6. In relation to European Community Law, explain the meaning of "dominant position". (Page 214)

CHAPTER EIGHTEEN

Hire-Purchase and Consumer Credit

```
CHAPTER OBJECTIVES

After studying this chapter you should be able to:
*  describe the characteristics of hire-purchase and related
   agreements; and
*  outline the main provisions of the Consumer Credit Act
   1974.
```

INTRODUCTION

The buyer under a contract of sale of goods is under an obligation to pay for them in accordance with the terms of the contract (s.27, Sale of Goods Act 1979). Consequently, the contract may entitle the seller to demand payment of the price in full in return for granting the buyer possession of the goods (in fact, unless otherwise agreed, payment and delivery are concurrent conditions (s.28, Sale of Goods Act)) or the seller may have agreed to accept the price in instalments whilst allowing the goods and the property in them to pass to the buyer in the usual way (*see* the definition of credit sale agreement, p. 223). Alternatively, in agreeing to the postponement of payment, the seller may have stipulated that the property in the goods should not pass to the buyer until payment of all the instalments (conditional sale agreement). In both cases, there is a contract of sale therefore the provisions of the Sale of Goods Act apply.

The possession of goods may also be acquired under a contract of hire and a contract of hire purchase. In the latter instance, it is in fact possible for the hirer to acquire also the property in the goods he has possession of under the agreement but, as we shall see, this is not an inevitable consequence of the initial transaction.

The Consumer Credit Act (replacing, *inter alia*, the Hire-Purchase Act 1965) provides for the regulation of transactions under which goods are acquired on credit and will therefore apply to the agreements specified in the above paragraphs provided they are regulated agreements as defined in the Act (*see* Consumer Credit Agreement below). The Act also establishes a system of licensing of those persons concerned with the provision of credit and this and other matters are referred to in this chapter. Responsibility for overseeing the working of the Act is conferred in the Director-General of Fair Trading who, in conjunction with the local trading standards authorities, has a duty to enforce the Act and regulations made under it.

Specimen credit sale and hire-purchase agreement forms are reproduced in Appendix II.

REGULATED AGREEMENTS

The regulatory provisions of the Consumer Credit Act 1974 as described in various parts of this chapter are principally concerned with this category of agreement which is defined to mean a consumer credit agreement or a consumer hire agreement other than an exempt agreement (s.189).

Consumer credit agreement

A consumer credit agreement is a personal credit agreement (i.e. one made between an individual (the debtor) and the creditor) by which the creditor provides the debtor with credit not exceeding £15,000 (s.8). The definition of individual includes a partnership or other unincorporated association (s.189) and credit includes a cash loan and any other form of financial accommodation (e.g. acceptance by a seller of goods of payment by instalments) (s.9).

The agreements which fall within the definition of consumer credit agreement include credit sale, conditional sale and hire-purchase agreements, and running account credit agreements (see below). In addition, transactions not directly involving the supply of goods and which are essentially straightforward loans of cash are included such as those made by a bank and other moneylenders and also agreements under which bank cheque cards are issued.

In relation to credit, the Act draws a distinction between fixed-sum credit (e.g. that provided under credit and conditional sale agreements and also hire-purchase agreements (s.9(3)) and running account credit (s.10). Whereas a fixed sum credit is provided in one amount or by instalments, a running account credit operates where a debtor is able to obtain from time to time from the creditor (or some third party) cash, goods and services (or any of them) to an amount or value which does not exceed an agreed credit limit and subject to the payment, by the debtor of regular instalments of cash (s.10). Retailers often provide this facility but a running-account credit may for instance also take the form of a bank overdraft.

Consumer hire agreement

This is an agreement for the hiring of goods made with an individual (as defined above) being one which:

(*a*) is not a hire-purchase agreement, and

(*b*) is capable of subsisting for more than three months, and

(*c*) does not require the individual (the hirer) to make payments exceeding £15,000 (s.15).

The point to emphasise about this form of regulated agreement is that, although the hirer is given possession of the goods, the property in them remains with the owner.

Credit-token agreement

This is defined as a regulated agreement for the provision of credit in connection with the use of a credit token (s.14(2)). Any card, cheque, voucher or similar document is a credit token where

(*a*) the person issuing it agrees to supply cash, goods and services on credit on production of the card by the individual to whom it is issued or

(*b*) the person supplying the cash, goods and services on production of the card is some third party, whom the person issuing the card has undertaken to reimburse in return for payment by the individual. Within this category are credit cards and trading checks, but bank cheque cards are not included.

It should be noted that the issuing of unsolicited credit tokens is prohibited (s.51).

HIRE-PURCHASE, CONDITIONAL SALE AND CREDIT SALE AGREEMENTS

As indicated above, these agreements will fall within the statutory definition of consumer credit agreement where the credit provided does not exceed £15,000.

The nature of hire-purchase

A hire-purchase agreement (*see* Appendix II) is one by which a person (the hirer) is granted the possession of goods in return for a deposit and a commitment with respect to periodic payments and, in addition, is given an option to acquire the property in the goods once he has performed the agreement in accordance with its terms. It must be emphasised that a hire-purchase agreement does not amount to an agreement to buy the goods, because the hirer can if he so wishes decline to exercise the option. In *Helby* v. *Matthews* (1895), the hirer of a piano under a hire-purchase agreement pledged the article with the defendant pawnbroker. Because the hirer had not agreed to buy the piano within the meaning of s.9 of the Factors Act 1889 (for which *see* Chapter 7, p. 92), no title passed to the pawnbroker against whom the owner's claim to possession succeeded. It should be noted that it is nevertheless possible for the hirer in these cases to pass a good title to a third party under the market overt exception and also, under the provisions of the Hire-Purchase Act 1964 (*see* Chapter 7).

The Consumer Credit Act defines a hire-purchase agreement as an agreement, other than a conditional sale agreement (for which *see* below), under which:

(*a*) goods are bailed in return for periodical payments by the person to whom they are bailed; and

(*b*) the property in the goods will pass to that person if the terms of the agreement are complied with and one or more of the following occurs:

(*i*) the exercise of an option to purchase by that person,

(*ii*) the doing of any other specified act by any party to the agreement,

(*iii*) the happening of any other specified event (s.189).

This definition is appropriate where the Act applies which will be the position in many cases of course but not necessarily all: thus, the provisions of the Act do not regulate a hire-purchase agreement where the hirer is a registered company.

There are frequently (although not necessarily) three parties involved in a hire-purchase transaction and the function of each should be considered. The parties are the dealer (with whom the goods originate), the owner (usually a finance company) and the hirer. The terminology adopted in the Consumer Credit Act is credit-broker, creditor and debtor respectively. A credit-broker is a person who introduces individuals wishing to obtain credit to those carrying on businesses by which credit is provided (s.145). Instead of acting as a credit-broker, a dealer may finance a hire-purchase agreement himself in which case he assumes the function of creditor.

The dealer will usually sell the goods which are to be subject to the hire-purchase agreement to the creditor (finance company) by whom they are then bailed to the debtor (hirer) (or, alternatively, the dealer may initially become party to the hire-purchase agreement but then assign his rights as owner under the agreement to the finance company).

The liability of the dealer

Because it is with the finance company and not the dealer that the hirer contracts under the hire purchase agreement, there is no con tract of sale as such between the dealer and the hirer. Consequently, the dealer cannot be held responsible to the hirer for breach of the implied conditions as to quality and fitness which are contained in the Sale of Goods Act 1979 (*Drury* v. *Victor Buckland Ltd.* (1941)). This is not to suggest however that there can never be a contractual relationship between the dealer and the hirer since the court may be prepared to enforce collateral promises made by the dealer the consideration for which being the hirer's entry into a hire-purchase agreement with the finance company. Thus, in *Andrews* v. *Hopkinson* (1957), the defendant car dealer was held liable in respect of injury sustained by the hirer whilst driving a faulty motor vehicle, where the dealer had earlier stated that the vehicle was "a good little bus" and that he would stake his life on it.

The position of the creditor

Apart from the possible liability of the dealer at common law under a collateral contract, it should be noted that the creditor has obligations with respect to the ownership of the goods supplied, their description and quality and fitness which are implied in every hire-purchase agreement by virtue of the Supply of Goods (Implied Terms) Act 1973 (as amended) (*see* Chapter 10, p. 124). Liability for breach of these obligations may not be excluded or restricted as against a person dealing as consumer (Unfair Contract Terms Act 1977). At common law, a dealer is not normally regarded as agent of the creditor (*Branwhite* v. *Worcester Works Finance Co. Ltd.* (1969)) except that an agency relationship may be held to exist with respect to a particular matter (*Financings* v. *Stimson* (1962)—dealer deemed to be finance company's agent for the purpose of receiving the hirer's revocation of his offer to enter into a hire-purchase agreement). However, under the Consumer Credit Act, a credit-broker (defined above) is deemed to act as the creditor's agent with respect to "antecedent negotiations"; that is, negotiations conducted by the credit-broker in relation to the goods sold to the creditor before forming the subject matter of the hire-purchase agreement (s.56). Antecedent negotiations are defined to include representations made by the credit-broker to the debtor. The effect of this section is that the creditor becomes responsible as principal for statements made by the dealer about the quality and fitness of the goods.

On the matter of agency, it should perhaps be noted further that, under the Consumer Credit Act, the credit-broker is deemed to be the creditor's agent for the purpose of receiving a notice of withdrawal from a prospective regulated agreement (s.57) and also for the purpose of receiving a notice of cancellation (s.69). In addition, if the debtor wishes to exercise a right to rescind the hire-purchase agreement, the credit broker is deemed to be the creditor's agent for this purpose as well (s.102).

The position of the debtor

The contractual position of the debtor is governed by the terms of the hire-purchase agreement. If the debtor is in breach of his agreement (by, for example, not taking proper care of the goods whilst they are in his possession or failing to pay the instalments) the creditor may bring an action for damages in the usual way (*see* Chapter 16). Thus, in *Yeoman Credit Ltd.* v. *Waragowski* (1961), the owners terminated a hire-purchase agreement and repossessed the goods after non-payment of instalments by the hirer over a six month period. On their claim for damages, the owners were allowed the full hire-purchase price less the amount of deposit and the proceeds from the sale of the goods. In a similar case, though (*Overstone Ltd.* v. *Shipway* (1962), the damages awarded were reduced by a further sum in recognition of the fact that the owners were obtaining the benefit of the repayment of their capital at a time earlier than that originally provided for under the hire-purchase agreement.

Damages will only be calculated in this way where the debtor's conduct is such that he may be taken to have repudiated the agreement. In *Financings Ltd.* v. *Baldcock* (1963), after failure by the debtor to pay the initial instalments, the owners terminated the agreement and repossessed the goods. The court limited their damages to the amount of the outstanding instalments (plus interest) only because, unlike the position in the *Waragowski* case, there was no evidence that the debtor had repudiated the agreement.

The hire-purchase agreement may confer on the debtor the right to terminate the agreement prematurely in which case the owner may be given a corresponding right to recover a minimum payment. A matter of concern in this context is whether the amount agreed as the minimum payment is subject to the rules relating to penalties (for which, *see* Chapter 16, p. 197). In *Associated Distributors Ltd.* v. *Hall* (1938), the Court of Appeal decided that the question whether or not a minimum payment constituted a penalty (penalties are of course irrecoverable) was irrelevant where the debtor did not break his contract but terminated in accordance with a term of the agreement.

The rules on penalties will apply where the hire-purchase agreement provides for the application of a minimum payment clause in the event of the debtor's breach of contract (*Bridge* v. *Campbell*

Discount Co. Ltd. (1962)) and, furthermore, in order to effectively exercise a right of termination (and thereby activate the minimum payment clause unhampered by the law on penalties), it would appear that the debtor must be fully aware of the consequences of his action (*United Dominions Trust* v. *Ennis* (1968)).

A statutory right to terminate is provided by the Consumer Credit Act. Thus, the debtor under a regulated hire-purchase or conditional sale agreement (but not a credit sale agreement) may terminate the agreement at any time before final payment (s.99). If he does terminate, he may be liable to pay to the creditor the amount (if any) by which one half of the total price exceeds the aggregate of the sums paid and the sums due in respect of the total price immediately before the termination (s.100). In addition to this payment, the creditor is of course entitled to recover possession of the goods.

Apart from termination, the debtor is given the right to discharge his indebtedness under the agreement by early repayment to the creditor (s.94) and the Act makes provision for the allowance of a rebate to the debtor in such cases (s.95).

Termination and recovery of possession by the creditor
It will be apparent from earlier paragraphs that an additional course of action which may be available to the creditor following a breach by the debtor is termination of the hire-purchase agreement and recovery of the goods (as in the *Waragowski* case, above). This right of termination may arise at common law (*see* Chapter 10, p. 118) or it may be expressly provided for in the agreement itself. Furthermore, the creditor is entitled at common law to immediate possession of the goods where the debtor is guilty of some act in relation to them which is not consistent with the creditor's interest—(by, for example, disposing of the goods to some third party (*Union Transport Finance Ltd.* v. *British Car Auctions Ltd.* (1978)).

In any event, the Consumer Credit Act requires the creditor to first serve on the debtor a default notice before he may become entitled to terminate the agreement or recover possession of the goods (s.87). The default notice must specify the nature of the alleged breach by the debtor and, if the breach is capable of remedy, the action which is required to remedy it must be stated together with the date before which such action must be taken. If the breach is not capable of remedy, the default notice must specify the sum which is required as compensation for the breach and the date before which it is required to be paid (s.88). The breach is to be treated as not having occurred where the debtor takes the necessary remedial action or pays the required compensation before the date specified (s.89). This date must not be less than seven days after the date of service of the default notice (s.88).

The right of the creditor to recover possession of the goods following a breach by the debtor is further limited by the Act in that a court order must first be obtained where the debtor has paid to the creditor one third or more of the total price of the goods (referred to as "protected goods"). This protection does not apply where the agreement is terminated by the debtor (s.90).

Conditional sale and credit-sale agreements

A conditional sale agreement with respect to goods is very similar to a hire-purchase agreement but, unlike the latter, it is subject to the Sale of Goods Act 1979 because it is a contract of sale. The Consumer Credit Act defines a conditional sale agreement as an agreement for the sale of goods (or land) under which the purchase price or part of it is payable by instalments and the property in the goods (or land) is to remain in the seller (possession being given to the buyer) until such conditions as to the payment of instalments or otherwise are fulfilled (s.189). A credit-sale agreement is similarly defined by the Act in that it is an agreement for the sale of goods under which the purchase price or part of it is payable by instalments but which is not a conditional sale agreement (s.189). Under this form of agreement, the property in the goods does pass to the buyer along with possession.

Because conditional sale and credit sale agreements may fall within the definition of consumer credit agreement (*see* p. 217) they are subject generally to the same provisions of the Consumer Credit Act as affect hire-purchase agreements. However, s.90 (the retaking of protected goods) and s.99 (the debtor's right of termination) do not apply in the case of credit sale agreements.

OTHER FORMS OF CLASSIFICATION OF REGULATED CONSUMER CREDIT AGREEMENTS

Restricted- and unrestricted-use credit agreements

Restricted-use credit agreements comprise those which:

(*a*) finance a transaction between the debtor and the creditor, whether forming part of the agreement or not (e.g. hire-purchase agreements), or

(*b*) finance a transaction between a debtor and a person (the supplier) other than the creditor (as in the case of credit token agreements; *see* p. 218), or

(*c*) refinance any existing indebtedness of the debtor's (s.11).

In the above cases, the credit is made available in such a way that the debtor is unable to use it for any purpose other than that for which it is earmarked. On the other hand, if the credit can be used for a purpose not orginally stipulated for (where the cash is actually given to the debtor as in the case of a bank loan), then, even if that use amounts to a breach on the debtor's part, the agreement is known as an unrestricted-use credit agreement (s.11(3)). An agreement falling within this category is that under which a cheque card is issued by a bank.

Debtor–creditor–supplier agreements

These embrace the following:

(*a*) restricted use credit agreements where either the supplier (of goods or services) also furnishes the credit (as in the case of hire-purchase and credit sale transactions) or the creditor is a person other than the supplier but there are pre-existing arrangements (or future arrangements are contemplated) between the two (the position for instance between the issuers of credit tokens and those suppliers who have agreed to accept the tokens in exchange for goods or services); and

(*b*) unrestricted use credit agreements made by the creditor under pre-existing arrangements with the supplier in the knowledge that the credit is to be used to finance a transaction between the debtor and the supplier (s.12).

Debtor–creditor agreements

Unlike the agreements described above, there is in the case of debtor–creditor agreements no business relationship between the person providing the credit and the supplier. That is, the agreement (whether for restricted use credit or unrestricted use credit) is not made by the creditor under pre-existing arrangements (or in contemplation of future arrangements) (s.13). Thus, loans made by banks and other lenders of money in circumstances where there is no pre-existing arrangement between the lender and the supplier with whom the debtor deals fall within this category.

The importance of the presence or otherwise of a business relationship lies in the fact that the creditor under a debtor–creditor –supplier agreement may be held liable for breach by the supplier (*see* p. 226). There may also be liability in respect of antecedent negotiations (discussed in relation to hire-purchase at p. 220).

Small agreements

These are either:

(*a*) regulated consumer credit agreements where the credit does not exceed £50 (other than hire-purchase or conditional sale agreements); or

(*b*) regulated consumer hire agreements where the hirer is not required to make payments in excess of £50.

In both cases, the agreement may be unsecured or secured by a guarantee or indemnity only (s.17).

Non-commercial agreements

These are consumer credit or consumer hire agreements not made by the creditor or owner in the course of a business carried on by him (s.189).

ENTRY INTO CREDIT AND HIRE AGREEMENTS

The main statutory provisions affecting entry into regulated agreements are as follows.

(*a*) Regulations may be made with respect to (*i*) the information which must be disclosed to the debtor or hirer before a regulated agreement is made and (*ii*) the form and content of documents embodying regulated agreements (ss.55 and 60). (*See* the Consumer Credit (Agreements) Regulations 1983.)

(*b*) The agreement document must contain all the terms of the agreement (other than implied terms) and be signed by the debtor or hirer and by or on behalf of the creditor or owner (s.61).

(*c*) The debtor or hirer is entitled to copies of the agreement (ss.62 and 63).

(*d*) If the agreement is one which may be cancelled by the debtor or hirer under s.67 (*see* below), there must be supplied to him in the prescribed form a notice of his rights in this respect (s.64).

(*e*) A regulated agreement is not properly executed if the various requirements relating to its formulation are not observed; in this case the agreement may be enforced against the debtor or hirer only by court order (s.65).

(*f*) The debtor or hirer has in certain circumstances a "cooling off" period; that is, the right to cancel by notice a regulated agreement which he has entered into at premises other than those at which the creditor or owner is carrying on any business (e.g. agreements signed at home). This right will normally be exercisable until the end of the fifth day following that on which the debtor or hirer received a copy of the agreement (ss.67 69).

(*g*) The effect of cancellation is that sums paid by the debtor or hirer became repayable and those which would have become payable under the agreement cease to be payable. Further, in the case of a debtor–creditor–supplier agreement, sums paid by the creditor to the supplier became repayable to the creditor (s.70). For his part, the debtor or hirer comes under an obligation to restore any goods which have been acquired under the agreement, pending which reasonable care must be taken of them (s.72).

(*h*) The creditor may be liable in respect of antecedent negotiations (*i*) conducted by a credit-broker in relation to goods eventually forming the subject matter of a debtor–creditor–supplier agreement, or (*ii*) conducted by a supplier in relation to a transaction financed by a debtor–creditor–supplier agreement (s.56, discussed also in relation to hire-purchase agreements at p. 220).

(*i*) With the exception of s.56, the above provisions do not affect (*i*) non-commercial agreements or (*ii*) debtor–creditor agreements which enable the debtor to overdraw on a current account (s.74 as amended by the Banking Act 1979) and, with the exception of ss.55 and 56, the provisions outlined do not apply to small debtor–creditor–supplier agreements for restricted-use credit (e.g. small credit-sale agreements).

MATTERS ARISING DURING THE CURRENCY OF CREDIT OR HIRE AGREEMENTS

Various provisions relating to the operation of regulated agreements have been considered in the context of hire-purchase transactions (*see* pp. 000–00). The matters already discussed are the statutory right of termination (s.99), early repayment (s.94), default notices (s.87) and protected goods (s.90).

As noted earlier, ss.90 and 99 are inapplicable in the case of credit-sale agreements but s.94 applies to all consumer credit agreements and s.87 applies to consumer hire agreements.
Other matters to note are as follows.

(*a*) In the case of debtor–creditor–supplier agreements (e.g. credit token agreements) any claim which the debtor has against the supplier of goods or services in respect of a misrepresentation or breach of contract may be asserted also against the creditor who, with the supplier, becomes jointly and severally liable (s.75). (Claims under non-commercial agreements and a claim relating to any single item to which the supplier has attached a cash price not exceeding £30 or more than £30,000 are excepted from this provision.)

(*b*) With the exception of non-commercial agreements, a creditor under a regulated agreement for fixed sum credit (*see* p. 217) must, at the request of the debtor, provide information as to:

(*i*) the total sum already paid under the agreement,

(*ii*) the total sum which has become payable but which remains unpaid, and

(*iii*) the total sum which is to become payable under the agreement.

A similar duty with respect to the provision of information devolves on the creditor under a running account credit agreement and the owner under a regulated consumer hire agreement (ss. 77–79).

EXEMPT AGREEMENTS

We have seen that various provisions of the Consumer Credit Act do not apply to certain categories of regulated agreement. In addition, the Act specifically provides that a consumer credit agreement is exempt from regulation where the creditor is a local authority, a building society, or a body specified by order by the Secretary of State (being either an insurance company, a friendly society or one of several other bodies) and the credit agreement is secured by a land mortgage for the purpose of financing, *inter alia*, the purchase of land (s.16 and Consumer Credit (Exempt Agreements) Order 1980).

Also exempted from regulation are:

(*a*) debtor–creditor–supplier agreements for fixed sum credit under which the number of payments to be made by the debtor does not exceed four (conditional sale and hire-purchase agreements are not included within this exemption);

(*b*) debtor–creditor–supplier agreements for running account credit where the whole amount of the credit provided in any one period is repayable by not more than one payment;

(*c*) debtor-creditor–supplier agreements to finance the purchase of land under which the number of payments made by the debtor does not exceed four;

(*d*) debtor–creditor agreements where the rate of the total charge for credit does not exceed thirteen per cent;

(*e*) agreements made in connection with overseas trade and the debtor receives the credit in the course of a business carried on by him;

(*f*) consumer hire agreements made with gas, electricity or water undertakings in respect of the hire of the meters or metering equipment and those made with the Post Office in connection with telecommunications apparatus (Consumer Credit (Exempt Agreements) Order 1980).

It should be noted that, although the above agreements are classified as exempt, they are nonetheless subject to those provisions of the Consumer Credit Act dealing with extortionate credit bargains (considered in the next section).

EXTORTIONATE CREDIT BARGAINS

Any credit agreement (irrespective of amount) may be reopened by the court where the overall bargain:

(*a*) requires an individual (the "debtor") to make payments which are grossly exhorbitant, or

(*b*) otherwise grossly contravenes the ordinary principles of fair dealing.

The matters to be taken into account in determining whether a bargain is extortionate include interest rates; personal factors relating to the debtor such as age, experience, state of health and degree of financial pressure; factors relating to the creditor such as the degree of risk accepted by him; and any other relevant considerations (s.137 and 138). A high rate of interest in itself does not necessarily give rise to an extortionate credit bargain since even a rate of 48 per cent may be fair in the particular circumstances of the case (*Ketley* v. *Scott* (1981)). Furthermore, the statute presupposes some inequality of bargaining power which is taken advantage of by the lender. If the terms of the loan are not oppressive or objectionable and the borrower is of full age and capacity the transaction will not be reopened (*Wills* v. *Wood* (1984)).

On reopening the credit agreement, the court has power to:

(*a*) set aside the whole or part of any obligation to which the debtor is subject,

(*b*) require the creditor to repay sums paid by the debtor, and

(*c*) alter the terms of the credit agreement (s.139).

LICENSING

With some exceptions, a licence must be obtained from the Director-General of Fair Trading in order to carry on a consumer credit business or consumer hire business (s.21) otherwise an offence is committed (s.39). The licence may be a standard licence (i.e. issued by the Director to a named person) or it may take the form of a group licence (i.e. covering such persons and activities as are described in the licence) (s.22).

An applicant for a standard licence must satisfy the Director that he is a fit person to engage in the activities to which the licence relates and further, the name by which he proposes to be licensed must not be misleading or otherwise undesirable (s.25). The Director is empowered to revoke or suspend a licence at any time during its currency (s.32).

SEEKING BUSINESS

The Act provides for the regulation of the form and content of advertisements which indicate that the advertiser is willing to provide credit or to enter into an agreement for the hiring of goods by him (s.44). Detailed requirements are in fact contained in the Consumer Credit (Advertisements) Regulations 1980. Thus, certain categories of credit advertisement must show the cash price of the goods or service the acquisition of which the credit is intended to finance, the rate of the total charge for credit and the total amount which the debtor will be required to pay.

An offence is committed if an advertisement to which the Act applies conveys false or misleading information (s.46).

A credit advertisement is not subject to the provisions of the Act where it indicates:

(a) that the credit provided must exceed £15,000, and that no security is required, or the security is to consist of property other than land, or

(b) that the credit is available only to a body corporate (s.43).

SUMMARY

On completion of this chapter you should be able to:

(a) Understand the nature of and differences between hire-purchase, credit sale and conditional sale agreements.

(b) Define the term "regulated agreement" and outline the provisions of the Consumer Credit Act 1974 relating to such agreements.

(c) Understand the different methods of classifying regulated agreements.

SELF-ASSESSMENT QUESTIONS

(Relevant page numbers are given in brackets.)

1. What is a consumer credit agreement? (Page 217)

2. Distinguish between hire-purchase and credit sale agreements. (Pages 218 and 223)

3. Outline the position of the debtor under a hire-purchase agreement. (Pages 221–3)

4. Can a penalty clause ever be effective in relation to contracts of hire purchase? (Page 221)

5. Define the following: (*a*) restricted-use credit agreement; (*b*) debtor–creditor agreement; (*c*) conditional sale agreement. (Pages 223–4)

6. What powers does the court have in relation to extortionate credit bargains? (Page 228)

Assignments

1. On Monday, Fred advertises reconditioned washing machines for sale at £50 each in a local newspaper. In the advertisement, it is stated that the appliances will be available at Fred's warehouse the following day and that each purchaser will be given a free bottle of wine. At midday, Susan is told that she may have a washing machine but no wine is available. Later that day, Irene and Pat are told that the stock of advertised washing machines is exhausted. Both are offered a different make of washing machine for £60. Irene accepts the offer but Pat rejects it. Mary takes delivery of her washing machine but, some days afterwards, finds that it will not heat water as the water heating element is faulty. On raising the matter with Fred, Mary is told that the washing machine is still "usable" since she can obtain hot water from her domestic supply.

As the parties' legal adviser:

(*a*) Advise Fred on his contractual obligations (if any) to each of Mary, Susan, Irene and Pat.

(*b*) Advise Mary as to the remedies (if any) available to her against Fred with respect to the defective washing machine. (Chapters 9, 10 and 16)

2. Tim purchases a new radio for £20 from Bill, a radio and television dealer, having been assured by Bill that the radio is suitable for reception on all wavebands. Before leaving Bill's shop, Tim notices a sign on the counter advertising a scheme Bill has for accepting goods back and repairing them if they prove to be faulty. An additional charge of £1 is payable for this service. Tim pays Bill £1 and is given in return a receipt which contains a clause stating as follows: "Apart from repair, no liability can be accepted for any statement or breach of any obligation relating to the condition of the goods sold." On using the radio, Tim discovers that it is unsuitable for "short-wave" reception and, furthermore, it has a faulty tuner. Tim returns the radio to Bill's shop and demands a refund. Bill insists that Tim's only legal remedy is the right to have the radio repaired.

(*a*) Explain to Bill the legal significance (if any) of his statement to Tim regarding the suitability of the radio and advise him whether he is entitled to rely on the clause in the receipt in resisting any claim made by Tim. Would your advice in the latter instance differ if the clause were contained in a notice situated in a prominent place in the shop and Tim's attention were drawn to it by Bill before the purchase of the radio?

(b) Advise Tim on the courses of action which are available to him and, in particular, whether he may claim a refund of the purchase price. (Chapters 10, 11, 16 and 17)

3. Ben is the proprietor of a petrol filling station. He has a mortgage agreement with the Happy Petrol Co. which includes provisions (a) requiring Ben to purchase all his supplies of petrol and oils from Happy Petrol for fifteen years; and (b) prohibiting Ben from reselling these products at prices lower than those specified by Happy Petrol. Ben's business is very slack because his competitors are charging lower prices, therefore he reduces his prices to a much more competitive level. Happy Petrol retaliate by threatening to cut off supplies totally if Ben does not keep to the agreement. Ben is considering obtaining his supplies of petrol and oils from another source.

(a) Advise the Happy Petrol Co. on the legality of the provisions in the mortgage agreement and indicate the remedy they might seek to compel compliance by Ben with these provisions.

(b) Advise Ben on the legality of the Happy Petrol Co.'s proposed course of action in withdrawing supplies.

(c) Assuming that the happy Petrol Co. have similar agreements with filling station proprietors in other member states of the Common Market, consider the circumstances in which European Community law might be infringed. (Chapters 11, 16 and 17)

4. Arthur is a heating engineer. He enters into separate lump sum contracts to install central heating systems in factories belonging to Tom, Frank and Harold. During the course of installing the heating system for Tom, Arthur claims an additional payment to cover unforeseen costs. There is nothing in the contract allowing for this but Tom agrees to make the payment because his employees are threatening to strike unless conditions at the factory improve and he does not want any disruption. Arthur starts but is unable to complete the work for Frank because the latter's factory is totally destroyed by fire. Arthur *is* able to complete the work at Harold's factory but the boiler he installs is faulty and is incapable of heating the premises to the levels of temperature required by current legislation. Following the above events, Tom demands that Arthur refund the additional payment and Frank and Harold refuse to pay anything at all.

(*a*) Consider whether Arthur is entitled to any payment under each of the contracts made with Tom, Frank and Harold.

(*b*) Advise Tom on whether he is entitled to recover back the additional payment made to Arthur. (Chapters 11 and 12)

5. Henry is looking for a plot of land near the south coast on which to build a bungalow for his retirement. He instructs Tony, a local estate agent, to find and acquire a suitable plot but tells Tony that he is to pay no more than £2,000. Henry agrees to pay Tony's "usual" commission. Tony is certain that a plot of land owned by his friend, Dave, will be suitable and, on Henry's behalf, agrees in writing to purchase the plot from Dave for £3,000. Dave pays Tony £100 for arranging the transaction. At first, Henry is both pleased with and agreeable to the arrangement but, on finding out about the payment of £100 by Dave, changes his mind and tells Tony that he wishes to have nothing further to do with the matter.

(*a*) Explain to Dave whether the circumstances give rise to a binding contract with Henry.

(*b*) Explain to Henry whether he is obliged to pay Tony's usual commission which he has been advised amounts to £500. (Chapter 14)

6. Sid retails furniture and household appliances. He contracts to sell a washing machine to Fred for £200; Fred pays a deposit of £50 and undertakes to pay the balance at the rate of £15 per month. In addition, Sid hires a suite of furniture to Susan for £500. This sum is repayable by instalments over a two year period at the end of which ownership of the furniture will pass to Susan.

(*a*) Identify clearly the nature of the agreements made by Sid with Fred and Susan, explaining the differences between them and indicating whether the agreements have anything in common.

(*b*) If Susan were to default under her agreement, advise Sid on the remedies available to him if Susan had (*i*) repaid £400, or (*ii*) repaid only £100.

(*c*) Explain to Sid where the loss would lie if both the washing machine and furniture were damaged before completion of the payments by Fred and Susan. (Chapter 18—See also Appendix II)

CHAPTER NINETEEN

Non-Contractual Liability

CHAPTER OBJECTIVES

After studying this chapter you should be able to:
* discuss the forms of liability which may devolve on a business organisation other than that following a breach of contract; and
* consider the position of suppliers of goods and services under the Trade Descriptions Act 1968.

INTRODUCTION

Tort

In earlier chapters we have considered how liability to another person can arise by the breach of obligations voluntarily undertaken; the liability of a seller of goods for breach of the implied obligations of fitness for purpose and merchantable quality is just one illustration of this (*see* Chapter 10). We are concerned in this chapter with categories of liability which may arise independently of contract. Thus, in addition to whatever might be his position in contract, a supplier of goods may be liable in the tort of negligence to those persons who suffer harm as the result of defects in such goods. A case in point is *Malfroot* v. *Noxal Ltd.* (1935). The defendant repairers fitted a side-car to the plaintiff's motor cycle but did so carelessly. The side-car subsequently broke loose and both the plaintiff and a passenger were injured. The defendants were clearly liable to the plaintiff in contract since it was he who had commissioned the work but they were also found to be liable to the plaintiff and the (non-contracting) passenger in the tort of negligence.

The same set of circumstances may then give rise to different headings of liability. This point is further illustrated by *Esso Petroleum Co. Ltd.* v. *Mardon* (1976). In this case, M was induced to take a lease of a petrol filling station following a representation by one of Esso's representatives that the anticipated annual turnover of petrol would be 200,000 gallons. The actual sales of petrol were nowhere near this figure therefore M claimed damages. No remedy could be awarded under the Misrepresentation Act, 1967 (*see* Chapter 11, p. 000) because the representation complained of was made before the Act came into force. Nevertheless, the Court of Appeal decided that Esso should compensate M:

(*a*) for their breach of a collateral promise (these are discussed in Chapter 10, p. 116), and

(*b*) in negligence for their breach of a duty to take reasonable care with respect to the accuracy of the statement.

The importance of establishing this alternative (tortious) category is especially apparent in those cases where there is lacking the necessary relationship of privity to found an action for breach of contract (this was in fact the position of the passenger in *Noxal's* case, above). It should be noted though that, whereas a successful action in contract is dependent simply on establishing non-performance or some other breach by the defendant, an action in tort will (with some exceptions) only succeed provided the defendant is shown to be at fault. This latter qualification is particularly evident with respect to the tort of negligence. Thus, in *Daniels* v. *R. White and Sons Ltd. and Tarbard* (1938), the plaintiff purchased a bottle of lemonade which contained carbolic acid. The defendant manufacturers were not liable in negligence because they were found to have taken reasonable care. However, despite the fact that she had not been careless, the retailer from whom the product had actually been purchased was liable to the plaintiff in contract for breach of the implied obligation of merchantable quality (*see also Frost* v. *Aylesbury Dairy Co. Ltd.*, Chapter 10, p. 123).

Crime

In his business dealings, a person may also be subject to criminal liability. A good example occurs under the Trade Descriptions Act 1968 which creates various offences with respect to false statements and descriptions accompanying the supply of goods and services (*see* later in this chapter).

Another statute which imposes criminal liability is the Consumer Safety Act 1978. This Act empowers the Secretary of State to make "safety regulations" covering a wide range of matters relating to the supply of goods including their composition, contents, design and provisions for testing and inspection (s.1). The Secretary of State can also make orders and notices prohibiting the supply of goods which he considers to be unsafe (s.3). It is a criminal offence to infringe a prohibition notice or order or any provision in the regulations prohibiting the supply of particular goods (ss.2 and 3).

What is particularly interesting about this statute is that any obligation imposed by a regulation or by a prohibition order or notice is deemed to be a duty owed to any person who is likely to be affected by the non-observance of such obligation. Consequently, the person who is in breach may be liable civilly (i.e. tortiously) to the person affected and such liability may not be excluded or restricted by agreement to the contrary (s.6).

Personal and vicarious liability

The liability which may devolve on a business organisation may be a consequence of what is to be regarded as its own personal wrongdoing or such liability may arise as the result of the wrongdoing of another person; that is, vicariously (*see* below). Personal liability is easily seen and appreciated where the business is controlled by a single proprietor who may himself be directly responsible for the tortious or criminal act in question (for instance, a small shopkeeper infringing the Trade Descriptions Act). It is also possible, however, for personal liability to come about as the result of the act of another. Thus, in *Clode* v. *Barnes* (1974), the defendant was convicted of supplying goods to which a false trade description had been applied contrary to s.1 of the Trade Descriptions Act 1968. He knew nothing about the matter because the wrongful act of applying the false trade description (a false representation as to mileage) had actually been committed by a co-partner in the firm. Nevertheless, the defendant could be regarded as having sold the goods and was therefore technically in breach of the statutory provision.

Where the wrongful act is a tort, all the partners in a firm are liable where the tort is authorised by them or is committed by one of their number in the ordinary course of the partnership business (s.10, Partnership Act 1890, and *see* Chapter 2).

Incorporated business organisations such as registered companies will in certain circumstances assume personal liability despite the fact that, as artificial beings, they must act through natural persons. In *Lennard's Carrying Co. Ltd.* v. *Asiatic Petroleum Co. Ltd.* (1915), the carelessness of a person who was the "directing mind" of the appellant shipping company was sufficient to render the company itself at fault with respect to damage to the respondent's cargo. Again, in *R.* v. *I.C.R. Haulage Ltd.* (1944), a company was convicted of conspiring with other persons to defraud (despite the absence of a dishonest mind). The reason for the conviction was that the acts of the company's fraudulent managing director were deemed to be those of the company. It should be emphasised that, in the aforementioned cases, the company's liability is not vicarious therefore the officer, agent or employee concerned must clearly be somebody of sufficient status within the organisation who can be identified with the company (for example, the company's managing director or some other person to whom managerial functions have been delegated). In *Tesco Supermarkets Ltd.* v. *Nattrass* (1972) the House of Lords decided that the relevant category excluded the shop managers in a supermarket chain therefore the appellants could avail themselves of a defence in the Trade Descriptions Act 1968 by establishing that the offence with which they were charged was due to the act of *another* person (*see* later). It may be noted that, under the Trade Descriptions Act, if the commission of an offence by a body corporate is shown to have been done with the consent of a director, manager or other officer or is attributable to such person's neglect, then that person is guilty of the offence also and may be proceeded against accordingly (s.20).

In the absence of personal liability for a wrongful act, the only other way in which liability may devolve is vicariously. Thus, an employer may be vicariously liable for the tortious acts of his employees. This responsibility for another's wrongdoing arises by virtue of the relationship created by the contract of service. The pre-conditions are:

(*a*) the person employed must be a servant and not an independent contractor, and

(*b*) the offending tort must be committed in the course of the servant's employment.

Whether or not an employee is a servant in a given case depends very much on the particular facts but the various factors which have been considered relevant for determining the question have included the degree of control exercised by the employer over the execution of the employee's work, the relationship between the employee and the business organisation, and the economic reality of the situation (*Argent* v. *Minister of Social Security and Another* (1968)). In some cases, the matter is beyond doubt. Thus, a clear distinction can normally be drawn between a chauffeur (a servant) and a taxidriver (an independent contractor *vis-à-vis* the employing passenger).

A servant will be deemed to act in the course of his employment despite the fact that he discharges his authorised duties carelessely (*Century Insurance Co. Ltd.* v. *Northern Ireland Road Transport Board* (1942)—employee lit a cigerette whilst delivering a consignment of petrol to a garage) and even an express prohibition may not be sufficient to prevent the employer becoming liable for his servants' wrongdoings. Thus, in *Rose* v. *Plenty and Another*

(1976), an employer was held to be vicariously liable for his milk roundsman's careless driving of a milk float which resulted in injury to a child passenger on the vehicle. The roundsman was held to be acting in the course of his employment in causing the injury despite that the practice of using children to help with the deliveries had been prohibited by the employer.

LIABILITY IN TORT FOR DEFECTIVE PRODUCTS

A manufacturer of dangerous or defective products may be liable in the tort of negligence to any person who eventually acquires them whether as purchaser or otherwise. The relevant principle was established in *Donoghue* v. *Stevenson* (1932) where Lord Atkin stated that a manufacturer owes a duty to a consumer to take care in the preparation and production of the goods "which he sells in such a form as to show that he intends them to reach the ultimate consumer in the form in which they left him with no reasonable possibility of intermediate examination . . ." In that case, a friend of the plaintiff purchased an opaque bottle of ginger beer which after being opened and partly consumed, was found to contain the remains of a snail. As a result of her experience, the plaintiff suffered shock and personal discomfort. The House of Lords decided that she had a cause of action against the defendant manufacturer.

The duty established in this decision is not confined to manufacturers *per se* but binds repairers and other persons who supply goods in the course of their business (*see*, for instance, *Malfroot* v. *Noxal Ltd.* (1935), p. 234). Furthermore, the category of individuals to whom the duty is owed embraces other people in addition to those who actually enter into contracts of purchase. This point is illustrated by *Stennett* v. *Hancock and Peters* (1939) where a pedestrian successfully recovered damages for injury caused by a wheel flange which had become detached from a motor vehicle after having been carelessly fitted by the defendants. Again, in *Hill* v. *James Crow (Cases) Ltd.* (1978), the manufacturer of a badly constructed wooden case was held liable for injuries sustained by a lorry driver when the case collapsed whilst the latter was standing on it.

An important point to bear in mind in this discussion is that a manufacturers' liability for injury, loss or damage caused by defective goods is not (as the law presently stands) automatic or strict. Before liability can be successfully established, the plaintiff must show that the harm was caused by the defendant's failure to take reasonable care (*see Daniel* v. *R. White and Sons Ltd. and Tarbard*

(1938), p. 235, and compare the position of a supplier of defective goods under the law of contract). In *Evans* v. *Triplex Safety Glass Co. Ltd.* (1936) a windscreen shattered a year after its production and injured the plaintiff and the occupants of his motor vehicle. An action against the windscreen manufacturers in negligence failed because it was possible that other factors might have caused the defect (for instance, bad fitting by the manufacturers of the vehicle).

There has been criticism in recent years of the fact that liability for defective products is fault based and various proposals for reform of the law have emerged. One such proposal is embodied in an EEC draft Directive on Products Liability which aims to impose strict liability on producers for damage caused by defective articles.

LIABILITY UNDER THE TRADE DESCRIPTIONS ACT 1968

In this section we are concerned with the principal provisions of the Trade Descriptions Act dealing with the control of false trade descriptions and other misstatements relating to the supply of goods and services.

The application of a false trade description

It is a criminal offence for any person in the course of a trade or business to:

(*a*) apply a false trade description to any goods, or

(*b*) to supply or offer to supply any goods to which a false trade description is applied (s.1). (Any difficulty with respect to the distinction between an offer and an invitation to treat (*see* Chapter 9) is avoided in that the exposing of goods for supply is deemed to amount to an offer to supply them (s.6)).

An offence under (*b*) will, for instance, arise where a motor vehicle is sold with an incorrect mileometer reading (whether the dealer is innocent in the matter or not) unless the false reading is sufficiently "neutralised" by a disclaimer (*Taylor* v. *Smith* (1974)). The definition of the offence requires that the trade description must be false to a material degree (s.3) and, further, the description must be related to any of such matters as the quantity or size of the goods, the method of their manufacture, their composition, fitness for purpose, strength and previous history (s.2). If therefore an attempt is made to conceal rust damage in a motor vehicle by means of plastic filler and paint, this will amount to a false description or indication of the strength of that vehicle (*Cottee* v. *Douglas Seaton (Used Cars) Ltd.* (1972)). In *British Gas Corporation* v.

Lubbock (1974), the court decided that there existed a false trade description relating to the composition of goods where a brochure in the defendant's showroom indicated that a particular make of gas cooker was supplied with a hand ignitor whereas the ignitor had in fact been withdrawn because of its unsuitability.

Liability under s.1 is strict in that, subject to s.24 (*see* below), a person may be guilty of an offence despite his lack of knowledge that a particular description is false (as in *Taylor* v. *Smith* above). It is, however, a condition of liability that a supplier of goods must be aware that a trade description has been applied to the goods (*Cottee* v. *Douglas Seaton Ltd.* (1972)—dealer unaware that defects in the car he was selling had been disguised by the previous owner).

No offence is committed if the application of a false description is unrelated to the provision of goods. In *Wycombe Marsh Garages Ltd.* v. *Fowler* (1972) a vehicle tester refused to award a certificate because he considered that the tyres of the vehicle under examination were unsuitable. Although the tester's decision was subsequently found to be unjustified, it did not amount to a false trade description because there were no goods provided in the course of trade to which the description could be applied. Further, no offence was committed in *Davies* v. *Sumner* (1984) where a person who used a motor vehicle in the course of his business as a courier failed to disclose the true mileage when exchanging the vehicle for a new one. There was no sufficient regularity of "trading in" vehicles to give rise to an act in the course of a trade or business.

Where goods are provided in the course of trade, the offending statement must be made in connection with their sale or supply and not afterwards (*Wickens Motors Ltd.* v. *Hall* (1972)—false statement as to fitness of motor vehicle made more than a month after its sale to a customer).

Disclaimers

Liability for breach of s.1 may be avoided by the use of a notice of disclaimer, but only if its effect is to cancel out the false trade description. Thus, in the case of the mileage of motor vehicles, a disclaimer to be effective must be of "equal power and penetration as the statement on the mileometer which it seeks to counter" (Lord Widgery CJ in *Waltham Forest L.B.C.* v. *T. G. Wheatley (Central Garages) Ltd.* (1978)). The point seems to be that it must be made absolutely clear to a customer that the offending statement should not be relied on. Thus, in *R.* v. *Hammertons Cars Ltd.* (1977), the Court of Appeal decided that a statement in small print in a contract for the sale of a motor vehicle was not adequate to displace the effect of a false mileometer reading.

Statements relating to the price of goods

False or misleading statements with respect to the price at which goods are offered for sale may give rise to liability under the Act. Thus, it is an offence for a person to give a false indication that the price at which he is offering the goods for supply is equal to or less than:

(*a*) a recommended price, or

(*b*) the price at which the goods were previously offered by him (s.11(1)).

It is also an offence for a person offering to supply goods to indicate that they are being offered at a price less than that at which they are in fact being offered (s.11(2)). An indication that the price of the goods was previously higher is deemed to be one that the goods were offered at the higher price within the preceding six months for a continuous period of not less than twenty-eight days, unless there is a statement by the seller to the contrary (s.11(3)).

A case illustrating the application of s.11(2) is *Doble* v. *David Greig Ltd.* (1972). A retailer displayed bottles of fruit juice on which was marked his selling price. The label of each bottle also carried a statement by the manufacturer that a deposit was repayable on the return of the bottle but, at the cash desk, there was a notice to the effect that the bottles were not returnable and that no deposit was charged at the time of purchase. The court decided that the display of the goods amounted to an offer (*see* s.6 above) and also an indication that was likely to be taken as an indication that the goods were being offered at a price less than the price marked on the bottles by the retailer. Similarly, in *Read Bros. Cycles (Leyton) Ltd.* v. *Waltham Forest L.B.C.* (1978) the defendants advertised for sale a motor cycle at a price of £540 (less than the list price of £580). A purchaser offered his own vehicle in part-exchange but the defendants sought to charge the full list price on the basis that their advertisement applied only to cash and hire-purchase sales. In deciding that an offence under s.11(2) was committed, the court stated that the relevant question was what would be understood by an ordinary person on seeing the advertisement. If the defendants wished to restrict the terms of their offer, this should have been made clear.

Statements relating to the provision of services

These are regulated by s.14 of the Act. This makes it an offence for any person in the course of a trade or business:

(*a*) to make a statement which he knows to be false, or

(*b*) recklessly to make a statement which is false in regard to the provision of any services, accommodation or facilities, the nature of such provision or related matters.

This offence can in certain cases give rise to strict liability. Thus, in *Wings Ltd.* v. *Ellis* (1984), a holiday was booked on the basis of a tour operator's brochure which in error contained a statement that certain accommodation was air-conditioned. The tour operator had earlier discovered the mistake and had made strenuous efforts to amend the many copies of the brochure since it would have been impossible to withdraw every one. Nevertheless, the House of Lords decided that an offence was committed when the unamended brochure was read by the holiday-maker concerned since, at that time, the tour operator knew that it contained an incorrect statement. However, in *Coupé* v. *Guyett* (1973), a question for consideration was whether the sole proprietor of a motor repairer's business could be guilty under s.14 in respect of reckless statements made by G, the person in effective control of the business. The court held that the mental state of the employee could not be attributed to the proprietor who had not therefore committed the offence (the position is to be contrasted with that obtaining under s.1 where it is possible for a person to be held to have personally committed the offence despite that the actual "wrongdoer" is another person—*see Clode* v. *Barnes* (1974), p. 236, above).

A statement made regardless of whether it is true or false is deemed to be made recklessly (s.14(2)(*b*)) and, for this purpose, it is not necessary that the person making the statement should act dishonestly (*M.F.I. Warehouses Ltd.* v. *Nattrass* (1973)). Liability under the section is nevertheless dependent on the making of a statement of fact since, provided they are honest statements of intention, the Act does not regulate promises or predictions about future events (*R.* v. *Sunair Holidays Ltd.* (1973)—statement in tour operator's brochure concerning proposed facilities at hotel in Spain not a breach of the Act when the facilities failed to materialise). (On this point, *see* the discussion of misrepresentation in Chapter 11, p. 130).

Finally, it may be noted that the fact of a conviction for a particular offence does not necessarily preclude subsequent convictions arising out of the same circumstances. Thus, in *R.* v. *Thomson Holidays Ltd.* (1974), the defendants were convicted of making false statements in their brochure with respect to (existing) facilities at an hotel in Greece. Some time later, they were prosecuted following complaints arising out of the same edition of the brochure and in relation to the same hotel. The Court of Appeal held that there could be more than one conviction in such circumstances because the number of offences was determined by the number of readers of the brochure.

Offences due to the fault of another and defences

If the commission by one person of an offence under the Act is due to the act or default of some other person that other person shall be guilty of the offence and may be charged and convicted irrespective of whether proceedings are taken against the first person (s.23). A prosecution under this provision will fail if the first person is found not to have committed an offence despite the fact that the person prosecuted might have been successfully convicted under some other section.

In *Coupé* v. *Guyett*, for example (*see* above), an employee who had made a false statement with respect to work he had done to a customer's vehicle was prosecuted under s.23 on the basis that his employer was in breach of s.14 (recklessly making a false statement) and that the commission of the offence was due to the employee's act or default. As we noted earlier, the court decided that the employer was not guilty of an offence under s.14, therefore it followed that the action against the employee should fail.

A person will have a defence under the Act provided it can be shown (*inter alia*):

(*a*) that the commission of the offence with which he is charged was due to a mistake or to another person's act or default; and

(*b*) that he took all reasonable precautions and exercised all due diligence to avoid committing the offence (s.24(1)).

This defence was relied on successfully in *Tesco Supermarkets Ltd.* v. *Nattrass* (1972) where, in connection with a prosecution under s.11(2) of the Act (indication that goods are being offered at a price less than that at which they are in fact offered) the defendants established to the court's satisfaction that:

(*a*) their commision of the offence was due to the act or default of one of their branch managers (*see* p. 237 above); and

(*b*) they had exercised due diligence by virtue of the system of supervision which existed within the organisation.

The taking of reasonable precautions and the exercise of due diligence was not established however in *Barker* v. *Hargreaves* (1981) where a dealer relied simply on the award of a motor vehicle test certificate in order to advertise a defective vehicle as "in good condition throughout". The s.24 defence was not resorted to in *Wings Ltd.* v. *Ellis* (above).

In addition to the above, a dealer who is charged with supplying or offering to supply goods to which a false trade description is applied will have a defence if he can prove that he did not know, and could not with reasonable diligence have ascertained, that the goods did not conform to the description or that the description had been applied to them (s.24(3)).

Enforcement

The duty of enforcing the provisions of the Trade Descriptions Act is imposed on local trading standards authorities (s.26) but, with certain exceptions, notice of a proposal to institute legal proceedings, together with a summary of the facts on which the charges are to be founded, must be given to the Director General of Fair Trading and the commencement of proceedings postponed either for twenty-eight days or until the Director has acknowledged the notification (s.130, Fair Trading Act 1973).

COMPENSATION ORDERS

It should be noted that where a person is convicted of a criminal offence, the court may, in addition to imposing other sanctions, make an order requiring him to pay compensation for any personal injury, loss or damage resulting from that offence (s.35, Powers of Criminal Courts Act 1973). A compensation order was, for example, made by the court on the occasion of the second conviction in *R.* v. *Thomson Holidays Ltd.* (above). In the case of a conviction by magistrates, the amount of compensation is limited to £1,000 (s.40, Magistrates' Courts Act 1980).

SUMMARY

On completion of this chapter you should be able to:

(*a*) Understand the difference between contractual and tortious liability in relation to the supply of goods and services.

(*b*) Appreciate the distinction between personal liability and that which may devolve vicariously.

(*c*) Describe the principal provisions of the Trade Descriptions Act 1968.

SELF-ASSESSMENT QUESTIONS

(Relevant page numbers are given in brackets.)

1. Why might it be important for a consumer to be able to establish liability in tort? (Page 235)

2. What are the main provisions of the Consumer Safety Act 1978? (Page 235)

3. Can a corporation be personally liable in tort and crime? (Page 236)

4. What conditions must be met for a person to be vicariously responsible for the wrongs of another? (Page 237)

5. To what extent may liability under the Trade Descriptions Act 1968 be described as "strict"? (Pages 240 and 242)

Assignment

Martin is a manufacturer of electrical goods. He supplies a batch of electric kettles direct to Tony, a retailer, but is unaware that they are faulty and unsafe. Jonah, one of Martin's employees and senior supervisor, failed to ensure that the kettles were properly insulated. In the window of Tony's shop is a large notice which reads: "Sale—all prices slashed". A customer, Linda, purchases one of Martin's kettles but is asked by a shop assistant to pay the manufacturer's recommended price because, she is told, the kettles are not included in Tony's offer. On using the kettle at home, Linda is electrocuted and suffers serious injuries.

(*a*) Explain to Linda whether Martin or Tony (or both) may be liable for her injuries and indicate what the nature of such liability would be in each case.

(*b*) Explain to Martin whether he could put forward as a defence to a claim by Linda the fact that Jonah is primarily liable for the defect in the kettle and that he (Martin) should not be held to blame.

(*c*) Advise Tony on whether he also could rely on Jonah's oversight with respect to the kettle.

(*d*) Consider whether any action could be taken with respect to the sale notice in the window of Tony's shop and, if so, indicate whether such action would be likely to succeed. (Chapter 19)

Appendix I

FORM OF MEMORANDUM OF ASSOCIATION OF A PUBLIC COMPANY

(*Sched. 1, Companies Act 1980*)

PART I

A PUBLIC COMPANY LIMITED BY SHARES

1. The name of the company is "The Western Steam Packet, public limited company".

2. The company is to be a public company.

3. The registered office of the company will be situated in England and Wales.

4. The objects for which the company is established are, "the conveyance of passengers and goods in ships or boats between such places as the company may from time to time determine, and the doing of all such things as are incidental or conducive to the attainment of the above object".

5. The liability of the members is limited.

6. The share capital of the company is £50,000 divided into 50,000 shares of £1 each.

We, the several persons whose names and addresses are subscribed are desirous of being formed into a company, in pursuance of this memorandum of association, and we respectively agree to take the number of shares in the capital of the company set opposite our respective names.

Names, Addresses and Descriptions of Subscribers			*Number of shares taken by each Subscriber*
"1. Thomas Jones	in the county of	merchant	1
2. Andrew Smith	in the county of	merchant	1
Total shares taken			2"

Dated   day of   19

Witness to the above signatures

A.B., 13, Hute Street,
Clerkenwell, London.
(Reproduced by permission of HMSO.)

Appendix II

SPECIMEN CREDIT SALE AND HIRE-PURCHASE AGREEMENT

(The following specimen credit sale and hire-purchase agreement forms are subject to copyright and are reproduced by kind permission of the Consumer Credit Trade Association, 3 Berners Street London.)

CSA
First

TERMS OF THE AGREEMENT

1 Payment

Before signing this agreement you must have paid the deposit shown overleaf. By signing this agreement you agree to pay the Balance Payable by making the payments set out overleaf, by their specified dates, to us at the address stated overleaf or to any person or address notified by us in writing. Punctual payment is essential. If you pay by post you do so at your own risk.

2 Right to demand earlier payment

If any amount is overdue for more than fourteen days we have the right, by sending you a notice of default, to require you to bring your payments up to date within seven days after service of the notice. If you do not do so, the whole of the balance remaining unpaid on the agreement shall then become due and payable immediately.

3 Earlier payment by you

If you pay off the balance on this agreement before the date on which the final payment falls due you will usually be entitled to a rebate of part of the charges.

4 Interest on sums overdue

We have the right to charge interest at the annual percentage rate shown overleaf on any amount payable under this agreement and not received by us by the date on which the final payment falls due. This interest will be calculated on a daily basis from that date until it is received.

5 General provisions

(a) No relaxation or indulgence which we may extend to you shall affect our strict rights under this agreement.

(b) We may transfer our rights under this agreement.

(c) You must inform us in writing within seven days of any change of your address. If you fail to do so you must repay on demand our reasonable costs in finding your new address.

(d) Where two or more of you are named as the Customer you jointly and severally accept the obligations under this agreement. This means that each of you can be held fully responsible under this agreement.

6 When this agreement takes effect

This agreement will only take effect if and when it is signed by us or our authorised representative.

CSA **Credit Agreement** *regulated by the Consumer Credit Act 1974*   Original
No right of cancellation

Agreement No. _____

This credit sale agreement sets out below and overleaf the terms on which you (the customer) agree to buy the goods described below from us (the sellers).

The Sellers
Name and address

The Customer _____
Full names please

Address _____

Particulars of Goods		Cash Price Incl. VAT	
Qty.	Description	£	p
	Total Cash Price (incl. VAT)		

Financial Details and Payments		£	p
Total Cash Price	(a)		
Less: Deposit			
= Amount of Credit			
Add: Charges	(b)		
= Balance Payable			
Total Amount Payable	(a) + (b)		
A.P.R.			%
Number of monthly payments			
Day of each month on which payable			
First Payment Due (month and year)		19	
Amount of each payment			
Amount of final payment (if different)			

IMPORTANT — YOU SHOULD READ THIS CAREFULLY YOUR RIGHTS

The Consumer Credit Act 1974 covers this agreement and lays down certain requirements for your protection which must be satisfied when the agreement is made. If they are not, we cannot enforce the agreement against you without a court order.

The Act also gives you a number of rights. You have a right to settle this agreement at any time by giving notice in writing and paying off all amounts payable under the agreement which may be reduced by a rebate.

If you would like to know more about the protection and remedies provided under the Act, you should contact either your local Trading Standards Department or your nearest Citizens' Advice Bureau.

Witness: Signature _____

Name _____
Block letters please

Address _____

Witness: Signature _____
Second witness required in Scotland only

Name _____
Block letters please

Address _____

DECLARATION BY CUSTOMER

By signing this agreement you are declaring that:

★ Your particulars given above are correct

★ All the information you have given us is correct

★ You realise that we rely on that information when deciding whether to enter into this agreement.

> This is a Credit Agreement regulated by the Consumer Credit Act 1974. Sign it only if you want to be legally bound by its terms.
>
> Signature(s) of Customer(s) _____

Signature of (or on behalf of) Sellers

_____

Date of Sellers' Signature (Date of Agreement)

Hire Purchase Agreement *regulated by the Consumer Credit Act 1974*   Original

No right of cancellation

Agreement No. _____

This agreement sets out below and overleaf the terms on which we (the owners) agree to supply the goods described below on hire purchase to you (the customer)

The Owners _____
Name and address

_____

The Customer _____
Full names please

Address_____

_____

Particulars of Goods		Cash Price Incl. VAT			Financial Details and Payments		£	p
Qty.	Description	£	p		Total Cash Price	(a)		
					Less: Deposit			
					= Credit Extended			
					Add: Charges	(b)		
					= Balance Payable			
					Total Amount Payable	(a) + (b)		
					A.P.R.			%
					Number of monthly payments			
					Day of each month on which payable			
	Identification Nos:				First Payment Due (month and year)		19	
					Amount of each payment			
	Total Cash Price (incl. VAT) (a)				Amount of final payment (if different)			

TERMINATION: YOUR RIGHTS

You have a right to end this agreement. If you wish to do so, you should write to the person authorised to receive your payments. We will then be entitled to the return of the goods and to half of the total amount payable under this agreement, that is £   .[1] If you have already paid at least this amount plus any overdue instalments, you will not have to pay any more, provided you have taken reasonable care of the goods.

[1] Insert one-half of the total amount payable.

REPOSSESSION: YOUR RIGHTS

If you fail to keep to your side of this agreement but you have paid at least one third of the total amount payable under this agreement, that is £   ,[2] we may not take back the goods against your wishes unless we get a court order. (In Scotland, we may need to get a court order at any time.) If we do take them without your consent or a court order, you have the right to get back all the money you have paid under the agreement.

[2] Insert one third of the total amount payable.

Witness: Signature _____

Name _____
Block letters please

Address_____

_____

Witness: Signature _____
Second witness required in Scotland only

Name _____
Block letters please

Address_____

_____

Signature of (or on behalf of) Owners

_____

Date of Owners' Signature (Date of Agreement)

_____

DECLARATION BY CUSTOMER

By signing this agreement you are declaring that:

★ Your particulars given above are correct

★ All the information you have given us is correct

★ You realise that we rely on that information when deciding whether to enter into this agreement.

> This is a Hire Purchase Agreement regulated by the Consumer Credit Act 1974. Sign it only if you want to be legally bound by its terms.
>
> Signature(s) of Customer(s) _____
>
> The goods will not become your property until you have made all the payments. You must not sell them before then.

HPA   **TERMS OF THE AGREEMENT**

1 Payment

Before signing this agreement you must have paid the deposit shown overleaf. By signing this agreement you agree to pay the Balance Payable by making the payments set out overleaf, by their specified dates, to us at the address given overleaf or to any person or address notified by us in writing. Punctual payment is essential. If you pay by post you do so at your own risk.

2 Failure to pay on time

We have the right to charge interest at the annual percentage rate shown overleaf on all overdue amounts. This interest will be calculated on a daily basis from the date the amount falls due until it is received and will run both before and after any judgment.

3 Ownership of the goods

You will become the owner of the goods only after we have received all amounts payable under this agreement including under Clauses 2 and 11. Until then the goods remain our property.

4 Selling or disposing of the goods

You must keep the goods safely at your address and you may not sell or dispose of them or transfer your rights under this agreement. You may only part with the goods to have them repaired. You may not use the goods as security for any of your obligations.

5 Repair of the goods

You must keep the goods in good condition and repair at your own expense. You are responsible for all loss of or damage to them (except fair wear and tear) even if caused by acts or events outside your control. You must not allow a repairer or any other person to obtain a lien on or a right to retain the goods.

6 Change of address

You must immediately notify us in writing of any change of your address.

7 Inspection

You must allow us or our representative to inspect and test the goods at all reasonable times.

8 Insurance

You must keep the goods insured under a fully comprehensive policy of insurance at your own expense. You must notify us of loss of or damage to the goods and hold any monies payable under the policy in trust for us. You irrevocably authorise us to collect the monies from the insurers. If a claim is made against the insurers we may at our absolute discretion conduct any negotiations and effect any settlement with the insurers and you agree to abide by such settlement.

9 Your right to end the agreement

You have the right to end this agreement as set out in the notice 'Termination: Your Rights' overleaf. You must then at your own expense return the goods to us.

10 Our right to end the agreement

We may end this agreement, after giving you written notice, if:

(a) you fail to keep to any of the terms of this agreement;

(b) you commit an act of bankruptcy (such as failing to pay a debt ordered by a court) or have a receiving order made against you;

(c) you make a formal composition with or call a meeting of your creditors;

(d) execution is levied or attempted against any of your assets or income or, in Scotland, your possessions are poinded or your wages arrested;

(e) the landlord of the premises where the goods are kept threatens or takes any step to distrain on the goods or, in Scotland, exercises his right of hypothec over them;

(f) where you are a partnership, the partnership is dissolved;

(g) you have given false information in connection with your entry into this agreement;

(h) the goods are destroyed or the insurers treat a claim under the above policy on a total loss basis.

If we end this agreement then, subject to your rights as set out in the notice 'Repossession: Your Rights' overleaf, we may retake the goods. You will also then have to pay to us all overdue payments, and such further amount as is required to make up one half of the Total Amount Payable under this agreement. If you have failed to take reasonable care of the goods you may have to compensate us for this.

11 Expenses

You must repay on demand our expenses and legal costs for:

(a) finding your address if you change address without immediately informing us or finding the goods if they are not at the address given by you;

(b) taking steps, including court action, to recover the goods or to obtain payment for them.

12 General provisions

(a) The word 'goods' includes replacements, renewals and additions which we or you may make to them with our consent.

(b) No relaxation or indulgence which we may extend to you shall affect our strict rights under this agreement.

(c) Where two or more persons are named as the customer, you jointly and severally accept the obligations under this agreement. This means that each of you can be held fully responsible under this agreement.

(d) We may transfer our rights under this agreement.

13 When this agreement takes effect

This agreement will only take effect if and when it is signed by us or our authorised representative.

IMPORTANT — YOU SHOULD READ THIS CAREFULLY

YOUR RIGHTS

The Consumer Credit Act 1974 covers this agreement and lays down certain requirements for your protection which must be satisfied when the agreement is made. If they are not, we cannot enforce the agreement against you without a court order.

The Act also gives you a number of rights. You have a right to settle this agreement at any time by giving notice in writing and paying off all amounts payable under the agreement which may be reduced by a rebate.

If you would like to know more about the protection and remedies provided under the Act, you should contact either your local Trading Standards Department or your nearest Citizens' Advice Bureau.

Appendix III

TOUR OPERATORS' CODE OF CONDUCT AND GUIDELINES FOR BOOKING CONDITIONS

(The following extract is reproduced by kind permission of the Association of British Travel Agents, 55–57 Newman Street, London.)

4.4 Booking Conditions

(*i*) Booking conditions, if any, shall define the extent of the responsibilities as well as the limits of the liabilities of tour operators towards clients and shall be so designed that they are easily read and understand.

(*ii*) Booking conditions shall not include clauses:–

(*a*) purporting to exclude responsibility for misrepresentations made by the tour operator, his servants or his agents;

(*b*) purporting to exclude responsibility for the tour operator's contractual duty to exercise diligence in making arrangements for his clients or for consequential loss following from breach of his duty; and

(*c*) stating that complaints will not be considered unless made within a fixed period after the end of a tour or holiday if such a period is of less than 28 days' duration.

(*iii*) Booking conditions (and/or brochures) shall prominently indicate the circumstances in which and the conditions on which surcharges may be made to clients.

(*iv*) Where booking conditions (and/or brochures) give a tour operator the right to make surcharges in the event of unfavourable variations in the rates of exchange, such booking conditions (and/or brochures) shall prominently indicate the tour operator's general policy in the event of favourable variations in the rates of exchange.

(*v*) Booking Conditions shall clearly indicate the tour operator's general policy in the event of his cancelling or altering a tour, holiday or other travel arrangements.

(*vi*) Booking Conditions referring to arbitration in accordance with paragraph 4.11 or this Code shall not deny to clients the option of taking action in the Courts if they so wish.

(*vii*) A tour operator shall not print his booking conditions (or insurance details) on the front or on the back of booking forms unless all such conditions (and insurance details) are provided separately to every client on or before confirmation of the booking.

(*viii*) Booking conditions shall conform with all relevant provisions of this Code.

(*ix*) Tour operators shall in practice interpret their booking conditions in accordance with the provisions of this Code.

Index

Accord and satisfaction, 155
Agency
  actual authority, 177
  agent's duties, 173
  agent's rights, 175
  apparent authority, 177
  breach of warranty of authority, 181
  creation of agency relationship, 172
  del credere agent, 101
  necessity, 179
  ratification, 178
  relations between the parties, 179
  undisclosed principal, 180
Agreement
  acceptance, 107
  certainty, 109
  discharge of contract by, 155
  intention, 113
  mistake and, 109
  offer and invitation to treat, 106
Agreements in restraint of trade, 140
Anticipatory breach, 152
Assignment of contractual rights, 83
  absolute and conditional, 84
  equitable assignments, 84
  requirements, 83

Bailment, 93
  duties of bailee, 93
  private carriers and, 161
Banking transactions, 184
  banker customer relationship, 185
  collecting banker, 191
  crossed cheques, 189
  definition of banker and recognition
    as such, 184
  deposit-taking controls, 193
  documentary credits and, 193
  garnishee proceedings, 192
  paying banker, 190
Bankruptcy, 57
  acts of bankruptcy, 57
  adjudication of, 58
  bankrupt, discharge of, 61
  creditors' claims, 60
  distribution of bankrupt's property, 59–61
  fraudulent preference, 59
  partnerships and, 61

  receiving order, 57
  relation-back, doctrine of, 59
  trustee in bankruptcy, 58
Bills of exchange, 70
  bearer bills, 71
  cheques as, 73
  function of, 73
  holder in due course, 85
  holder for value, 85
  negotiation of, 85
  order bills, 71
  parties to, 72
Business property, 67
  classification of, 67
  copyright, 77
  distribution of on winding up and
    bankruptcy, 55, 59
  goods, 69
  land, 68
  negotiable instruments, 70
  patents, 78
  securities, 95
  shares and debentures, 74
  trade marks, 79
  transfer of, 81

Capacity to contract, 112
Carriage of goods, 158
  carriage by air, 162
  carriage by land, 161
  carriage by sea, 163
  common carriers, 158
Carriage of goods by sea, 163
  bill of lading, 164
  charterparties, 163
  c.i.f. contracts, 165
  f.o.b. contracts, 166
  freight, 168
  general average, 169
  shipowner's liability, 166
  shipping documents, 164
Cheques, 73
  "account payee", 189
  bankers and, 184, 189, 190
  bills of exchange and, 73
  crossed cheques, 189
  forged indorsement, 190
  forged or unauthorised signature, 186

Common carriers, 158
    definition, 158–9
    liability of, 159
Condition precedent, 118
Condition subsequent, 118
Conditional sale agreements, 223
Consideration, 110
    privity of contract and, 111
Consumer credit agreement, 217
Contract
    agency, 172
    assignment, 83
    collateral, 116, 156
    creation of, 105
    elements of, 105
    exclusion clauses, 125
    formalities, 81, 105
    guarantess and indemnity, 100
    implied terms, 117
    performance and discharge of, 145
    privity and, 111
    remedies for breach of, 196
    rights and obligations under, 115
    sale of land, 81
    sales of goods, 88, 120
    standard form, 125
Contractual relationships
    creation of, 105
Contractual terms, 115
    conditions and warranties, 118
    express, 115
    implied, 117
    "intermediate" terms, 119
Copyright, 77
Corporate personality, 3
Corporations, 4, 113
Credit sale agreements, 223
Crime, 235
    liability under Consumer Safety Act,
        235
    registered companies and, 236

Damages, 196
    liquidated and unliquidated, 197
    nominal, 196
    penalties and, 197, 221
    remoteness of loss and, 198
    substantial, 196
Debentures, 36, 56
    debenture holders, 36
    floating charges and, 56, 76
    mortgages and, 75
    transfer of, 86
Derivative actions, 49

Directors, 36
    agency law and, 43
    appointment and disqualification,
        37
    delegation of powers to, 37, 44
    duties of, 39
    insider dealing and, 41
    managing director, 38
    number of, 21
    relations with members, 43
    removal, 42
Discharge of contracts, 145
    agreement to, 155
    breach, 150
    frustration, 152
    performance, 145
    waiver, 156
Divisible contracts, 147, 148
Documentary credits, 164, 193
Duress, 134

Entire contracts, 147
Exclusion clauses, 125
    common law and, 126
    contra proferentem rule, 127
    fundamental breach, 127
    Unfair Contract Terms Act and, 128

Fair trading, 204
    anti-competitive practices, 211
    Business Advertisements Order, 206
    consumer trade practices, 205
    Consumer Transactions Order, 206
    detrimental and unfair conduct, 206–7
    Director General of Fair Trading, 204
Fixed charge, 76–7
Floating charge, 26, 56, 76
    crystallisation, 76
    registration, 77
Frustration
    effect of, 153
    nature of, 152

Gaming and wagering contracts, 141
Goods, 69
    bailment of, 93
    carriage of, 158
    definition of, 69
    delivery of, 149
    hire purchase and, 218
    implied terms relating to, 120
    nemo dat rule and exceptions thereto,
        90–2
    non-contractual liability and, 234, 239

property in, 88
remedies relating to, 199
reservation of title, 55, 89
specific, 69
specific performance and, 201
title to, 88
unascertained, 69
Guarantees, 100
distinguished from indemnity, 101
formalities, 101

Hire purchase agreements, 218
Consumer Credit Act and, 219, 225–7
creditor, 220
dealer's liability, 219
debtor, 221
parties, 219
termination and recovery of
possession, 222

Illegal contracts
categories of, 139
effect of, 142
meaning, 130
Incorporation
effects of, 4
methods of, 4
Injunction, 202
Mareva injunction, 192
Intention to create a legally binding
agreement, 113

Lien, 99
agent's lien, 176
possessory, 99–100
sale and, 100
Limitation of actions, 203
Limited companies, 21, 36, 55
Limited partnerships, 18

Misrepresentation, 130–4
effect of, 132
silence and, 131
Mistake
effect on agreement, 109
fundamental, 136
non est factum, 138
Monopolies and mergers, 212
European Community Law and, 214
Mortgages, 95
Consumer Credit Act and, 97
goods, 97
land, 95
shares and, 95

Negotiable instruments, 70
bills of exchange, 70–1
cheques, 73
definition of, 70
promissory notes, 74
Novation, 85, 155

Organisations, 1
incorporated, 3
unincorporated, 1

Part performance, 82
Partnership, 8
contractual liability of, 13
definition, 9
dissolution of partnership, 16
distinguished from incorporated
associations, 2
duty of good faith, 12
features of, 8–11
general partners, 18
limited partners, 18
non-contractual liability of, 13
partnership agreement, 9
partnership property, 12
relations of partners to each other,
11
relations of partners to outsiders, 13
Patents, 78
Penalties, 197, 221
Performance of the contract
complete performance, 145
Sale of goods Act and, 149
substantial performance, 147
Supply of Goods and Services Act
and, 150
time for performance, 146
Pledges, 98
Consumer Credit Act and, 98–9
nature of, 98
Private companies, 21
distinguished from public companies,
21
Promissory notes, 74
Property, 67
equitable interests in, 69
legal estates, 68
personal, 67
real, 67
things in action and possession, 67
transfer of, 81
Public companies, 21
distinguished from private
companies, 21

Registered companies, 20
  articles of association, 29, 47
  classification of, 20
  Company name, 21
  company secretary, 46
  directors, 36
  dissolution of, 52, 56
  formation, 22
  guarantee company, 21
  liability of members, 21, 55
  majority rule, 48–9
  managing director, 38
  meetings, 31
  membership of, 34
  memorandum of association, 27
  minority protection, 49
  objects clause, 27
  promoters, 23
  prospectus, 24
  raising of capital, 26
  relations between members and the
    company, 47
  resolutions, 32
  share capital, 21, 29, 74
  shareholders, 34
  shares, 21, 34, 74
  ultra vires rule, 27
  winding up and, 52
Regulated agreements, 217
  advertisements, 229
  consumer credit agreement, 217
  consumer hire agreement, 217
  credit-token agreement, 218
  debtor-creditor agreement, 224
  debtor-creditor-supplier agreement,
    224
  entry into, 225
  exempt agreements, 227
  extortionate credit bargains, 228
  licensing, 228
  non-commercial agreements, 225
  restricted- and unrestricted-use credit
    agreements, 223
  small agreements, 225
Remedies for breach of contract, 196
  equitable remedies, 201
  Sale of Goods Act and, 199
Representative actions, 3, 49
Restrictive covenants, 69, 112
Restrictive trading agreements, 142, 207
  European Community Law and, 211
  references to Restrictive Practices
    Court, 208

  registration of, 207
  resale price maintenance, 209
Rights and obligations of contracting
    parties, 115

Securities, 95
  guarantees, 100
  lien, 99
  mortgages, 95
  pledge, 98
Share capital, 29–31
Shares, 21, 34, 55
  definition of, 74
  ordinary shares, 75
  preference shares, 74
  shareholders, 34
  transfer of, 86
Specific performance, 82, 201

Tort, 234
  defective products, 238
  vicarious liability, 236
Trade descriptions
  compensation orders, 244
  defences, 242
  disclaimers, 240
  false trade description, 239
  statements as to price, 240
  statements as to the provision of
    services, 241–2
Trade marks, 79

Undue influence, 134
  effect of, 136
Unlimited companies, 21

Void agreements
  categories of, 140
  effect of, 142
  meaning, 130
Voidable contracts
  innocent party and, 132, 136, 138
  meaning of, 130

Winding up of registered companies, 52
  by the court, 53
  distribution of assets, 55
  "just and equitable" ground, 53
  liquidators 54, 55
  preferential claims, 56
  secured and unsecured creditors,
    55–6
  voluntary, 54